The Equity Premium Puzzle,
Intrinsic Growth & Monetary Policy

Third Edition

Robert Shuler

Paperback ISBN 978-1-5061-4465-8
eBook ISBN 978-0-9911130-1-9

Published by Robert Shuler, Friendswood, TX
Distributed by CreateSpace, North Charleston, SC

Additional book information & resources at
http://mc1soft.com/books/EquityPremium

Publishing History:
First Edition December 2013
Special Investor's Edition 2014
2nd Edition, 2015 (Tate Publishing)
3rd Edition, 2016

Other books by Robert Shuler:

Money, Wealth & War

The Economic Optimization of Innovation & Risk

A Summer Night
(The illustrated children's poems of Pauline S. Shuler)

Table of Contents

Introduction

This book in a nutshell

No central bank (in USA "the FED") ever prints enough money to cover the increasing output of goods and services from mass production and automated productivity. Sure, they sometimes print too much for reasons like financing socialist governments or escaping from debts. This causes disasters which stick in people's minds and undermine the insight and the will to print the money to cover increases in production.

But economies don't function when production overruns the currency. Instead of a modestly growing standard of living, there is a sudden surplus, devastating prices, to which consumers may think they should cheer. But this results in massive layoffs, permanent dislocation, social strife, and even war. The middle class finds their savings destroyed to meet unemployment living expenses and by market losses. The poorer class finds it impossible to get ahead or even get a job, despite low prices. The wealthy class finds no opportunity to invest and create jobs, because with declining prices they can never recover their investment. The economy stops moving.

Even though no central bank adequately addresses this problem, their attempts to, along with certain other factors, ensure that ordinary borrowing and lending rates will be less than equity return rates. The uncertain commitment of central banks results in ordinary people and shop owners losing ground to large businesses and wealthy investors. This shows up as the Equity Premium at long time horizons which the individual investor finds hard to capture.

This book will explain money as no other book has and you will understand it clearly, and even know how to calculate how much money is enough. We do the calculation for Japan's long running deflationary spiral, a mistake the US is making even now.

Why write (or read) this book

I know of no way to soft pedal this, no way to sneak up on you and persuade you gently:

> **The ideas which work very well for you in business and**
> **family matters will lead the country to war and ruin!**

Businesses and investors do not print money, but the government establishes and issues money. Families do not "layoff" members expecting them to find another family. The trouble is we apply these principles to candidates of either party. There are significant differences in the positions of the parties. One presumes generally that the Democrats would advocate deficit spending on social programs, in other words print or borrow money to finance the government, which leads to inflation and can lead to bankruptcy, just as it can with families.

And one presumes generally, though certain historical presidents have been notable exceptions, that modern Republicans advocate austere government spending, and some of them even extreme measures like sequestration and, in the Libertarian subset, abolishing the Fed, which leads to not printing enough money to cover productivity increases, and to deflation and layoffs and bankruptcy. So, both policies lead to bankruptcy.

You probably vote for what would improve your personal position, so that your company can complete that trade deal, or so that you can have cheaper gas or clothes. The result is that you or your fiends are laid off and cannot find work at half the salary they used to.

The most shocking response I got from the first edition of this book was that there was no particular response to the radical view of the role of the Federal Reserve that I proposed. People would read the book, and the expected arguments would not begin. Instead, they would intellectualize, perhaps even agree, and later in discussions of current events they would *resume their same old views about lending, inflation, trade and productivity.* I might have reached their minds, but I had failed to penetrate their deeply held instinctual thoughts.

An internet search for "equity premium solutions" produces twenty-one million hits. The top three academic papers which propose solutions are cited over five thousand times, presumably by scholars offering better solutions. There are 114,000 papers on the subject found by Google Scholar.

Large numbers of papers and books attempt to survey and compare this vast literature. Not only has no consensus emerged, and no "close" solutions, but papers appear regularly denouncing most or all of them as completely at odds with real data,[1] or having no ability to predict future premiums.[2]

Do you, or should you, care if interest and bond rates are noticeably lower than stock returns – or if the effect is predictable or not? Let me ask you a few questions that might elucidate whether this is something you care about, and whether you think understanding "why" is interesting or important, other than perhaps just an afternoon's entertainment, which it certainly is.

Who or what do you think sets interest rates?

---

[1] Zheng, L., "A Survey of the Empirical Difficulties of the Consumption Capital Asset Pricing Models," J. Mod. Econ. Manag., vol. 2, no. 1 (2013). http://scik.org/index.php/jmem/article/view/665
[2] Welch, I., Goyal, A., "A Comprehensive Look at the Empirical Performance of Equity Premium Prediction," The Review of Financial Studies, v. 21 n. 4, 2008

If you are an investor, banker or ordinary citizen with money in a bank or in stocks who reads the financial news, you probably answered "The Federal Reserve," and added some comment like "of course."

But if you are an economist, you probably answered "the market." There is a big difference. Who is right? Does it matter?

What is the value of long-term growth? How much confidence do you have in long-term growth? How do you capture that in a portfolio?

Unless you have some answer to these questions, you probably don't invest in stocks and are reading this book only for the politics, social policy or the entertainment of understanding and solving famous puzzles, all good reasons. That is fine. You will get your money's worth. But the answers are *critical* to someone thinking of investing.

The point is, equity markets more or less define our way of life, making capital from households available to businesses to produce goods and services, the profits from which will be shared with the equity owners and in turn provide for the future needs of households.[3]

If the reasons for prices and returns are unknown, it is hard to imagine the market, or the act of investing, being rational. And the process might break down at critical times, such as during a crisis.

Economists have shown, at least to their own satisfaction, that flow of capital from households to markets during a crisis benefits the households (investors), the economy, and the country. Yet that is exactly the point at which confidence is lowest, and when policy makers are most likely to tinker with the rules of the game.

Understand this very clearly. Without knowledge of the rationale for the prices of equities, there is no possibility policy makers are using any kind of valid theory to guide their tinkering. History, which we will get into, shows 250 years (in this country alone) of arguing one dogmatic position against another, the same old positions in fact.

Here is the problem. Rational investor theory suggests all types of investments should "equalize" in price so that the returns from them are basically the same, except for a slight premium for those more risky. That is because rational investors would pile on the better one driving its price up until the two are comparable. The equity premium puzzle, discovered by a friend of mine and published in 1985,[4] reveals that this is not the case. The returns from stocks over long periods of time are much higher than the

---

[3] At least this is the theoretical view of economists. For example, see Zheng, L., "A Survey of the Empirical Difficulties of the Consumption Capital Asset Pricing Models," Journal of Modern Economy & Management, vol. 2, no. 1 (2013) available open access at http://scik.org/index.php/jmem/article/view/665

[4] Mehra, R. and Prescott, E., "The Equity Premium A Puzzle," Journal of Monetary Economics, North-Holland, 15, 145-161 (1985) http://www.academicwebpages.com/preview/mehra/publications/

returns from other kinds of investments, in particular bonds. So economists have no theory that explains the real world.

Here is how it relates to interest rates. Economists use the interest rates, usually based on Treasury bills with some adjustment for the amount of risk involved, as a discount rate to figure the fair present value (NPV or *net present value*) of the future reward of investments. Bond returns are pretty well explained by this method. Why aren't stocks?

For that matter, a companion puzzle exists which is "Why is the risk-free interest rate so low?"[5] Bonds are volatile too, and go up and down when interest rates change or confidence changes. What Mehra and Prescott found was that the long-term difference in risk between bonds and stocks only justified at most a 1% higher return for stocks (equities), but the measured difference including dividend reinvestment and compounding over long periods was more like a 7 to 8% annual rate (though not of course reliable in a given year).

Obviously you care about such matters if you are an investor. But even if you are only an ordinary job holder, whether you can keep your job is intimately connected to policy decisions made about the national economy. And even if you don't have a job or investments and are living from Social Security, welfare or other government payments, the ability of the government to pay you, and the value of what you can buy, is determined by the fate of our economy.

And you vote for these guys. Maybe you are more interested in immigration reform or military spending, etc. None of those things will work very well without an economy. You vote for the President of the United States, and he chooses the Chairman of the Federal Reserve, and the chairman pretty much runs fiscal policy. It's a much more direct connection than other political choices, where you vote for someone who then must fight with other elected politicians to get anything accomplished.

You probably have some opinions. Maybe you like the idea of a gold standard, or abolishing the Federal Reserve. What you probably don't have are facts. Most people studied American History when they were too young to think about money, and do not connect Andrew Jackson's abolition of the Second Bank of the US with how they feel about the Federal Reserve. Abolishing the Fed has essentially been tried. But do you remember what the results were? Do you remember the era of free banking? The different methods of financing that the North and South used during the Civil War?

---

[5] Weil, P., "The equity premium puzzle and the risk-free rate puzzle," Journal of Monetary Economics, 24 (3), 401-42 (1989) available from Weil's website at http://www.philippeweil.com/research/riskfree%20rate%20puzzle.pdf

Do you think the US was historically on a gold standard, which was only removed partly by Roosevelt in 1933 and fully by Nixon in 1971? You remember reading about William Jennings Bryan, right? What was the main point of his campaign? But McKinley won, and what did he do in 1900? That's right; the United States was not even on a gold standard until the beginning of the twentieth century. And what was the end result?

What kind of money did Henry Ford and Thomas Edison advocate in the 1920s? What kind of money do we have today?

If stocks return such high amounts, why do individually managed investment accounts return on average barely more than money market accounts?[6] How do you pick stocks? How do you make a portfolio that will actually produce the equity premium that you've read about?

This book will give answers for those questions, good answers that while surprising, you will understand. And even if you never vote or invest, you will have the satisfaction of many eureka moments, and of understanding financial puzzles that have eluded generations and set the trajectories of nations up or down.

Lessons from events since the first edition

During 2014 the Fed ended its quantitative easing (QE) program, and the market seemed at first to take it in stride. But then there was a resounding crash in the energy markets just a few weeks after QE ended. No one but me seems to have put the two together.

Of course there are other significant factors. Many big companies invested hugely in increasing the supply of oil through relatively more expensive extraction methods, from "fracking" to tar sands. But do you suppose the bean counters at these companies did not estimate what the price of oil would be after their oil hit the market? I would assume they did.

Did they "assume" without justification that Saudi Arabia would just suck up the difference by cutting production, and their own market share? Not if they assumed Saudi Arabia was rational.

It is likely investors in these new methods anticipated some reduction in price, but not as much as there has been. Of course it might be temporary. We don't know yet. But I am concerned.

One of the most astonishing conclusions of this book is that productivity must be compensated not just by a onetime increase in the money supply, to account for the greater quantity of goods in circulation, but a permanent increase in the rate of growth of money supply.

---

[6] Physsis Borzi, Asst. Secy. Of Labor testimony to Congress, "From 1998 to 2007 the average annual returns for IRAs were 4.5%," posted by Steve Beck at http://www.marketriders.com/investing/expected-rate-of-return-nail-it-or-else/

Productivity is a production *rate* increase. QE amounted to a continual monthly increase in the money supply, probably just about right to counter the vast increases in productivity that resulted from employers figuring out how to increase production after the financial crisis without hiring more workers. Now that it's gone, something had to give. Oil wasn't in a bubble. The current price just isn't supported anymore.

Now maybe this will all have a fairytale ending. Maybe around the world money that would be spent for oil can now be spent for consumer goods. We shall see.

There is a further and surprising reason that in January 2015 as the price of oil dropped below $50 a barrel, American companies continue to pump and do not reduce production. They are not getting the return on their investment they expected, and if they would decrease production only slightly, the price would rise and the total profit they would reap from their oil reserves would be much higher over time.

However, they did not make all this investment with equity. They increased their borrowing dramatically. This was as the FED intended. Interest rates were lowered, making borrowing attractive.

But now interest payments are due whether they pump oil or not. As notes expire they must be renewed based on current ability to pay, which depends on continuing to pump oil. The companies cannot reduce production noticeably without coming up short on their payments. So they must continue to pump oil, even though they make very little profit margin between the payments and other expenses, and what they get for the oil. In fact, they might have to pump oil at a loss rather than come up short of the cash to cover their debts.

In the long-term the cheap supply of energy will greatly stimulate economic growth, probably all around the world. The return on debt will have been held quite low by the FED. The short-term return on equity will be low, almost matching it. But in the long-term, the new growth will greatly increase the value of stocks (equities).

As of January 2016, the price of oil was in the mid-$30s and dropping even as a serious dispute broke out between Iran and Saudi Arabia. The Saudi's executed a leading Shiite Cleric along with a bunch of terrorists. After an initial attack on the Saudi embassy in Tehran, the Iranians were oddly conciliatory. They also promised to increase their oil sales modestly if sanctions are lifted – the first sign of "rational behavior" I have seen in the oil market. If supply were reduced only 6%, by 4 million barrels per day, the current 2 million barrel per day surplus would be wiped out immediately and soon prices would double or triple and everyone would make double or triple the money they are currently making.

While this would be rational, the countries involved – the US, Iran, Russia, Saudi Arabia, Iraq, ISIS, Venezuela – cannot cooperate. Oil is priced in dollars, and the disorder in the market, the wild swings and layoffs, are caused by a stubborn Fed that wants to prove it can eliminate QE and raise rates as planned, even when the rest of the world is falling into recession and easing monetary policy.

Russia has certainly made some changes, entering the war in Syria, damping down conflict in Ukraine, but has not yet convinced the West to lift sanctions. It has been forecast that some countries, maybe even Saudi Arabia, will begin to experience internal social turmoil due to cutbacks in social programs. Saudi Arabia has a new and untested King, and has already cut social programs. Are the executions a response to increased unrest in this opaque kingdom? Will they raise oil prices to finance a nuclear program with which to deter Iran? Here we have examples of the interlocking of military, social and economic policy, together with the actions of central banks.

Lessons from Rome and the Bronze Age

Also since the first edition I read a book about the economy of the period of the Republic, when Rome was growing into a world dominating force. The most astonishing thing was the sentence that opened the book. No significant amount of gold was ever found in Italy!

Rome was not built on gold. It was built on wheat. Rome never used a significant amount of precious metal coinage. The largest and longest lived empire in the history of the world did not have gold-backed money. They had better concrete than we do, sophisticated contracts and "stock," plumbing and aqueducts, but not gold-backed money. Apparently it is necessary neither for empire nor civilization.

The Bronze Age ended in such complete chaos that of the four great empires, memory of all but one was lost until the mid-19th century. The age had lasted for thousands of years. During that time grain was money. It was stored in temples, with little protection except the wrath of the god. Money was represented in trade caravans by copper bars. So copper money was backed by grain.

Then one day in about 1200 BCE Tulkuti-Ninurta (known in the Bible as Nimrod) sacked the temple at Babylon and took everything there. Our modern telling of this has been amended to emphasize that maybe the temples contained a lot of gold, because we don't see how grain could be that important. That is only because we have a lot of grain, especially in America. Ask the Ukrainian farmers about the importance of grain when one is starving.

Nothing happened to Nimrod. He was not struck dead by the god. He kept whatever he took. Uh-oh! The money was no longer worth anything. No one could be sure that some armed gang had not already retrieved the deposits represented by the copper bars. Trust was gone.

In Lydia, a region of modern Turkey, a few hundred years later, kings with names such as Croesus and Midas started to mint coins out of a gold and silver alloy. This was not because gold or silver were scarce. There was a river flowing down out of the mountains containing so much of the alloy that it would coat anything placed in it! Gold might have been scarce elsewhere, but the Lydians had so much of it that they decided to make coins out of it. You may have heard the expressions "rich as Croesus" or "the Midas touch"? Is the fable about Midas' touch intended to teach us the value of gold? Hardly. It was to teach us that almost anything else is worth more. Midas' touch was a curse.

And so the Lydians cursed the rest of the world with the idea of gold as money. It worked for the Lydians because they had plenty of it. We will learn how this was like silver in the American west, which they found plenty of, and how the national dispute between western ranchers and miners, and eastern bankers and traders, led to the unfortunate adoption of a gold standard in 1900, followed by two world wars and a great depression.

The repair of that mistake led to the greatest century of economic growth the world has ever known. And if we can avoid lapsing back into that mistake, the economic miracle will continue. But if we go back to making gold and debt our guiding moral principles, they will drive us into serfdom and poverty that will make the Middle Ages look positively bright, and into global conflict with terrible weapons that will make past wars look like a Sunday outing.

PART ONE

MONEY & RATIONAL MARKETS

A BRIEF HISTORY & INTRODUCTION

Portfolio Logic

Everyone is an Investor

We all make investment decisions, whether it is deciding on a career, a house, a school or a spouse; to hold cash, bonds, a mortgage or gambling debts. Any of these things is a gamble that affects our happiness, wealth, health and survival. It is pitifully inadequate to measure all these things with one yardstick, money, but that is largely what our culture and common law does. If someone unjustly deprives you of any of them, the remedy is to sue in court and if you prevail you get money.

The question of the equity premium asks us to compare, in our judgment as investors, two very different things: a past debt of a specific amount of money, and ownership of a future activity that has broad possibilities for impacting everything we care about. Hardly a fair comparison. The one is a legal contract with well-quantified assessment of its enforcement. The other doesn't exist yet and estimates of what it is are just vague promises. But equity (stock) ownership has been around long enough that we ought to have a handle on what it's worth, and there ought not be a documentable discrepancy in this comparison over periods of hundreds of years. That is the dilemma.

Consider the following statement: "Investors care about *portfolio* returns, *not* about the behavior of specific assets."[7] Imagine that. John Cochrane, the *asset pricing specialist* at the National Bureau of Economic Research, asserts basically that he does not care about particular stock prices, and presumes "investors" do not care about such details either.

When Cochrane uses the word "investor," who is he talking about? Obviously not someone buying a house or selecting a career. Are you within his definition of investor? Some readers will be and some won't. This book is for all of you, and I'll show you what you have in common and how you differ.

What is your salary and net worth? According to SEC rule 501(a) of Regulation D, an *accredited investor* is "(a) any natural person whose individual net worth, or joint net worth with that person's spouse, *exceeds $1 million* at the time of purchase; or (b) any natural person who had an individual income in excess of $200,000 in each of the two most recent years or joint income with that person's spouse in excess of $300,000 in each of those years and who reasonably expects reaching the same income level or greater in the current year."

---

[7] New Facts in Finance, June 1999, http://www-gsb.uchicago.edu/fac/john.cochrane/

These two requirements together, portfolios (Cochrane) and net worth (the SEC), eliminate many people as investors. In fact the dividing line roughly corresponds to "the one percent" we have heard so much about in political discourse of the last decade. The 99% generally invest in a career in *one* industry, perhaps one company. Some of the 1% choose to do this, such as Bill Gates and Rupert Murdoch. But the best examples are diversified into a portfolio of companies, for example Warren Buffet.

Even if an employed person owns index funds in a retirement account, most of his or her income is from a specific job. Things like education, housing, transportation and children absorb earning power until late in most careers, when finally funds may be available for diversified investing. Small business owners are very non-diversified. CEOs, however, are reasonably well off. They have excess income for investing earlier than most, and often their skill can transfer to another industry.

The Lopsided Money Tree

Consider the alternate possible "returns," future gains or losses from the growth (or not) of your business or investments, as the *branches* of a money tree. I say "alternate possible" because you don't know what they are going to be. Each alternative that will be decided by future events is a "branch." Some years you will do well, from luck or careful planning or consumer whim, and some years poorly. For simplicity, let's say there are two branches (possibilities) each year, one fat and one lean, depending on whether next year is a good or bad year. To keep the numbers simple, let's say that in a good year you will go 20% ahead, and in a bad year 20% down. If we look out just two years in the future, there are four possible branches, like this:

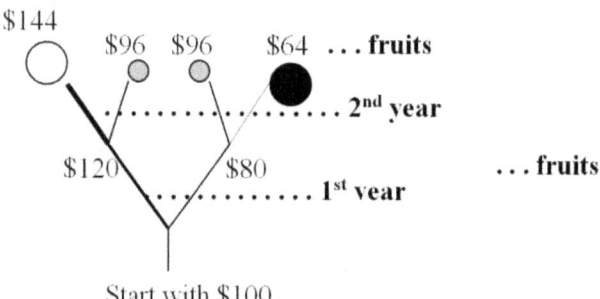

Start with $100

Right away you see the tree is lopsided. Only one of four branches is profitable, three are not. With the prospect of equal gains or losses of 20%, you might think the most likely gain would be zero, but it's not. A gain of 20% followed by a loss of 20%, or vice versa, amounts to a loss of 4%. This is called *compounded returns*. Alternately it may be called a *geometric return*. Do the math with any percentage you care to use, it's always the same. The bigger the percentage, the bigger the loss in the middle branches.

So the likelihood is that three out of four investors, given such circumstances, will experience a loss. But the *average* return is not a loss. If you had owned four separate businesses, and the future of each one followed a different growth path through the money tree, ending in a different branch, you would not have a loss. The gain from the winner offsets all three losers. Try it. Add 144 + 96 + 96 + 64 and you get 400. Divide by 4 and that's an average end result of $100.

Obviously to make money the gains in good years must be greater than the losses in bad years, or the good years must be more likely than bad years, or both. But the principle of the portfolio still holds true. The lucky business owner whom fortune favors will look like a genius. Most business owners, or stock pickers, or gamblers, will make *less than the market average*. And "investors" who own a portfolio with many businesses will make about the market average.

So which are you? Are you the gambler, business owner, stock picker? Or are you the investor with a portfolio?

Mutual and Index Funds

Ah, perhaps you protest that you own mutual funds? Professor Cochrane unfortunately has nothing good to say about mutual funds. The average fund underperforms the market by about 1%. And generations of careful empirical analysis have found no persistence in the performance of particular fund managers. Cochrane admits:

> *"This fact is surprising. Professionals in almost any field do better than amateurs. . . Apparently the vast majority of funds are not holding well-diversified portfolios on behalf of their clients, but rather loading up on specific bets."*

You can of course buy index funds. Even that will not capture average returns for an index dominated by a small number of very large companies, such as the NASDAQ 100. Even the S&P 500 can wind up with 5% in only three or four companies. For an index where the companies are similarly sized, it should work. But capturing average returns is not very exciting. In any other walk of life, it is considered dull and even marginal to be "average."

Efficient Markets vs. Private Returns

That brings us to the second aspect of being a investor. Not only must you have a balanced portfolio, which disqualifies all small business owners since they are over-weighted in the business they own, but you must be accredited. You must have a very high income or a net worth over a million dollars. Why?

To cash in on private returns, that's why. Economists classify returns on investments as either public or private. Different rules apply to each.

Public returns result from investment in the shares of public companies, available to everyone. The trouble with public investments is something called the Efficient Market Hypothesis, or EMH, originally postulated by Eugene Fama in 1970,[8] and popularized by Burton Malkiel in "A Random Walk Down Wall Street." As defined by *investopedia.com*, EMH states:

> *"... It is impossible to beat the market because prices already incorporate and reflect all relevant information."*

EMH arises from competition among investors, and from the unfortunate fact that returns are relative to current price. If investors know a company will do well, they bid up the price of its shares until the returns that can be realized by buying them are comparable to other companies. Without stopping to ponder the subtleties of this surprising assertion, let's see how a wealthy accredited investor avoids being trapped into mediocrity by EMH.

Private returns result from proprietary investment opportunities. These may be protected by anything from a de facto monopoly to a patented process, from a secret formula to the simple time lag a competitive startup would require. The important thing is that in the end, the shares are not sold to the public. They are only available to accredited investors, that is, to people who are already wealthy. The public is not allowed to bid up their price, reducing their returns to the efficient market average.

You can of course start your own business, and that is proprietary. But unless you are very wealthy, you can only start one business, not a portfolio of them, and the lopsided money tree effect will destroy 80% of small businesses in the first 5 years. In order to feasibly have a portfolio of proprietary investments, you must be able to buy into other people's proprietary businesses. Whether you approach this from the point of view of venture capital or hedge funds, you will find the entrance requirements are the same. You must already be wealthy.

At least, that was the theory a number of years ago. There are signs of some change, which probably represent market pressure on private returns, pushing them toward efficiency. Congress has authorized a class of investments called Business Development Companies. These

---

[8] Eugene F. Fama. Efficient capital markets: A review of theory and empirical work. Journal of Finance, 25:383-423, 1970.

are a little bit like Real Estate Investment Trusts (REITs) or Royalty Trusts or Partnerships in that as long as the company passes along most of its income as dividends, it is not double taxed by the government.

Examples of BDCs include companies such as Hercules Technology Growth (HTGC) and Horizon Technology Finance (HRZN) and many others that you can find with a simple search. They are not exactly the same as venture capital funds. VC funds don't pay dividends, betting entirely on the growth of their startups. BDCs may hold equity in small or startup companies, but in addition are likely to make loans to such companies. For example, the two I cited are somewhat different in this regard.

Trading vs. Investing and Zero-Sum Games

We have seen that the returns of a stock, or a portfolio for that matter, over time suffer a loss due to compounding. Over the space of available investments (companies) a portfolio is a tool to reduce this effect and capture something closer to the true average return. Even the portfolio approach suffers if over time the whole economy and thus the whole market fluctuates up and down. Such fluctuations are known as volatility, and compounding losses are one of the reasons volatility is considered bad.

Inflation-adjusted price of gold[9]

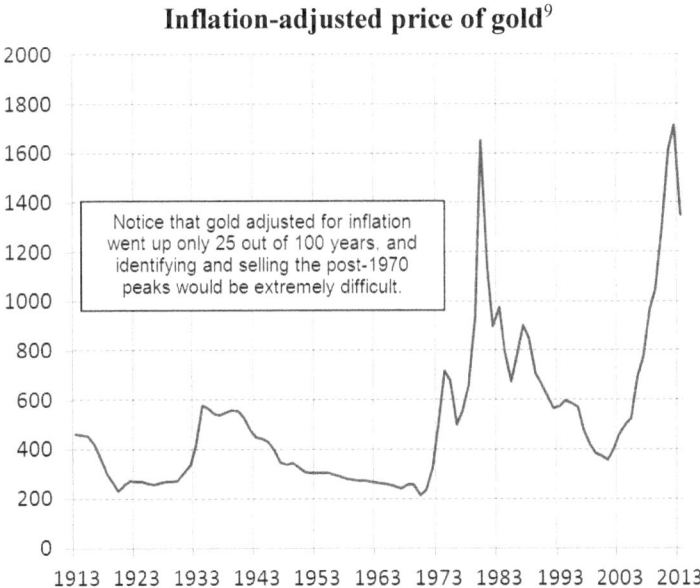

Notice that gold adjusted for inflation went up only 25 out of 100 years, and identifying and selling the post-1970 peaks would be extremely difficult.

[9] Data sources: CPI from Bureau of Labor Statistics, Gold prices from
http://www.measuringworth.com/datasets/gold/result.php

Not everyone considers volatility bad. Traders and speculators depend on it. Traders are not investing in the long-term business and do not care about future returns. Traders often invest in commodities such as wheat, sugar, coffee, copper, oil or gold (not the companies that produce these things). These are not business activities and over the long-term produce no returns in excess of simple inflation. Economists consider such activities to be zero-sum games. The total sum of all gains has to be zero. That sum includes presumably the profit of one trader, the loss of another trader, and the commissions and fees charged by trading exchanges and brokers. So from a trader's perspective, it is a slightly negative sum game. If one believes in efficient market theory there is no money to be made. Obviously, traders do not believe in EMH.

In fact, there is another puzzle involved in efficient market theory. Why is there so much trading? Some transactions are just liquidation to meet expenses, or represent investment of new funds. A few traders probably are acting on inside information. But the large volume of trading, often driven by automated algorithms, is derisively called *noise trading* by EMH theorists, and considered uninformed.

The trading puzzle can be re-stated somewhat obliquely to the effect that all capital is not efficiently allocated. There is some inefficient capital. Perhaps even a majority of capital is inefficient. Capital is constantly being generated as business profits, savings from salaries, contributions to pension funds, etc. There are two things to note about this capital.

First, if it is truly uninformed then its effect on markets is roughly neutral. It should not prevent equalization of returns, for example, by itself. If there is a large flow, it might create a general asset bubble but it would either affect assets randomly, or through the erroneous belief in a fad, which would end dismally for most participants. Or it would affect all assets similarly, as in a general boom. It would not explain a long-term favoring of bonds over stocks, necessarily, as would be required to explain the equity premium.

Second, it suggests the adoption of a weaker form of the EMH, one based not so much on knowledge as on evolution. Capital that is efficiently employed tends to increase, and other capital tends to decrease as it earns lower returns. This *adaptive market hypothesis* was proposed by Andrew Lo.[10] But there is not general agreement that it is a valid viewpoint. We assume it produces a weaker form of the EMH because it does not guarantee the immediate results we would expect from "knowledge," but in a sense it is stronger because it works regardless of

---

[10] Lo, Andrew W., "The Adaptive Markets Hypothesis: Market Efficiency from an Evolutionary Perspective," Journal of Portfolio Management, Forthcoming. Available at SSRN: http://ssrn.com/abstract=602222

whether the complete knowledge assumption of traditional EMH is true or not.

Steady State

Above we discussed booms and fads. These are examples of transient effects in markets. Obviously during a transient one asset or another may perform better, and then when the transient is ended this does not continue. We've also mentioned volatility, which can include very short-term transients, some never explained – even computer glitches.

In the equity premium puzzle, the problem is to determine a cause for a very long-term, presumably permanent state of affairs. This is called steady state, or equilibrium. And it is much easier than working with transients. For example, periods of inflation and deflation can last a couple of decades, and have serious effects on the returns of bonds and stocks. Wars also have a large effect. It can be very hard to quantify the driving forces or the effects of such transients.

But to analyze the equity premium we really only have to consider periods greater than 20 years, or perhaps centuries. Very simple mathematical models can be used. Generally speaking, without transients differential equations are not necessary. Even currency fluctuations are not very important. If a currency trended steadily down for centuries, for example, it would essentially go out of existence.

There are some things which do trend for centuries. At least since the Renaissance, there has been a trend of increased travel and communication, bringing trade. And there has been a trend of increased industrialization and automation. These very long trends are fair game. The rate of change in the trend becomes a steady state parameter of a roughly constant value.

Even though a particular transient is not eligible for consideration because of its shortness compared to our time horizon of interest, might the general level of such transients, for example volatility, play some role? Possibly, but it does not seem so. I spent a lot of time chasing this idea. But at the end of the day, compounding losses due to volatility amount simply to a reduction in average returns, and possibly an increase in risk. But many authors have already modeled this risk in a variety of ways, and Mehra and Prescott argue none of them explain the equity premium.[11]

[11] Mehra, R. and Prescott E., "The equity premium in retrospect," in: G.M. Constantinides & M. Harris & R. M. Stulz (ed.), Handbook of the Economics of Finance, edition 1, volume 1, chapter 14, pages 889-938, Elsevier (2003).

Borrowing and Equalization

Mehra at one time considered whether borrowing constraints might influence the equity premium.[12] The idea is that young people who have the time horizon necessary to realize the equity premium (which can disappear for a decade or two at a time) might like to do so, but their income is in the future, and they do not have sufficient credit to borrow enough to make much difference in markets. Middle-aged consumers do not have the investing time window to guarantee they will capture the equity premium, and hold a balanced portfolio of equities and the more predictable bonds – thus reducing interest rates and contributing to the equity premium.

It is an interesting idea, and indeed later we will use a much stronger form of it (which has nothing to do with young people). But it brings up the question of how equalization works, and its relation to borrowing. The non-economist reader may be assuming that the natural demand for investments will be proportional to their value as recognized by all or most investors. Indeed, as we saw earlier even if investors do not recognize the demand, over time a kind of adaptive selection corrects the market by granting superior returns to the investors whose preferences are rational, even if they do not know why. But the premise of equalization in standard efficient markets theory acts more quickly. Only one or a few investors can accomplish equalization through arbitrage. You see this when a corporate acquisition is announced at a premium price over the current market price. If it is believed the acquisition will go through, the market price immediately jumps close to the offered price. Professional arbitrageurs will buy arbitrary quantities of stock, and make a profit on the small difference that remains between the price they offer, and the acquisition price.

The key fact is that the arbitrageur does not have to have in reserve the amount of money needed to make such an arbitrarily large purchase. He or she can borrow any amount necessary, because lenders are very confident they will be repaid. Borrowing is the key to classical equalization theory, and anything which interferes with borrowing will interfere with equalization.

Where do lenders or banks get arbitrary amounts of money to lend, or who do they in turn borrow it from? That is another question. Of course, for transactions such as described above they can use short-term money. Short-term money cannot capture the equity premium. In the very short-term, during a financial crisis, lenders (depositors) may even have to

[12] Constantinides, G., Donaldson, J., Mehra, R., "Junior Can't Borrow: A New Perspective on the Equity Premium Puzzle," The Quarterly Journal of Economics, February (2002).

pay (a kind of negative interest) to keep their money safe, especially for large deposits.

Non-linearity

The term *linear* refers to addition, and also multiplication by a constant as in algebra equations which describe a straight line. In a linear system, things add up. The returns of the combination of A and B would be equal to the returns from A plus the returns from B. This is certainly true for data expressed in currency amounts such as dollars. If A pays $X dividends and B pays $Y, and I own one share of each, my total dividend is X + Y.

If, say, shares in both A and B are $50, so that I have a $100 portfolio, and A goes up 10% and B goes down 10%, then the 10% gain on A is $5 and the 10% loss on B is -$5 for a net of zero. So far all is linear.

But suppose both A and B go up 10% one year (plus $10, so I now have a portfolio value of $110), and down 10% the next (down 10% of $110 is $11). Now I have a portfolio value of only $99. This can be obtained by adding $10 and -$11. But it cannot be obtained by adding 10% and -10%. With respect to percentage returns, the combination of the two years is non-linear.

Business returns are fairly expressed as percentages because generally they are proportional to the size of the business. A small business with a small inventory and few stores is limited in both its upside and downside. A large business with many stores (or whatever its profit units are) and a large inventory has both larger upside and downside. Percentages are the reasonable way to look at business returns.

Compounding is especially evident in the long-term returns of so-called *ultra* or leveraged Exchange Traded Funds, which offer 2x or 3x times the price movement of the basis asset. For example, UPRO offers 3x the S&P 500 index on a daily basis. Consider 3x (three times) the + and − 10% example above. That would be a gain of $30 the first year, and a loss of $39 for the second year, with a final portfolio value of $91, nine times the loss of the underlying asset. Not three times. The 3x is only per *day*. In this example over two years it was 9x down.

This particular kind of non-linearity will not explain the equity premium. But it is a simple example of something more complex that we will investigate later. It will turn out that the kinds of portfolios (e.g. index based) used in the equity premium are highly non-linear over long periods, and their value is simply not equal to the sum of their asset values, *strange as that may seem.*

Summary

Whether we purposely invest in the stock market, or whether we accidentally invest wherever our job or pension plan takes us, we are all investors. A successful investor must have a strategy for dealing with the naturally lopsided distribution of future returns based on growth. This is an artifact of the mathematics of proportional returns (i.e. percentage based), and runs somewhat contrary to the expectation of "average" returns. More complex non-linear properties of portfolios will be developed later for dealing with equalization pressures on one side of the equity premium.

The efficiency of markets is a separate issue, which is influenced by borrowing costs and constraints, and influences the equity premium from another direction.

This chapter has explained the basic mechanics of portfolios and returns which we will need. However many other factors are needed – inflation, productivity, politics, growth. Next let's peak into the origin and meaning of money.

Finance Dawning

What is Money?

You can't eat it or wear it. It won't keep you company. And even in urban settings money may be augmented by barter or by an intrinsically valuable trading commodity such as salt.[13] Defining money is a hard problem. So, why do we care? Everyone uses it well enough.

Here's a reason. Economists model investor behavior as "rational decision making." They assume investors maximize risk-adjusted returns based on all known information. They model consumer behavior in a similar fashion, substituting some other maximizing function. Do you make rational decisions about money? Or are you influenced by hidden feelings and attitudes?

Marketers don't believe in a rational model. When was the last time you saw an automobile ad that presented charts and figures that would support rational decision making?

Somehow I don't think psychologists will go along with rational decision theory either. They will say we make decisions based on emotion and belief. Hotter personalities will go with emotion, and cooler heads will ponder their well-considered beliefs. From the sea of available facts, both types are more likely than not to select information that supports their decision.

Since an investor is a consumer of investments, and since the future return on investments isn't nearly as certain as the performance of an automobile, investment decisions are even more likely to be made based on emotion and belief. Systems of investing, capital markets, ways of thinking about business and growth, notions of fair business practices, feelings about trade and competition are partly matters of emotion and belief.

Belief about what?

Some beliefs will be about money specifically. But if we can pin down what money is, we'll identify a broader set of beliefs. We'll notice factors such as trust, expectation, how we feel about obligations, whether we return favors, confidence in finding help when we need it.

Let's start with a barter transaction, stretch it so that we need money, and see if we can identify what money is. Say you help your neighbor build a fence, and he gives you some chickens. I'm going to go to money in three simple steps.

In step one, say you don't need anything from your neighbor today but wish him to repay the favor in the future. Or say he doesn't have

---

[13] The 1999 Iranian film "Children of Heaven" illustrates use of barter and salt-based transactions in an urban setting.

anything for you right now. In either case, he can "promise" to repay the favor at a future time. If your neighbor forgets a few of these favors you may ask him to write down the promise, so he hands you an IOU specifying what he has promised.

Debt, Risk and Returns

The IOU is money that is good only between two people. It is like two things we routinely use. First, it is a contract, an agreement between two parties, which requires something from each of them – in this case the help with the fence from you, and the chickens from your neighbor. But it is also a debt, because you have already delivered your end of the deal. By giving you the IOU, your neighbor becomes a debtor, and you become a lender.[14] But unlike such formal instruments as bonds or loans, the IOU probably doesn't specify exactly when the debt is to be paid. It will be paid whenever your neighbor has chickens and you want them.

What do you think is the earliest IOU we know of? Is it a piece of parchment or a stone tablet with something written on it? Do we have an example that old?

If that's what you guessed, guess again. IOUs are older than writing. In fact, shortcuts in the creation of IOUs are thought to have precipitated the invention of writing.

In 1929 German archaeologist Julius Jordan dug a trench into the Inanna temple precinct in the ruins of Uruk, city of ancient Sumer, now in Southern Iraq. In addition to the goddess' home and storehouse, an elegantly decorated colonnade, and stone steps of the temple, he found a number of small tokens "shaped like commodities of daily life: jars, loaves and animals."

It appears these tokens were kept in hollow clay envelopes about the size of softballs, called bullae. In order to keep from having to break open the envelopes every time someone wanted to check the contents, marks were made on the outside, probably by imprinting the tokens in the clay. Thus the symbol for "lamb" was the imprint of a small carved lamb in the clay. Eventually more abstract symbols developed, for example the symbol for "sweet" developed from the imprint of a jar of honey, and finally a stylus was used to directly make the imprints, skipping the step of first carving tiny figures.[15]

---

[14] Paul Millett proposed in *Lending and Borrowing in Ancient Athens* that lending did begin as neighborly reciprocation in rural societies.

[15] A detailed theory of the co-development of money and writing has been put forward by Denise Schmandt-Besserat in *Before Writing*, and *How Writing Came About*. You can also find a concise summary in Harriet Crawford's *Sumer and the Sumerians* in the chapter on writing and the arts, or online in the first chapter of

The bullae are interesting for their role in the development of writing, but were they the first money or IOUs? Prior to writing, usage of objects must be inferred from the context of archaeological finds, so we cannot be entirely certain. But it seems as though grain and other food items were lent and used as money beginning between 8000 and 5000 BCE. If so, then at one time you *could* eat money! Before that, perhaps shells were used.[16]

With any debt or contract there is a risk of non-performance. Your neighbor may meet with some unfortunate accident, or move away. Or he may issue IOUs to other neighbors for the same chickens, which is kind of like a country printing more money than it has goods and services. Of course if the neighbor's chickens multiply, all the IOUs are good, so money can expand with growth. To the extent IOUs are like fiat paper money (or stone or clay as paper precursors), then fiat paper money is very old and natural.

If you sense the risks are significant, you may request and your neighbor may consent to give you an extra chicken beyond what was originally agreed. You could probably work this out so that on average, in dealing with all your neighbors, the extra chickens you'd get would balance the chickens you lost on bad IOU's.

This is a bit like "interest," but notice it is not like "investment." You have no expectation of net profit from this sort of lending.[17] You may benefit from the trade, but you are only just breaking even on the risk adjusted lending. The purpose of the "extra" chicken is to get what you are entitled, so that on average favors are returned as often as given. Also notice that I just used the word "return" to describe the repayment of the debt, comparing it to the return of a favor.

Since we presupposed a barter economy, it will be evident to the holder of an IOU that he can exchange it with a second neighbor for something else, provided the second neighbor is acquainted with the first, and feels confident the first will provide him the chickens.

We may find that other chicken ranchers generally are willing to honor the IOU, enabling you to redeem it for chickens as specified, but from someone else. Suppose the first neighbor has gone hunting for two

---

William Goetzmann's *Financing Civilization*. See
http://viking.som.yale.edu/will/finciv/chapter1.htm

[16] See *A History of Interest Rates* by Sidney Homer & Richard Sylla, 3rd ed. revised 1996, pgs. 19-20.

[17] Millet [see earlier footnote] also confirms that profit-oriented interest developed later, in connection with explicit contracts and urbanization.

weeks just when you have an appetite for chicken dinner. You may seek to trade the IOU to the second neighbor for chickens. She may honor it for reasons already stated, or for the additional reason that she would like to encourage you to trade regularly with her. She promises she does not care for hunting and will always be available whenever you are hungry. She takes the IOU and replenishes her chicken stock from the first neighbor when he returns. A chicken economy develops.

Trading Commodities and Unlike Goods

A barter economy naturally trades unlike goods, such as fence work for chickens, and so at first I didn't think the development of a trading commodity was part of the story of money. But in a barter economy we might have all sorts of rules or superstitions about what kinds of things could be traded for what other kinds of things, and what could not, and even who could trade them. In a money economy, the idea that *"everything has a price"* is a principal feature, and one which generates strong feelings, often negative. So I'll propose step two on the road to money is the establishment of a universal trading commodity.

We began by mentioning salt as a trading commodity. Salt would have the advantage that it is relatively imperishable and portable, as compared to chickens. Later we'll discuss the use of scarce commodities such as silver or gold.

The unique feature of a trading commodity is that it universally equates all things. If we can convert chickens into salt, and salt into hogs, then we can indirectly convert chickens into hogs, even if there is a local prohibition against trading chickens for hogs. To give this example more weight, suppose neighboring tribes agree to loan each other warriors when needed for self defense. This is a delayed barter transaction, like our original fence work now for chickens later. The tribe first needing help would present an IOU to the helping tribe good for one battle. Lives may be lost in battle. It is a very serious thing. Unless the second tribe were starving, it is unlikely they'd accept chickens for their help. But if the first tribe had been accumulating a universal trading commodity for decades, it might be equivalent to chickens for a lifetime, and they might be able to pay for mercenary help with it.

To re-state so this is absolutely clear, so many chickens all at once would not be useful. They would have to be housed and looked after, which is impractical. An IOU for that many chickens is not credible. The other village might not last that long, or might try to back out of the deal in a bad year. But by using a non-perishable trading commodity, suddenly we can have the trading equivalent of a lifetime supply of chickens or other food, and can purchase human help at risk of their lives. In other words, we begin to be able to equate this precursor to money with human life. It is a strange twist on so simple and convenient an idea.

Another interesting feature of the ability to accumulate a large amount of a universal trading commodity is its attractiveness to thieves and military adventurers. Probably it wasn't the cause of warfare. Perhaps it added a new reason. Possibly it made warfare less deadly if the thief was content to carry off the trading commodity, leaving the chickens and people behind.

Every trading commodity has some source, and not only would stocks of the commodity be coveted, but also the sources. While there are many reasons for the acquisition of land this adds another one, which can become strong enough to impact history, as for example in providing a large part of the Spanish motive for colonization.

It appears universal trading commodities would have large advantages. For example, a traveler could carry a little salt or some jewels, and trade for supplies along the way, not having to carry everything on his back. Along with these advantages came some liabilities. The traveler, already wary of thieves, would have added substantially to the criminal motive by carrying a large quantity of the trading commodity.

Investing, Business and Growth

The IOU of the first step is not quite modern money, but already we have familiar concepts like debt, contracts, risk, and interest or return. We even have monetization problems, like inflation which occurs when too many IOUs are issued against the same chickens or some of the chickens die, and the remaining chickens must be divided among the outstanding IOUs. We are most of the way toward money, though a difficult step remains.

What we don't have is the concept of excess returns, the kind investors seek. We won't get it in the next step either because it doesn't come from money. It comes from the operation of a business. For example, you find you can acquire chickens by breeding, barter or the redemption of IOU's. Instead of eating the chickens you feed them, and barter away the eggs. Or you can invest further by keeping and hatching the eggs and bartering away the young chicks. The idea of investment, or excess return, seems to come from the excess productivity of animal husbandry and intensive agriculture, both of which developed about 10,000 years ago. If the idea wasn't around before, it surely developed at that time. Barter is probably an older notion, along with some limited ideas of money.[18]

---

[18] Theories of the development of money (see earlier footnote) deal with a period well after intensive agriculture and animal husbandry, which both originated 10,000 years ago at the end of the last ice age. My statement about some idea of

In ancient Sumer, where as we have seen writing seems to have been invented as an outgrowth of financial contracts, the word for "interest" [*mash*] is "calves." In ancient Greece interest [*tokos*] also refers to cattle offspring. The Egyptian word for interest [*ms*] means "to give birth." The productivity of intensive agriculture gave rise to cities because the surplus allowed some people to specialize into non-farming trades. Urban centers, where not everyone knew each other and where various specialized trades were not as interchangeable as farm skills, probably gave incentive to the use of explicit contracts like our IOU, and also the promise of interest returns as a "sweetener" to motivate transactions.[19] This idea is distinct from the idea of "risk" interest we discussed earlier, which accounts only for the possibility of not being paid.

Interest in Sumer was well established and regulated by the government at a maximum of 20%.[20] At times no "period" was specified in the regulation, and lenders worked around the regulation by lending for shorter and shorter periods. Longer loans up to thirty years with a type of compound interest were also known, along with methods for calculating their total return.

The idea of barter exchange increased the well-being of both parties. But the surpluses from "growth" of crops or animals, if they can be accumulated, can be used to gain a large amount of power. A Hebrew story tells of how Joseph foretold of coming famine in a dream, and advised the Egyptian pharaoh to place excess grain in storehouses. Archaeology cannot confirm this specific legend, but it does suggest Egypt used such storehouses. According to the legend, the Hebrews became dependent on Egyptian grain, and eventually became slaves. That's a good point to remember.

If you always have to take chickens, or help with fences, or something tangible in return, your favor-performing will be limited to what you need, or you might perform favors just because you have the time and like to be helpful. But if you can accumulate IOUs which are easily exchanged, and easily stored, this gives you power. Your neighbors may be willing to do some pretty strange things for you if it will keep you

---

money likely being older is conjecture based on the observation that pre-agricultural hunter-gatherer cultures are known to use beads or tokens as an exchange medium.

[19] See William Goetzmann's *Financing Civilization*,
http://viking.som.yale.edu/will/finciv/chapter1.htm

[20] In the Hammurabi law code, circa 1800 BCE, loans of silver were regulated at 20% and loans of grain at 33 1/3%, repayable in kind. *A History of Interest Rates* by Sidney Homer & Richard Sylla, 3rd ed. revised 1996, pg. 3.

from calling in all your IOUs at once. Or they may stay out of your way, not wanting to remind you of their debt.

Confidence

Step three is to increase confidence in repayment. A simple way to do this is to use a Big man. If the Big man is known to keep his or her word, has loyal servants and guards, extensive holdings, and is owed favors by many neighbors, your favor to this person is likely to be repaid. If the big man's heir promises to maintain the obligations of the estate, even death will not cheat you. Other neighbors who depend on the goodwill of the Big man are more likely to repay both you and the Big man, since they could suffer substantial loss of goodwill. The Big man serves as a kind of credit bureau. Of course if he's a mean jerk, the idea could backfire.

Reputation would be very important in an IOU-based economy, whether it was reputation among a network of friends, or with a Big man, chief, or temple priest. But in an urban environment, reputations would be harder to keep up with.

A modern example of money backed by the reputation of a Big man is the issuing of currency by local warlords in Afghanistan during the chaotic period after the Russians withdrew, and before the American invasion. The money would typically carry the name and picture of the man who guaranteed its value.

Another way to increase confidence would be for a group of neighbors or a community to agree to back one another's IOUs. Modern examples include the practice among airlines of honoring each other's tickets in emergency or in case of default. This is done precisely to increase confidence, encouraging more people to fly. Another example is the practice among dry cleaners of honoring each other's coupons. This is done for competitive reasons. But it has the secondary effect of increasing confidence in the coupons, and increasing their utility.

Problems immediately arise in community backed money that discourage the use of easily created paper IOUs or coupons. The system is open to abuse by someone who prints a lot of coupons, inflicting the burden of honoring them on competitors, resulting either in higher prices (inflation) to offset the coupon losses, or in refusal to honor the coupons. The coupon problem can be solved with "hard currency." Hard currency uses various methods to prevent unwarranted creation of surplus IOUs. A simple example is something scarce, such as silver or gold, which perhaps is already in use as a trading commodity. A design pattern can be added which is hard to duplicate, further discouraging copying.

In the hard currency system, your neighbor with the fence cannot just write an IOU. He would either use money on hand, say from selling chickens last year, or he would borrow money from someone keeping a store of it. This moves the "borrowing" from random and unreliable transactions between individuals, to organized borrowing from a Big man, who is probably associated with the religious or political authorities, and who is better able to know reputations and demand repayment. So the community-backed and Big man systems of increasing confidence can work together.

Sumerians later used silver disks with holes punched in them as money. Civilizations such as Greece and Rome used coins stamped with the images of emperors or deities. Pull a nickel out of your pocket and look at the flip side. There is an engraving of Monticello, which in stylized form looks much like a temple.

The big men pictured on American money are all dead. Why is this? Recall that one of the advantages of money backed by a Big man is the promise of the heirs to maintain all the obligations. So on the dollar and the quarter we have a picture of George Washington, first president and symbol of the unity and strength of the USA. On the five dollar bill and the penny we have Lincoln, who also preserved unity and thus the promise of fulfilling obligations. Jefferson, on the nickel, acquired the Louisiana purchase and Jackson, on the twenty, secured it. Feminine impressions on US money seem to be most common on the silver dollar, and include lady liberty (who might be compared to goddess images on ancient money), and Susan B. Anthony, who secured women's role in maintaining the obligations of the country. Citizens of other countries will, I'm sure, be able to construct their own similar examples.

A final aspect of confidence building is to make money "legal tender." This happens when the backer, community or Big man, insists that money be accepted in payment for all debts. We find money being accepted not just for material debt, but for crimes and damages.

Some Consequences of Money

So, money really wasn't very complicated. Rural barter exchange was transformed in obvious ways by the needs of an urban environment into thoroughly modern money, in just three simple steps. But along with money came debt as an intrinsic part of what money is. And along with building confidence in money came an increase in the coercive power of the temple and later the government, as well as the potential for individuals to accumulate enormous power.

As agricultural surpluses allowed cities to develop, and as religion was viewed as important in assuring favorable weather and advancement of agricultural seasons, people built temples in the cities. These came to hold as much as 20% of the land in ancient Sumer,[21] and much of the silver.

It has been suggested that the government of Sumer actually preferred its citizens in debt, as they were more productive and crop yields were higher. This does not quite square with the fact that they periodically declared general debt relief, much to the consternation of creditors. By 2000 BCE default on loans to farmers was the chief cause of land transfers, and it is still a cause of the loss of family farms today. If one accepts the idea of making large profits from lending, it seems one must also accept the idea of foreclosing on an unfortunate debtor, and to some extent repudiate the original idea of reciprocal mutual aid.

The practices both of lending with interest, and of periodic debt relief, spread widely in the ancient Near East. We have some interesting records from the Hebrew culture in what Jews call the Torah or what Christians call the Old Testament. Debts are forgiven at regular intervals of seven years,[22] although this seems to apply only to Hebrews and not to foreigners.[23] Every fiftieth year there is to be a "jubilee" in which land is returned to its original owner,[24] though houses inside walled towns are excluded.[25] Advice is given not to co-sign a loan,[26] and in giving a loan to

---

[21] At one time it was thought the Temple owned all the land in a Sumerian city state, but this has been shown to be incorrect, a result of not having a full estimate of the size of the city state.

[22] "At the end of every seven years there is to be a general forgiveness of debt. (Deut. 15:1)

[23] "2 This is how it is to be done: every creditor is to give up his right to whatever he has let his neighbor have; he is not to make his neighbor, his countryman, give it back; because a general forgiveness has been ordered by the Lord. 3 A man of another nation may be forced to make payment of his debt, but if your brother has anything of yours, let it go;" (Deut. 15)

[24] "And let this fiftieth year be kept holy, and say publicly that everyone in the land is free from debt: it is the Jubilee, and every man may go back to his heritage and to his family." (Lev. 25: 10)

[25] "And if a man gives his house in a walled town for money, he has the right to get it back for the space of a full year after he has given it up. 30 And if he does not get it back by the end of the year, then the house in the town will become the property of him who gave the money for it, and of his children for ever; it will not go from him in the year of Jubilee." (Lev. 25: 29)

[26] "1 My child, if you co-sign a loan for a friend or guarantee the debt of someone you hardly know – 2 if you have trapped yourself by your agreement and are

require collateral from co-signers.[27] People can become slaves as a result of debt.[28] [29] Debtors can be roused into an army of rebels.[30]

The Phoenicians are credited with not only spreading alphabetic writing to the Greeks, and hence to the rest of the western world, but also the idea of mercantile interest. It seems to have been thought more suited to dealings with foreigners than fellow citizens, as evidenced in Hebrew culture, and so the Phoenicians *did not spread the idea of debt relief to the west.* The condition of debtors became a severe problem in Greek and Roman culture.[31] Westerners took up the practice of throwing people into prison until they paid their debt – a notion that did not diminish in some quarters until the 1800's.

By the Christian era, debt loomed so large in the human psyche that it was the central metaphor of man's relationship with deity. Humans are in debt to God because of universal sin. The debt is forgiven only when paid by another party, Jesus, probably reflecting hundreds of years of Greek and Roman culture and the demise of the idea of ritual debt

---

caught by what you said – 3 quick, get out of it if you possibly can! You have placed yourself at your friend's mercy. Now swallow your pride; go and beg to have your name erased. 4 Don't put it off. Do it now! Don't rest until you do. 5 Save yourself like a deer escaping from a hunter, like a bird fleeing from a net." (Prov. 6)

[27] "Be sure to get collateral from anyone who guarantees the debt of a stranger. Get a deposit if someone guarantees the debt of a foreigner." (Prov. 20: 16)

[28] "A thief who is caught must pay in full for everything that was stolen. If payment is not made, the thief must be sold as a slave to pay the debt." (Exod. 22: 3)

[29] "And you mix the wheat you sell with chaff swept from the floor! Then you enslave poor people for a debt of one piece of silver or a pair of sandals." (Amos 8: 6)

[30] "Then all the people in distress, in debt or embittered began gathering around [David], and he became their leader; there were about four hundred with him." (1 Sam. 22: 2)

[31] The classical history of Greece began with the laws of Solon in 600 BCE, drastic reforms necessitated in part by widespread debt and personal slavery for debt. Limits to interest were abolished, but so was personal slavery for debt. Rome's legal history began with regulation of debt, in about 450 BCE, also precipitated by excessive debt. Interest was limited to 8 1/3%. Personal slavery for debt was allowed but physical well-being protected. *A History of Interest Rates* by Sidney Homer & Richard Sylla, 3rd ed. Revised 1996, pg. 3.

relief. No mention is made in the Christian era of a seven year release from debt or a fifty year return of land. Instead we have cancelled debt being equated to love.[32] Children are said to owe a debt to forebears.[33] Failure to forgive debts is equated with sin.[34] Paradoxically, we have demand for high returns[35] alongside exhortations to lend expecting no return.[36]

---

[32] "A certain creditor had two debtors; one owed five hundred denarii, and the other fifty. 42 When they could not pay, he canceled the debts for both of them. Now which of them will love him more?" 43 Simon answered, "I suppose the one for whom he canceled the greater debt." And Jesus said to him, "You have judged rightly." (Luke 7: 14)

[33] "3 Show respect to widows who are really in need. 4 But if a widow has children or grandchildren, first let them learn to do their religious duty to their own family and thus repay some of the debt they owe their forebears, for this is what is acceptable in the sight of God." (1 Tim. 5)

[34] "24 When he began the reckoning, one who owed him ten thousand talents was brought to him; 25 and, as he could not pay, his lord ordered him to be sold, together with his wife and children and all his possessions, and payment to be made. 26 So the slave fell on his knees before him, saying, "Have patience with me, and I will pay you everything.' 27 And out of pity for him, the lord of that slave released him and forgave him the debt. 28 But that same slave, as he went out, came upon one of his fellow slaves who owed him a hundred denarii; and seizing him by the throat, he said, "Pay what you owe.' 29 Then his fellow slave fell down and pleaded with him, "Have patience with me, and I will pay you.' 30 But he refused; then he went and threw him into prison until he would pay the debt. 31 When his fellow slaves saw what had happened, they were greatly distressed, and they went and reported to their lord all that had taken place. 32 Then his lord summoned him and said to him, "You wicked slave! I forgave you all that debt because you pleaded with me. 33 Should you not have had mercy on your fellow slave, as I had mercy on you?' 34 And in anger his lord handed him over to be tortured until he would pay his entire debt." (Matt. 18)

[35] "15 "To one he gave five talents, to another, two, and to another, one, each according to his own ability; and he went on his journey. 16 "Immediately the one who had received the five talents went and traded with them, and gained five more talents. 17 "In the same manner the one who had received the two talents gained two more. 18 "But he who received the one talent went away, and dug a hole in the ground and hid his master's money. ... 24 "And the one also who had received the one talent came up and said, `Master, I knew you to be a hard man, reaping where you did not sow and gathering where you scattered no seed. 25 `And I was afraid, and went away and hid your talent in the ground. See, you have what is yours.' 26 "But his master answered and said to him, `You wicked, lazy slave, you knew that I reap where I did not sow and gather where I scattered no seed. 27

Without doubt, people today in every culture are influenced by strong feelings about debt, and since everyone possesses an intuitive grasp of money's origin as a kind of re-marketed interchangeable debt, those feelings must also influence how we view, accumulate, use or lose money.

Novel Uses of Money

Sumerian records show that about the same time high interest loans were catching on, some people got the idea of pooling resources in a partnership to fund a high risk venture, often a maritime trading expedition, with the expectation not of return in the form of fixed interest, but of a share in the profits of the venture. As with many new business ventures, expectations were often not met, and the practice fell out of favor. It would be revived later by the Romans to provide services to military expeditions, and Europeans to finance the trading companies formed for European expansion.

Still another novel use of money was to pay wages for labor. Traditionally people have organized themselves for work along lines of kinship, tribute or slavery. Instead of wages, dependents might receive "rations," kind of like a child receives an allowance. In the Hebrew story of Jacob and Rachel we have a situation in which Jacob lives with and works for Laban in this capacity for a month as a relative on rations. But then Laban inexplicably says, "Because you are my relative, should you therefore serve me for nothing? Tell me, what shall your wages be?" Still, in the vast majority of the rural world, wages were the exception until the decline of slavery in the 1800's, and were reserved mostly for dangerous jobs such as mining, where one would prefer not to risk the affection of relatives or the capital of slaves. This expendability of wage earners is an interesting point to keep in mind if your life financial plan is based on wages.

A final novel use of money was to obscure its own meaning as a debt contract. Instead, money is viewed as the solution to debt. But the lender does not really create a loan when the lender makes money available to a debtor. The lender actually transfers debts he is owed to the debtor, who is expected to transfer them back with interest. The lender remains aware that he must eventually, and perhaps unpleasantly, collect the debt. But the holder of the anonymous debt contract of money, with no

---

`Then you ought to have put my money in the bank, and on my arrival I would have received my money back with interest. 28 `Therefore take away the talent from him, and give it to the one who has the ten talents.' " (Matt. 18)

[36] "But love your enemies, and do good, and lend expecting nothing in return; and your reward will be great and you will be sons of the Most High; for He Himself is kind to ungrateful and evil men." (Luke 6: 35)

specific repayment schedule, may easily forget its essential debt nature. He or she may even resent debt collectors or slave owners or land usurpers, and not wish to be like them.

Trust and Coercion

Debt is coercive. Assets can be confiscated, and for much of history people could be thrown in jail for debt. Reciprocal favors are usually not coercive, but are based on trust. They might be thought of as debt which is only repaid voluntarily. Since money is derived from reciprocal favors, it too is voluntary. Prices and exchange rates may vary, or a person from whom you want something may simply be unwilling to part with it, or with their time and labor, for any reasonable price. For money to have value, we must trust that someone is willing to make repayment on the debt it represents. The motto on our money might more appropriately be *"In each other we trust."*

Some societal functions are compulsory. For example taxes. Early governments confiscated part of the annual harvest, and conscripted soldiers for armies. If citizens are going to be allowed to more conveniently meet these obligations with money, then steps have to be taken to make the value of money less voluntary, and ensure that money paid in taxes will be able to induce someone to perform the services we collectively require, whether building roads or providing defense.

Where societies have wished to avoid compulsion, the solution that has evolved is a culture of "jobs."

In a society that uses money, some people will become poor and feel like debtors whose surplus will be confiscated. In their experience it has been pointless to work hard. They will work only enough to meet immediate subsistence needs. Other people will work and save and eventually become rich, and will not need to work. So no one in this "free" society will feel compelled to do much work, neither the rich nor the poor.

But if a culture of jobs and a work ethic develop, certain benefits accrue only to those who have jobs. Retirement benefits are an example. Although the government provides a retirement program, Social Security, it is tied to jobs or at least to paying taxes as a self-employed person. Investors and the unemployed do not accrue any Social Security benefits.

Access to credit is another benefit of a job. Every credit application form asks about job history and status as a primary criterion for granting credit. And of course, once you have credit you will have to keep your job so you can make the payments. Jobs become mandatory for most people. In fact it is difficult to fill out a credit application and explain that you are wealthy but unemployed.

Prior to adoption of the Affordable Care Act the most practical way to obtain healthcare was by having a job that provided it as a benefit. Doctors and hospitals charge up to four times as much to the uninsured, so it's risky to simply do without. At the time of this writing some in the country would prefer to change or repeal this law, a debate beyond the scope of this book.

One further detail is needed to understand the jobs based culture. Money is "zero sum." To get some, you have to take an equal amount away from someone else. The sum of both sides of the transaction is zero. When we have a money based culture, we are constantly confronted with this zero sum nature of money.

In general, human transactions are not zero sum. When we engage in reciprocal favors, our focus tends to be on the positive sum. Your neighbor gets his fence, you get your chickens, both of you are better off. Your community grows stronger, and is better able to defend itself, or engage in competitive commerce.

But when we use money, even though the same thing could happen, what's most visible is the zero sum financial transaction. You could use the money from the fence to buy chickens. In this case the result would be the same. But you might not get the chickens from the same neighbor, and your relationship would not experience the same reinforcement. You also might foolishly squander the money in a gambling hall and have nothing to show for it. This would not be as likely in a reciprocal favor economy. Your neighbor might indulge you in a wager, and you might wind up fencing for him two days in a row. But when he saw you were not having time to tend your own place, and that without harvesting your crops he would likely wind up having to feed you, your neighbor would put a stop to it.

In a money based culture, where everything is for sale and people are not tied to their family plots of land, the neighbor might just decide to press his luck, take over your land, and evict you. In that case it could not be said you were both better off, or that the net social gain was greater than zero. It might well be less than zero. It might be negative.

Money is not only zero sum in transactions. It is even zero sum in creation. If more money is created than products, the money everyone has becomes worth a little less, and everyone gets a little poorer. This keeps the job culture going. Some people get richer and richer, making the rest of us poorer and poorer, so we cannot just quit our jobs when we have enough. We'd quickly fall behind. So we keep working even when we have enough.

Note carefully that I did not say simply *if more money is created* – only if more money is created than products are created. The creation of products behaves more like the exchange of favors. New wealth comes into existence. If the supply of money is not adjusted deflation can take hold. We'll look more into this later.

The Life of Money

The promise of a reciprocal favor does not have an indefinite life. In a few years, or even months, the memory of the fence help will grow dim in your neighbor's busy mind, and he will not think it worth so many chickens. Eventually he will move away or die and the favor will be worth nothing. If you are polite, you will waive it off if not collected promptly. There are exceptions when a critically important favor has a large effect on someone's life, but by and large I think it is as I have described.

Since money is derived from this reciprocal favor, it too has a limited life, more so because it is anonymous and loses identification with the original favor. To be sure, we have implemented confidence building measures to try and stabilize the value of money, but it is bound to erode with time. This is called inflation. It is a kind of natural inflation, progressing slowly, unlike the rapid inflation that results from product shortages or excess money creation. In fact money might be artificially engineered to behave differently than the underlying favors. The point here is that a certain slow inflation is a natural property of the underlying favors.

The idea of interest is opposed to inflation, and as we have seen, probably derives from agricultural surpluses. Subsistence economies that produce little surplus may have extensive systems of reciprocal favors, but do not have interest.

"Real interest" is the excess of interest over inflation. Oddly, during much of US economic history real interest has been very low, close to zero, despite high growth.

Because interest was [probably] based on the natural growth of crops and animals, it normally has a relatively stable and predictable value. Church "tithes" are similar to interest. One might think of them as the interest the deity charges for use of land and nature. Many religious sources are divided between the evils of debt, insistence on debt relief, and the requirement for interest-like productivity in support of the church or society at large.

Equity profits, unlike interest, are unpredictable. Partnerships specify a percentage of the net return after expenses, rather than a percentage return on investment. We have seen they were developed to finance less predictable exploits, such as maritime trading, military adventures, and competitive enterprise.

So money has a finite life, which confidence measures attempt to lengthen, and which exploitation of agricultural surpluses and business risks attempt to defeat. The many anecdotes saying how wonderfully a person would have done to invest such and such an amount in a certain way long ago are just that, anecdotes. How many banks, mutual funds or Dow 30 companies still exist from "long ago"? Not many. Most of the choices available 50, 75 or 100 years ago are out of business today.

Summary

Now you know what money is. Money has been made anonymous, compulsory and universal. Therefore giving from your supply is the same as issuing. Everyone in the society is responsible for performing services when called on to honor and maintain the value of the money. Recall my list of people whose picture is on the money? Each is there because of their contribution to ensuring the future value of American money.

Can you survive without money? There is no free land on which you can hunt or pitch your tent. You will have to pay someone rent. Collective social debt was created when money was issued, and you have the debt even if you have none of the issued money.

When you give money for any purpose you become more of a debtor than you were. The person who receives it becomes a lender, and negotiates to "collect" the debt when using the money.

Though initially money might represent a definite amount of labor, it comes to be worth only what others will give for it. And though the original deed may have been a personal and reciprocal favor exchange, once converted to money it becomes anonymous and interchangeable, quite convenient but losing its personal flavor.

How you use money depends on how you feel about money, and also how you feel about debt and the temple, big man, community, and the scarce material or trading commodity used to create and maintain confidence. If you are squeamish about collecting debts, you probably won't drive a very hard bargain when buying a car. If you have little faith in your government, you probably won't try very hard to accumulate the money it backs. If you don't have very much money, you may behave as a debtor and avoid accumulating more money because you feel it would only go to pay your debts. And if you have a lot of money, you likely have people working for you who behave as if they were in your debt.

Whether you have a lot or a little money, the way you use it reflects your unique personality and values. But money itself is anonymous. It doesn't have your name on it, and when you turn it over to a money manager or a corporation or a government for the promise of a return, one of two things will happen. Either it will be squandered, or it will be used to generate the promised return by any means necessary without regard to your personal values. The only measures applied to this transaction are risk and return. No other aspect of your personality survives the exchange.

You can avoid this, of course, by investing in your brother's business and helping him run it. Then you are likely to have some say in matters. But by and large most investing is as anonymous as money. You don't know, and probably don't *want* to know, what tactics are used to achieve the returns. At one time if a company was using questionable tactics the shareholders might insist on change. But at the present most investors don't invest directly in companies. They invest in pension funds and mutual funds, which own 60% of the shares of corporations.

A mutual fund manager is not at liberty to decide to sacrifice returns in exchange for more ethical or prudent business practices. And so the owners of business, like money, are to a great degree anonymous, and sometimes businesses behave "as if" their only "value" were return on investment.

Money arises from reciprocal favors, which are granted anonymity for convenience of exchange, and supported with confidence building measures. This in turn gives rise to businesses whose purpose is to make reciprocal favors more efficient and extract value from them for investors. The degree to which these activities succeed in increasing the value and quality of human life and environment is as varied as humans themselves, with the pull of the dark anonymous side of money in constant tension with the cooperative reciprocation it represents.

One side effect of the anonymity of money and investing, and the lack of personal characteristics involved, is that it may become possible to mathematically analyze the behavior of money and investments using simplified assumptions. We turn our attention to this analysis in the next chapter.

Minimally Rational

Rational Investors & Rational Markets

The idea is that if investors make only rational choices, these can be easily quantified in a mathematical model and theorems proved about investor behavior, individually or aggregated as in markets. A quick internet search is liable to reveal that a crisp definition of "rational investor" is hard to come up with.

Yet most of modern economic theory is either based on the idea of rationality, or is based in opposition to rationality under the heading of behavioral economics. Any extension of economic theory (such as this book) should specify from what it extends and how.

What a search might turn up is a discussion of different kinds or degrees of rational markets, and such a discussion might reference a 2001 paper by Mark Rubinstein, a long time financial economist at the University of California at Berkeley. His paper "Rational Markets: Yes or No? The Affirmative Case"[37] sums up the arguments he developed for a 1999 debate on the rational vs. behavioral view, and it is freely available online. It is a broad commentary touching intelligently on many of the ideas one will encounter in modern economics. Rubinstein defines three possible degrees of market rationality:

1. **Maximally Rational** – All investors are rational
2. **Rational** – Asset prices are set as if investors are rational
3. **Minimally Rational** – Markets are not rational but fail to supply opportunities for abnormal profits

Rubinstein observes that most economic *models* are based on maximal rationality, that is the rationality of individual investors. Surprisingly he dismisses this, saying economists "need only talk to their spouses or to their brokers to know it cannot be true." He makes no further comment on the implications of basing models and theory on a false premise.

The comments about choice #2 are not definitive and Rubinstein does not elaborate further. Instead he chooses in the remainder of the paper to defend minimal rationality, choice #3. He discusses and gives possible explanations for several supposed anomalies, including excess volatility, the equity premium puzzle which he significantly calls the *risk-premium puzzle*, the value vs. growth and size puzzles, closed-end fund

---

[37] Rubenstein, M., "Rational Markets: Yes or No? The Affirmative Case," Financial Analysts Journal, vol. 57 no. 3, May/June 2001.

discounts, calendar effects, and the 1987 market crash. For the most part, his comments are an excellent tutorial on how to think clearly and are worth a brief summary.

Volatility

"Asset prices vary far too much with respect to fundamentals," Rubinstein explains, citing Shiller[38] as the leading proponent of this puzzle. Shiller won the 2013 Nobel Prize along with two others holding conflicting views – more about that later. Then he gives a plausible explanation. It is due to changes in beliefs about the prices other investors are willing to pay.

I've tried to use that idea several times in economics since it is very familiar to me, having cut my logical teeth so to speak on Gödel Undecidability and Touring's Halting Problem, both of which use self-examining propositions to create interesting paradoxes. Certainly it has some role in the effect traders have on short-term price movements. Trading is not something we consider in this book. It is a zero sum short-term game, and the equity premium and its positive sum profits are a long-term proposition. Other possible explanations for both long and short-term volatility will emerge from our investigations.

Anomalies

Rubinstein rebuts several anomalies that are often cited as evidence or even proof that markets are inefficient and investors are irrational. The equity premium is one of these. Some have better explanations than others. All have points in common, along with differences.

Risk-Premium Puzzle

Misnaming the equity premium puzzle, Rubinstein equates it with the volatility puzzle. But economists generally agree the puzzle has not been solved with such thinking, and Rubinstein gives away that he has not carefully read the 1985 Mehra and Prescott paper, which clearly analyzes equity and bond volatility and determines the greatest reasonable risk premium to be less than 1%.

The name of the puzzle might be more clearly stated as regarding the *equity returns in excess of a risk-premium puzzle*. But to state it that way offends the assumptions of many economists that there can be no kind of difference in returns except based on risk.

Rubinstein correctly points out that the US market during the 20th century was the best performing market in the world. He then suggests the

---

[38] Shiller, R. 1981. "Do Stock Prices Move Too Much to Be Justified by Subsequent Changes in Dividends?" *American Economic Review*, vol. 71, no. 3 (July):421–436.

appearance of a premium for stocks in such a market could be accidental, an artifact of selection bias, or as he calls it survivorship bias (not quite correct usage). Excess return (of stocks over bonds) of *867%* over a century seems like quite a fluke if that's what it is. There might be more to it. Even if it is a fluke, the fluke might be in some other conditions that led to such excess returns, because a century is plenty of time for investors to figure out what is happening and equalize the returns of stocks and bonds.

Book-to-Market, Value vs. Growth, Size
Rubinstein continues with credible and clever explanations of these puzzles. Perhaps more clever than accurate.

Closed-End Fund Discounts
The trading value of a close-end fund is not explicitly linked to the sum of the values of the assets the fund holds. And they famously trade below their fair value according to the sum of the asset values. This is interesting for our purpose just to note the strange arithmetic that can occur with portfolios, for a closed-end fund is a kind of portfolio. Usually it is a proprietary selection of companies, and not an index or similar broad based portfolio. I would point out that the under-performance of actively managed portfolios is well-known, and that this rationally justifies the lower price for closed-end funds.

In fact, the only thing that saves an ordinary mutual fund from this fate is that it promises to liquidate or add to its position daily to account for sales or purchases, and these have to be done through the fund. In other words, there really is no market for mutual fund shares. You must sell to the fund and buy from the fund and the price is artificially set equal to the sum of asset values, less a trading commission. Exchange traded funds (ETFs) use a more complex and computerized scheme allowing them to be traded on open markets, but the computers effectively arbitrage any notable price differences so that large discrepancies in fund value vs. net asset value are minimized.

Calendar Effects
The one Rubinstein discusses is the Monday effect, which disappeared in 1987, convenient to his argument. But I do not dispute this argument. Many calendar effects have been known to disappear when discovered, exactly as efficient market theory says they should.

The 1987 Crash
Rubinstein repeats his volatility theory, more or less, using other words attributing it to interactions among different types of investors.

The Prime Directive

The most salient point Rubinstein makes is perhaps that it is "too easy" to come up with specific behavioral explanations of anomalies. And to do so doesn't prove they are correct. So he advocates a "prime directive" which I'll quote:

> *Explain asset prices by rational models. Only if all attempts*
> *fail, resort to irrational investor behavior.*

It seems like a good plan.

The Use of Behavioral Economics

It would be easy to explain the equity premium by irrational investor behavior. That's not even a puzzle. One could just point to any wealthy person who refuses to even consider buying stocks, believing it is a rigged game. But for every one of those there is someone who believes they can get rich quick with stocks. So it is not a quantitative theory.

Lest one might think I am implying the wealthy investor is simply risk averse, I hasten to add the same investor may be willing to sink millions into new or small business ventures which have a well-known failure rate of 80% within five years. Risk alone obviously does not explain individual investor choices.

Rubinstein would say that it only matters that on average for the entire community of investors risk explains investor choices (the minimally rational market). What is the use of models of individual rational investors – models which lead to predictions that trading volumes should be very low, for example – if one concedes that they are not accurate? No one has proved a theorem, after all, that maximally and minimally rational markets are equivalent in all important respects. Certainly they are not with respect to trading volume, and if one is engineering a trading website and inferring size parameters from rational investor models, the results will be worse than disappointing. However, rational does not mean identical, and economists are having some luck tweaking the models with preferences of different types.

So what is the use of behavioral economics? My opinion here is strictly personal. I have found it useful in gaining confidence once I have identified a workable investment strategy. Behavioral finance's best advice is to keep calm and execute your plan. Many investors will sell out of fear of loss when they should hold or buy, and buy out of greed (or fear of missed profits) when they should hold or sell. But it is no help in formulating or validating a plan. One leading behaviorist exhorts readers to hold in the face of fear and not trade so much, and a few chapters later advises that most investors hold too long and fail to sell when the market changes and an investment begins to decline. But there is no guidance as to how to distinguish these practically identical situations.

Performance of Individual Investors

The investor performance topic is here because it came up in the context of discussing behavioral economics. I was going to cite some study of how badly individual investors do, but it didn't work out!

The truth is, it depends on who did the study or who cites the study. Very comprehensive studies vary all over the place. Not being an expert on study methodology I cannot state precisely why. But I can state confidently that most authors will simply cite the study that supports their point and not mention the others. It is only by accident that I did not do the same. I could not find the reference I was looking for in which individual accounts did poorly, returning about 1% to 2% over long periods when the market at large returned 7% to 8%.

Had I found it I would have mistakenly stopped there because it supports the thesis of the equity premium, that there are excess returns to be had from market-representative portfolios held for long periods. I'm sure I found it in some literature on either the equity premium or index investing generally. The closest I can find now is a study by DALBAR[39] reported in Moneylife[40] stating that over the 20 years ending December 2011, the average investor in US equity mutual funds realized just a 3.5% annual return, while the S&P 500 index returned 7.8%. DALBAR is a financial services marketing research firm. Their customers provide financial services, and can use such data to entice customers who would otherwise manage their own money.

Contrast that with an academic paper by Ivkovic[41] showing that individual investors with portfolios concentrated in a few stocks, mostly small stocks not even listed in the S&P 500, and annual trading turnovers of 80%, did better than the market! Performance by category is even more intriguing:

---

[39] http://www.dalbar.com/News/DALBARintheNews/tabid/163/Default.aspx

[40] http://www.moneylife.in/article/why-people-lose-money-in-mutual-funds/30231.html

[41] Ivkovic, Z., Sialm, C., Weisbenner, S., "Portfolio Concentration and the Performance of Individual Investors," Journal of Financial and Quantitative Analysis, vol. 43, no. 3, Sept. 2008, pp. 613-656.
http://business.illinois.edu/weisbenn/RESEARCH/PAPERS/JFQA_Concentration_Sept2008_613-656.pdf

Investor performance in the year following purchase
Ivkovic et. al. 2008

Portfolio type	Portfolio size	Outperformance of market benchmark
Diversified	Any	-1% to -2%
Concentrated	0 to $25k	-1% to -2%
Concentrated	$25k to $100k	+1.3%
Concentrated	Over $100k	+2.2%

It is the opposite of what any portfolio theorist or efficient market theorist would expect. Notice also that the "rich get richer" effect shows up here. At first glance this might seem to contradict the idea presented in the first chapter on Portfolio Logic that the rich are able to invest more broadly and capture the statistically unusual cases, the upper branches of the binomial money tree. However there is really not sufficient data to support that conclusion. The larger portfolios, after all, can sustain losses and keep going more easily, and capture more of the exceptional cases over time. Just because they can, doesn't prove that is what's happening either, of course.

But I have seen over and over in my own investing that larger portfolios do better. Really large portfolios do a lot better. I have two retirement accounts in about the same range. The smaller one does poorly. The one that is about two times larger does well, perhaps because it is invested in a broad index. Before consolidation into the index fund its performance was mediocre, but in no case was it invested in individual small companies as in the concentrated portfolios examined by Ivkovic. I have two regular taxable accounts (for redundancy, actually, in case there is a problem with one broker). One is smaller and concentrated, and does not do quite as well. The main account, several times larger, and it has been doing very well for about 20 years, even though I have used various strategies from broad to concentrated. It fully recovered from more than a 40% loss in 2009 by late 2010. The two smaller portfolios with individual stocks (one IRA and one regular) still have not recovered. But the index fund has. One thing I find is that I cull only my best ideas from the large portfolio for use in the smaller one, and often it is my second best ideas that do well.

I've tried smaller accounts, less than $25k, for my wife and my sister (a joint account), again using my best ideas, severely culled to about 5 stocks. These have been able to generate dividends, but the capital value is always in the loss column. So I have developed a conviction, at least for myself, regarding portfolio size, but the verdict is still out on explanation.

How to reconcile this with Ivkovic? Ivkovic was studying short-term trading, and limited his evaluation to the first year – probably relevant for him given the 80% turnover. In early 2009 I tried day trading after studying it for a while. I was trading only on the up side, while the market was decidedly biased downward during early 2009. Without any special knowledge, just following trends and charts, I made money.

I hasten to point out that my average profits over about two months were only about 10% at best of the volatility in my daily earnings. In other words, I might be up $10k one day and down $20k the next. But by the end of two months I was something like $2k ahead, and this figure had been steadily increasing as long as I averaged over at least weekly intervals. That meant I was making about $250 a week, after transaction costs, which were not large. I was trading amounts of $100k to $200k. Had I kept this up for a year, if you are following the numbers, I would be making 1.5% annually – remarkable in a severely down market, but not worth the trouble. I could simply work at my day job and make about that much in a day, with little risk. I have known people who made much larger sums, usually either with special insight into foreign markets, or by locking themselves in the house during market hours and trading only during up markets.

The better performance of investors with special insight is consistent with Ivkovic. That is the thesis of his paper.

I switched back to longer term investing, and as usual, I noticed my timing was not good when I was not sitting in front of the monitor absorbed in trading. Initial investments would often decline. This is also consistent with Ivkovic's results, that diversified individuals experienced declines in the first year. I began to anticipate this. Initially I would purchase no more than half what I eventually planned to hold, and purchase the rest after it went down. But only once. To do this repeatedly can result in chasing a bad stock all the way to bankruptcy, as I did with a couple of airlines and two mortgage companies. But even with such mistakes, the long-term winners over two to three years dominated portfolio performance.

Since the time frame is different – within one year for Ivkovic vs. 2 to 3 years for me, there is not really any conflict in the two outcomes. It shows how tricky it can be to interpret and compare different studies.

The two results also show the first glimpse of a point that will be important later. The short-term performance of a portfolio or strategy may be very different than its long-term performance. The performance of a long-term portfolio is poor at first and better over time. This is the same as the characteristic of the equity premium. There is no premium over 2 to 3 years. But at 20+ years there usually is. Understanding the arithmetic of how this can be – it doesn't seem logical – may be more important than theories about investor behavior and markets, rational or irrational. You have to know what arithmetical properties you are dealing with, and this is the second time we have seen that returns don't add up. In the first chapter, the returns of a diversified portfolio were greater than the median return of the individual assets. Now we see that the sum of many short-term returns is, apparently, greater than the individual terms. But we don't yet have an arithmetical explanation.

Earlier we called these curiosities of arithmetic *non-linearities*. In a linear system, the value of A and B together is just A + B. Most of economics is based on linear theory. If there are non-linearities, then the rational market hypothesis may be usable, but may lead to different conclusions than expected in linear theory. Many physical systems are linear within certain operating regions, but non-linear over wider ranges. The equity premium considers a long time span, i.e. a wide range.

Sustainable and Unsustainable

To understand how the economy behaves over long periods, to produce something like the equity premium, we look at how things behave in *equilibrium*. This does not mean in a stationary state at all. It just means we ignore short-term ups and downs. In some ways it makes analysis simpler.

Suppose you think you see a trend that something like housing prices are going up and you want to know if it is sustainable, or if it is just a transient that will not last (unsustainable). Ask yourself what will happen if the trend continues to ridiculous extremes. Would the forces powering the trend still be in place?

In the 1970s I purchased a house because prices were going up so fast I thought I'd never own a home if I didn't get one right then. Within 18 months prices were 40% higher. Within a decade they were 150% higher, but notice that is a much lower rate per annum. The very rapid price increases were not sustainable. The value of that house peaked at about 300% above what I paid after 30 years and then actually began to slowly decline. Today it is about 200% over what I paid, which works out to a 2.7% per year increase. According to an online inflation calculator[42] the current value of my house is 41% *less* than inflation over the same period. This is not entirely attributable to the housing crisis of 2008-9 which is at least partly recovered. Even at the peak prices, the house had done no better than inflation.

---

[42] http://inflationdata.com/Inflation/Inflation_Calculators/Inflation_Calculator.asp

Inflation adjusted US Home Prices 1975-2012[43]

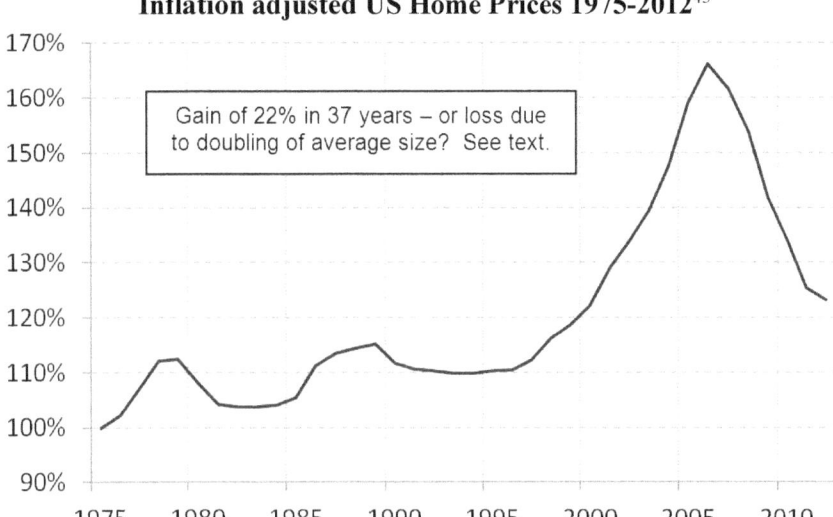

Gain of 22% in 37 years – or loss due to doubling of average size? See text.

But the average home size in 1970 was 1400 square feet, increasing to 2700 square feet in 2009[44], so in reality price per square foot fell!

Generally it is not sustainable for the price of anything people buy and use every day to go up, relative to other items, without limit or for a very long time. People simply wouldn't have the money to buy it, and demand would drop. In 2007-8 it looked like the price of gasoline was going over $5/gallon in the US and would keep going up. In the short-term people had to have it to get to work. But over a few years, people lost their jobs or moved or got more efficient vehicles, and quit buying gas. The price at this writing has again dropped to under $3 in many places and is still falling.

The only way a price can go up indefinitely is if it becomes a collectable item, and no one is actually using it any more. At that point, it isn't really a factor in the economy.

But some trends can be sustained indefinitely. How, you might ask. One simple way is if membership in the trending class keeps changing. For example, suppose there is a trend for small companies to increase in value faster than large companies. At times this has been a fact, and at times it seemed not so, and economists have wondered if it will continue. I don't know if it will, but it certainly can. If small companies

[43] St. Louis Fed http://research.stlouisfed.org/fred2/series/USSTHPI/
[44] Natl. Assoc. of Homebuilders via http://www.infoplease.com/askeds/us-home-size.html

grow faster, they become large companies. At that point if they grow more slowly, it counts against large companies not small companies.

Another way trends can continue is if something (e.g. money) is extracted or added to balance the trend. For example, value companies vs. growth companies. Value companies often pay dividends. If they pay enough dividends that they do not grow, value companies can provide higher returns indefinitely. Not that they will. But there is no law of math or physics preventing it.

A growth company cannot provide superior returns (compared to all other companies and compared to inflation) forever. If it did, it would become so large that by comparison the rest of the economy would not exist, and there would be no one for them to sell to.

However, it is possible that growth companies generally could provide superior returns. Not that they will, but here is how it is possible. Membership in the set "growth companies" can change. When a company gets very large, it can grow more slowly and begin to declare a dividend. At that point investors treat it as a value company, so its slower growth does not count against growth companies.

You the astute reader may wish to point out that it is not fair accounting to remove a particular growth company from the set of all growth companies until the final drop in share price associated with the transition is subtracted, and that in this case it seems like it is not sustainable that growth companies can grow forever by the trick of rotating membership in the portfolio, or set or growth companies. Feel free to do some figuring. You may be surprised. In the chapter on perpetual portfolios I will show you.

Is gold a useful commodity that cannot rise indefinitely, or a collectable that can? It has some uses, but it is also heavily collected, including by governments. So its history is some of both. Prior to 1980 it was rising faster than inflation. Since then it declined for many years, and has recently come back up to 1980 levels when adjusted for inflation.[45]

The same website from which I got the gold data also has a chart of the inflation adjusted US Real Estate Index confirming that my home value experience was pretty typical. There has been little change in home values when inflation adjusted, except for a recent spike, now retracted, corresponding to the late 2000's housing bubble.[46]

Returning to the example of the value companies that pay dividends, if you use these dividends to buy more shares of value companies, can you keep growing your net worth faster than average (assuming value companies are returning more than average)?

---

[45] http://www.aboutinflation.com/gold-vs-inflation
[46] http://www.aboutinflation.com/Home

For a long while, I suppose you can. But it does not leave the rest of the economy unchanged, and can't go on forever. It isn't that the companies are growing. It is that your share of ownership is growing. While *you* can do this, all investors *cannot*, because if your share of ownership is increasing someone else's share must be decreasing. If you live long enough you will eventually own everything, but no one will be able to buy it from you and you will have to settle for the dividends.

Efficient Markets and Equalization Revisited

Equalization, or the lack of it, is so central to the equity premium puzzle that we will discuss it several times with increasing degrees of understanding, and look at it from different angles. Economists believe that if investors are rational, they will not ignore opportunities to make more money. The consequence of this is that markets should be efficient, or at least approximately so. There should not be obvious opportunities lying around to make a greater return than the market average, regardless of what all those get rich quick flyers claim that you've been getting in the mail since you opened your brokerage account.

You will find in economic literature a great deal of discussion of efficient markets in terms of information. There was a scandal recently about a Federal Reserve announcement being made available to certain parties a few thousandths of a second before the public. While no one can read an announcement that fast, there was concern that computers may have been employed to scan the announcement, looking for keywords or perhaps doing artificial intelligence analysis, and automatically placing trades in index funds to benefit from the announcement.

It is actually debatable how much of an advantage the Fed announcement is, but trading firms who are able to get bid and offer prices microseconds ahead of the rest of us do gain an advantage. They can run in front of our trades scooping up the shares we were about to buy and selling them to us for a fraction of a penny more. Multiplied by large volumes this can be big money. Uneven distribution of information can be a market inefficiency that can be exploited for profit.

In most cases, though, it is not necessary for everyone to have all information for markets to be very efficient. The word "efficient" does not mean that market prices are correct in some absolute sense. It just means they are not predictable. You might think a company is undervalued, but the market might never recognize that. So you could not make any money from it. And most likely no information is available to you that is not also available to others.

Often you will find that there is a difference of opinion. One commentator or analyst will write about the poor prospects for a company, and another will write that while the information of the first analyst may be true, the price has already been lowered too much and is now likely to rise. Because information is already reflected in the price, and you are not sure to what extent it is reflected, and because the future is inherently uncertain, the future direction of share prices in the short-term is very uncertain. In fact the future of the company itself may be widely known, but if this is already priced in, the future price direction of its stock is uncertain.

As a practical matter, this means that no one should be able to enjoy a higher return and eventually wind up owning the whole world as in the example in the last section. Some other investors would notice, and begin asking more for their shares, to the point it was no longer worth your while to buy them.

Let's start with a simple example. A bank savings account is paying 4%, and a very large and stable company with a good future is offering bonds that will pay a coupon of $4 per year. What is a fair price for the bonds?

Assuming the big company is about as reliable as the bank (a bit of an oversimplification if the bank is insured), you should have said $100, because $4 is 4% of $100, and that would make the bond equally profitable as the bank account. The bond return has been equalized with comparable risk returns from bank accounts if its price is $100.

Risky Business

Interest Rate Risk and Discounting

Continuing with our example of a bank account vs. a $4 coupon bond, suppose next year the bank is only paying 2%. Actually, at the moment they are paying less than that, though 4% was common in the mid-2000's. When you try to sell this bond, what will you be offered for it? Assume it is a very long-term bond so that the termination date is so far in the future you don't care. Then to equalize with the now-current interest rates, you will be able to sell the bond for only about $50. You have just taken a large capital loss, -50%, on a bond from a very safe company. In fact, the stock in that company is probably doing a lot better than the bond, because low interest rates may allow consumers to finance purchases, and businesses to finance production.

Fortunately, the bond won't go down that much. If the maturity date is 10 years away, then over that 10 years only $40 in interest will be paid. Then the principle of $100 will be returned, and this principle is not a function of interest rates. However its present value is. The net present value, or NPV, of a future payment is the amount of money that would have to be invested today, at a comparable risk, to obtain that payment in the future. Well if the interest rate is now 2%, then some amount $X plus ten years of compound interest at 2%, will produce the final payment of $100. The trick is to find X. We can write:

$$X \times 1.02^{10} = \$100$$
$$X = \$100 / 1.02^{10} = \$100 / 1.219 = \$82.03$$

You can use the x^y key on the scientific version of a computer calculator to figure 1.02 raised to the 10th power. So the bond will be worth more than $82, the discounted value of the final return of principle, because in addition there are ten interest payments at $4 per year. The nearest one is worth almost the full $4, and the final one is worth $4 / 1.219 = $3.28 (same discount as the principal), so the interest payments in total are worth something like $36.40 discounted to the present day. Add that to the principle and the bond is worth $118.43. So if the bond maturity is not infinitely far away it may increase rather than decrease in value as interest rates go down, because the discount rate, which is generally taken to be the interest rate, is so much lower. It doesn't get discounted very much, and it still has the rather high interest (coupon) payments from prevailing conditions when it was issued.

Minimally Rational

We just went through the process of equalizing the bond through the mechanism of its price. The amount $118 for the old 4% bond with maturity still 10 years away produces an equivalent result to new $100 bonds being issued for 10 years at 2%. Other than a slight shift in when the money is paid back, there is no difference. In the long run, an investor should do no better or worse with one than the other.

What if interest rates do not remain at 2%? Well, then the bond is not really worth that amount, but without knowledge of the future interest rates, you don't know what it will be worth. This is interest rate risk. The closer the maturity date the less difference this will make, which is why money market funds buy only bonds with maturity dates days or weeks away, or even just one day.

The bank account does not have any interest rate risk. True, the amount of interest you collect will vary, but you can always withdraw your $100 and invest it somewhere else. The value of the principle will not go up or down as rates change.

In theory, stocks should be equalized in the same way. There should be a small premium for stocks due to their uncertainty. Mehra and Prescott figured no more than 1%, because while stocks are certainly volatile (variable in price), we have seen how easily bonds can have 18% volatility, and for longer term bonds it would have been higher and negative. The equity premium *puzzle* is why stocks should return 7 to 8% more than bonds, instead of the 1% that seems justified.

Bankruptcy Risk

Investment grade bonds have a very low bankruptcy rate, of the order of a tenth of a percent per annum. It is very straightforward to account for this in the same way we did with the chicken economy in chapter 2. We just add a tenth of a percent to the interest rate we ask bond issuers to provide, and it's covered.

Do investors really behave this way? So-called junk bonds have bankruptcy rates closer to 4%. Historically the rates of interest they yielded have run around 8% when investment bonds were yielding 4%. It seems a straightforward addition of the bankruptcy rate to the low risk rate, provided the bankruptcy rate is reliably known.

At present junk bonds are yielding closer to 6% (this may be entirely different by the time you are reading these pages, of course). That could mean one, some or all of the following:

- Investors think future bankruptcy rates will be lower
- Investors think investment grade bond rates will decline
- There is a bubble in junk bonds, i.e. investors are wrong

The point is, many common types of risk are not very mysterious and it doesn't take complicated math to effectively account for them.

For the last several hundred years, scientific statistics has used a *frequentist* approach. Take a representative sample and count the number of times per thousand (the frequency) that something happened. This works very well when you have a representative sample, such as for bankruptcy rates.

It does not work so well when you are wondering whether there will be a war or whether the Fed will contain inflation or whether consumers will start buying again. Recently an older method called *Bayesian* has been gaining in popularity, but it requires an initial guess which is hard to make scientifically. So it doesn't help if the original problem was guessing about the future.

Savage Statistics

Did you notice that we never did exactly specify what rational investor behavior is?

If you dug around on the internet, you might have found that it is based on the theory of *subjective expected utility* for which one of the most imminent developments is given by L. J. Savage in a 1954 book, *The Foundations of Statistics*.[47] And if you try to buy a copy you will find there is an expanded and revised Dover edition published in 1972, in whose preface you will find these remarks:

> *Today, as I see it, the theory of personal probability applied to statistics shows that many of the prominent frequentistic devices can at best lead to accidental and approximate, not systematic and cogent, success . . . Among the ill-founded frequentistic devices are minmax rules, almost all tail-area tests, tolerance intervals, and, in a sort of class by itself, fiducial probability.*

Savage goes on to admit that he has become something of a Bayesian, diverging from the unquestioned frequentist methods of the first edition.

The preface to the first edition is also interesting, as we find this unusually candid author stating:

> *A book about so controversial a subject as the foundations of statistics . . . cannot be a textbook, or manual of instruction, stating the accepted facts about its subject, for there scarcely are any. . . . it must, even more than other books, be an airing of its author's current opinions.*

---

[47] Savage, L. J., *The Foundations of Statistics*, John Wiley & Sons, NY 1954.

. . . Finally, he fears that he himself, and still more such public as he has, will forget that the book is tentative, that an author's most recent word need not be his last word.

The book begins with *Postulates of a personalistic theory of decision.* Well indeed, that does sound like it could be a basis for some kind of rational investor. It is rather amazing, though, to find that the purveyor of this theory viewed it so tentatively, has so accurately forecast that practitioners in another field (whom he refers to as readers) will "forget that the book is tentative."

I have never heard the word "Bayesian" mentioned by an economist. Not that I think Bayesian solves anything, but it's just interesting how prescient Savage was, and how thoroughly unaware economists seem of how the theory of the rational investor is built upon what its architect considered sand. Economists are fond of wagers. I would bet almost any amount that very few have read Savage, either edition, and almost none have read the tentative words in the preface.

Subjective Expected Utility

Rather than get lost in this subject, I'll try to briefly paraphrase and explain a rather ecliptic Wikipedia article on subjective expected utility.[48]

- You believe an uncertain event has possible outcomes *A, B,* etc. (the Wiki article uses a set-vector notation $\{x_i\}$) – for example, heads and tails.
- Each outcome has a utility to you which is personal, and you write this as a numerical function *u(A), u(B),* etc. – perhaps heads you win tails you lose. We will assign utility numbers later.
- Your choices can be explained by assuming you believe there is a *subjective* probability *P(A), P(B),* etc. for each outcome. For example 50% heads or tails (in this case not too subjective, but you can see that if it were regarding stocks going up and down it would be very subjective).
- Your *subjective expected utility* (SEU) is the *expected value* function, which is the sum of the utilities of each outcome times its probability, like this:

$$SEU = u(A)P(A) + u(B)P(B) + etc.$$

- You may be able to make a *decision* which changes the outcomes to something else – maybe you decide to bet on the coin toss, or not. Or to choose a particular investment.

---

[48] http://en.wikipedia.org/wiki/Subjective_expected_utility

- Which *decision* you prefer depends on which subjective expected utility is greater.

(Notice that the SEU function is *linear*. The utilities *u(..)* are constants you choose. But we know outcomes may not be.)

People may make different decisions because:

1. Their estimates of probabilities differ
2. Their utility functions differ

There is a little note at the bottom of the article that "*Experiments have shown that many individuals do not behave in a manner consistent with expected utility.*" Examples include such things as the preference among three choices depending on the order in which they are presented. In most cases I can manage to make sense of most any situation by choosing carefully the correct utility functions. But in economic models, there is often only one set of utility functions (homogeneous models) so there is no personalization at all, and at most there are two or three sets. Economists would prefer all rational investors behave identically, or at least in a meaningful average way.

Example – roulette in your favor

It's useful to work out an example. Suppose your net worth is $100,000, and an old college buddy who is very successful invites you to her private island for the weekend and the entertainment is gambling. The friend wants you to have a good time and offers to give you the house cut with any bet. So on roulette, betting on the red or black, you also get the green, the 0 and 00 belonging to the house. This makes your odds on any particular bet 20/38 = 52.6%. Not bad. The house limit is one million dollars per spin and you can play for one hour with unlimited credit. Your host assures you the wheel is honest, and she has always been reliable in the past. How much will you bet?

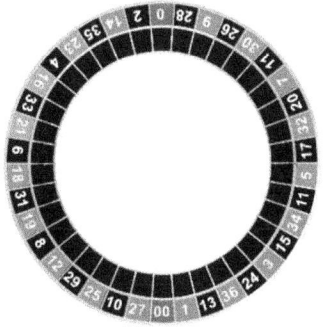

The bet is in your favor. What should you do? Will you limit your losses to your net worth? Some fraction of your net worth? Will you take a chance of losing more than your net worth?

According to Savage, it depends on your utility functions, and your probability estimates. But it depends on your *subjective* probability estimates, and I have given you something to think about. What is it?

It is not the probability of winning against an honest wheel. That is 52.6% on each spin. What are the subjective probabilities here?

What is the probability your host is telling the truth that the wheel is honest? *That* you must estimate. You have no prior data points, at least not of this magnitude, only some college drinking parties. Your host never did anything underhanded *that you know of.* You have to decide if anything else is fishy, maybe even a flaw the host doesn't know about.

And you have to estimate the probability and negative utility of losing more than you can pay. Will the host tear out your fingernails or torture your children? Or can you simply declare bankruptcy?

You also might want to make a quick calculation of the probability of being ahead or behind after some number of spins you can fit into an hour. Let's say 30 spins, allowing everyone time to place bets and a little showmanship. Few of us would know the exact odds and maybe not even immediately how to calculate them, so we might make a subjective estimate.

While you are thinking, let me propose a strategy for the sake of argument. Bet the full limit on every spin, and do not quit no matter how far behind you get.

Why? First, your net worth is probably similar to your annual earning power, maybe twice or half but close. If you lose it all, you can get it back. If you lose more, you can declare bankruptcy, because you don't think my friend is a mobster and you do think she does not want to go to jail. These are subjective probability estimates, and you can see how important they are.

That means there are no big negative utility functions. If there were, then you probably would sharply curtail your betting to avoid negative utility. More about strategy for this case in a minute.

Without big negative utility functions, you can pretty much just use the expected monetary value of the events, in place of the expected utility, and try to maximize your winnings. This becomes real simple. Since the odds are in your favor, bet the maximum allowed amount on each spin. Your expected winnings for the evening are something like:

$$30 \times (0.526 - 0.474) \times \$1,000,000 = \$1,560,000$$

Well, it seems there is a problem. An hour is not long enough. All might be going very well and you might be one or two spins (millions) ahead near the end of the hour. In the last two spins, there is a 24% chance they will both go against you. There is a 12% chance the last 3 spins will go against you. Since the odds are you will not be three million ahead by then, there is about a 1 in 8 chance you will have to declare bankruptcy.

Of course there is a similar chance you will walk away a multi-millionaire. Will you take it?

It's amazing how few spins it takes to completely change the outcome. This is the problem with short-term investing. If you could play all night, or all weekend, the odds would be overwhelmingly in your favor. One might ask then, when to quit? I think I would begin to consider quitting with a few hours left (if playing all night). If I got down to being only one million ahead with a couple of hours left, I would quit. No need to be greedy.

Notice one more thing about the probabilities in this example. This is not gambling. It is not a zero-sum game. The odds are in your favor. It is like investing.

The Impact of Personal Utility

Now let's go back to the case of negative utility functions. Suppose you are retired and your $100,000 net worth is all you have. If you lose it and go bankrupt, you are basically dead. It won't matter if your friend is a mobster or not. My suggestion would be for you to bet only $1000 mostly for fun, and quit if you get a couple of spins ahead. It's kind of like going to Vegas at that point. Even though the odds are slightly in your favor, the hour time limit is not long enough for you to be sure of getting the odds, and the price of losing is just too high.

This is the situation of many working class people. The time limit is imposed by their situation. They do not have investment capital they can part with for decades. Maybe they are saving for a child's college education, or an aunt's eye surgery, and need the money within two years. If the market goes down 20% this year and is flat next year, the planned expenses may not be covered. Even ten years is a marginal time limit. Investing is not the same as saving for planned expenses.

Sideways markets can easily last ten to fifteen years. The market went sideways basically from 1965 to 1982, and recently from 2000 to 2013. Investors got some dividends, but if they were holding companies that went out of business, were bought out at unfavorable prices, or if they had to sell to cover personal expenses, they had capital losses.

Dow Jones 30 Industrials (DJIA) 1896-2013[49]

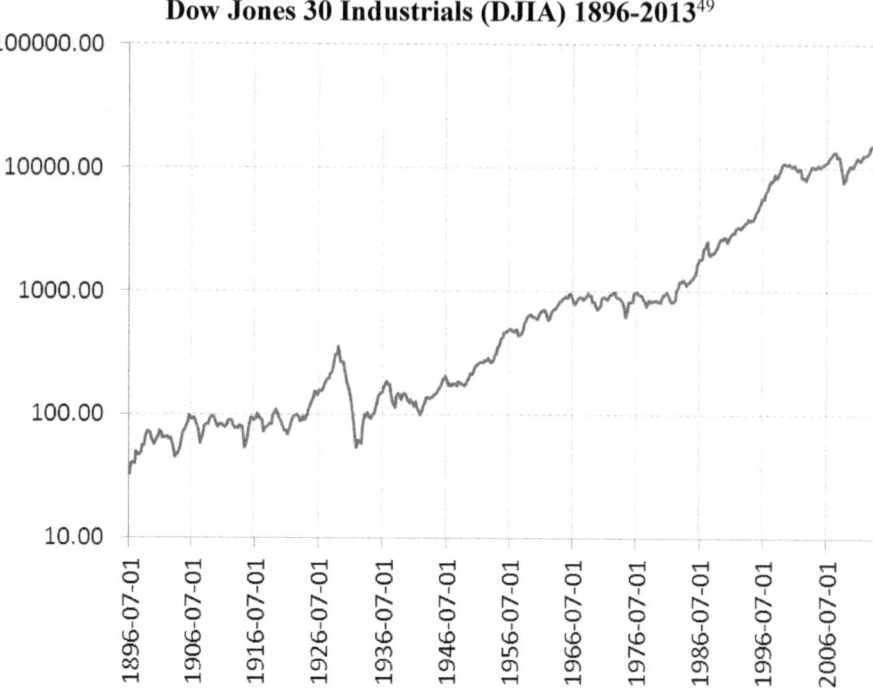

But I do not suggest doing nothing even in the case with large negative utilities lurking about. In the case of the hypothetical roulette game, bet $1000 and choose when to quit. In the case of the working class family, skip a vacation and put the money in an index fund and leave it to your children in your will. Many emotional characteristics are developed by such an exercise, such as dealing with overconfidence that comes after winning and panic that sets in with losing. It isn't easy to trust a random process. Maybe by seeing you do this, your children will decide to do a little more of it and at each generation the amount will increase, and one of your grandchildren will become a wealthy investor.

In the case of our friendly roulette game with the unusual odds, at the end of the evening your host says, "You did very well. I've been looking for someone I trust to manage my investments. Would you like the job?"

"Of course," you say. "But only if I can occasionally use the island." You don't want to appear too eager and give away all your cards. It would not be rational.

---

[49] Data from St. Louis Fed,
http://research.stlouisfed.org/fred2/series/DJIA/downloaddata

Weaknesses of Bayesian and Frequentist Methods

Using the common frequentist methods one cannot see the future. If examining a physical or biological process with repeatable behavior, the past is usually a good guide to the future. The exception is looking for rare correlations or events. If one looks at cross correlations with enough data, the probability of finding something by accident increases. For example, if one does thousands of experiments correlating whether different substances are associated with increases in cancer rates (or market returns), a certain number of positives will be due only to chance. If the study is simply repeated, the positive will disappear. (Calendar returns?)

So it is easy to look at financial data with respect to many different strategies, and some of them in retrospect will appear to have worked. But as financial advisors are quick to say, past performance is no guarantee of future results.

It is even possible to make this error when only looking at the future. First adopt several strategies, and set up a separate brokerage account for each. After a few years, pick the one that does best and write a book about it, or start a newsletter! But you will need to make your money from selling the newsletter because the strategy was probably just chance.

In this respect, finance and investing are frustratingly different from most other life activities. If analyzing a sports team or player, or even a business (not the stock, just the business itself), there are normally factors that can be identified which indicate future success. Most of science and all of engineering is predicated on this. But not the economics of investing in financial markets. Rational investors in efficient markets will, according to the theory, adapt to any known prediction by adjusting prices to equalize returns, taking all of the advantage out of traditional study, research, preparation and planning. Perhaps even removing the advantage of being smart? We will see.

A second weakness of frequentism, even when applied to deterministic processes, is that the past data may not be long enough or broad enough to include some rare event, such as a big market crash. Prior to 2008 most market models did not include depression era data, so these models did not estimate a fair probability of a highly correlated downturn in almost all investments.

It might be useful to some to digress briefly into the reason for correlated downturns. Investors tend to use a lot of leverage, or borrowed money. When such an investment declines dramatically, funds have to be withdrawn from good investments to cover the borrowed amount. So when a crisis reaches critical mass, the holding of different equities by the same pool of investors provides sufficient correlation for all to decline. But frequentist methods can only predict this if they see it in past data.

In Bayesian methods, one starts with an estimate of a future probably, presumably subjective, and updates this probability with each new event. It shares then the flaw that it cannot predict events that are not in the data it has examined. Even if some estimate of rare events is included in the initial subjective estimate, it can be gradually lost through the updating process. When humans do this informally, it is called being lulled into complacency.

Bayesian methods are particularly blind to one special and important kind of data: rare events with logarithmic intensity and probability, such as earthquakes. And market crashes. When frequentist methods are used over limited time periods, perhaps justified saying that something has changed and the remote past is irrelevant, then frequentist methods are being used in a Bayesian manner, weighting more recent events and therefore having the same blind spots.

For those interested in further insight into using data to make predictions, and the characteristics that make it successful or otherwise, I recommend Nate Silver's *The Signal and the Noise*.[50] One of the key qualities Nate identifies is feedback. Weather forecasters, who've made more progress than most people realize, are constantly reminded of their failures, and have quite a good idea of how accurate their forecasts are or are not. However, each consolidator who handles and passes on the forecasts makes modifications.

In the financial arena, few are taken to task for poor predictions. There are analysts who are paid by the companies they cover, perpetual bears who have a following and are right like a stopped clock whenever whatever they are predicting happens to happen, and government officials who always predict mild recovery and growth as long as the current administration is re-elected. Nate suggests not listening to financial gurus at all.

Markowitz vs. the Market

I mention Markowitz[51] portfolios, sometimes called *modern portfolio theory*, simply because you will encounter the idea. It is very popular with financial service providers who want to claim they have a scientific method for beating the market. Anyone familiar with efficient markets should be suspicious, but Markowitz used the terminology of efficiency, claiming there was an "efficient frontier."

The basic idea is to have a portfolio of uncorrelated assets so that some of them would always be going up, and to make the selection based

[50] Penguin Press, 2012
[51] Harry Markowitz won the Nobel prize in 1990, see
http://en.wikipedia.org/wiki/Modern_portfolio_theory

on frequentist analysis of past data to optimize the return. In other words, to beat the market.

One has to wonder, if there is anything at all to efficient market theory and returns are equalized, how can the market return be different than the return of any individual equity selected at random?

In fact the market return is different and we will get into that in the next chapter. But is it better to use statistical methods based on a few years' data? Or to use a portfolio representative of the whole economy, to which the voters and the government are committed and which they will defend with their lives? This is the primary difference between a Markowitz portfolio, and the portfolio of chapter one that recognized we don't know which company will provide the outsized returns in the future.

If it were possible to select a non-market portfolio by any means and reliably provide higher returns, a mutual fund offering this strategy would stand out in the statistical data, and as far as I know none does.

A minimally rational efficient market might allow such a portfolio to be constructed once, but soon the price of it would be bid up, reducing the returns to normal levels. Or so the theory says.

The Nobel Prize for Risk

In 2013 the Nobel Prize in Economics was split between Fama, Shiller and Hansen, for work in efficient markets, identifying bubbles, and new statistical methods respectively. Identifying bubbles and efficient markets would seem to be at odds. If the market is even minimally efficient, one should not be able to identify a bubble. The Nobel committee explained that *risk* was at the root of the work of all three prize recipients.

The committee released a scientific background paper explaining the significance of the prizes, with the title "Understanding Asset Prices."[52] The introduction takes us back to personal decision theory:

> . . . *The choice between saving in the form of cash, bank deposits or stocks, or perhaps a single-family house, depends on what one thinks of the risks and returns associated with these different forms of saving. Asset prices are also of fundamental importance for the macro economy because they provide crucial information for key economic decisions regarding physical investments and consumption.*

---

[52] http://www.nobelprize.org/nobel_prizes/economic-sciences/laureates/2013/press.html

What they mean by "asset prices . . . provide crucial information" is that investment is directed by prices. If home prices rise, that indicates a shortage or increasing demand and more homes are built in response to the rising prices. Continuing the quote:

> While prices of financial assets often seem to reflect fundamental value, history provides striking examples to the contrary, in events commonly labeled bubbles and crashes. Mispricing of assets may contribute to financial crises and, as the recent recession illustrates, such crises can damage the overall economy.

In other words, it now appears the glut of homes built during the supposed housing bubble is not actually needed. The pricing information was misleading. One could say this does not seem very "efficient," if we had not already defined efficiency in a narrow way to mean that the market is said to be efficient if we cannot determine when it is inefficient. [sic] Again continuing:

> If it is possible to predict with a high degree of certainty that one asset will increase more in value than another one . . . such a situation would reflect a rather basic malfunctioning of the market mechanism.

There seems to be an attempt here to link the two kinds of efficiency. We should be able to recognize bubbles. If it is possible to predict them, then we can say the market is inefficient in the narrow sense. There is an implication that when this is generally known, rational investors will fix the problem and restore efficiency in both senses. Though, I am reading a lot into just one sentence.

> In practice, however, investments in assets involve risk, and predictability becomes a statistical concept. A particular asset-trading strategy may give a high return on average, but is it possible to infer excess returns from a limited set of historical data? Furthermore, a high average return might come at the cost of high risk, so predictability need not be a sign of market malfunction at all, but instead just a fair compensation for risk-taking. Hence, studies of asset prices necessarily involve studying risk and its determinants.

There is a brief mention of frequentist methods – the use of historical data – which we already discussed. You can see that there is no clue where to look beyond the past, and in fact this is what Hansen's work is all about.

The quote ends with an emphatic declaration that the only excuse that will be allowed for being able to predict returns, high or low but especially high, is risk. It is a Nobel Prize for Risk.

To Risk or Not to Risk

The Nobel write up goes on to say:

In the longer run, compensation for risk should play a more important role for returns, and predictability might reflect attitudes toward risk and variation in market risk over time. Consequently, the interpretations of findings of predictability need to be based on theories of the relationship between risk and asset prices.

So they won't give the prize to me unless my analysis is based on risk? Does this extend to journal referees? Where is the discussion of the reason that only risk is a basis for returns?

It is not to be found. But it is the written law of investment economics. In their original paper Mehra and Prescott said the explanation of the equity premium was likely to be friction, not risk, but this has been ignored. No wonder it took seven years for their paper to be accepted.

Savage imagined unspecified personal utility functions. In market theory this has become personal risk preferences. If an investor objects to child labor, doesn't want a high rise apartment building to block her view of the mountains, or factories to pollute the air, these are not considered. The presumption is that some other investor will not care, and such personal preferences will have little effect. Risk is assumed to be universal, though in fact humans vary widely in risk preferences, from gambling addicts to money in the mattress.

I could make the case that the equity premium is due to risk preferences. I have laid groundwork that you probably thought was going in that direction, with the discussion about how middle class families saving for near term objectives should probably not be playing the market. For a long, long time I tried to make that the solution. It does certainly play a role. But the role is surprisingly small.

A good example of non-risk preferences are the so-called sin-stocks, such as tobacco, casinos, etc. Can the returns from Philip Morris remain low indefinitely? What we find is that the price to earnings (P/E) ratio can remain low, or high, indefinitely, until a company is merged or goes out of business. But the returns are about the same. Only if the P/E ratio suddenly changes to some other level will excess profit be made. One could argue that dividend yields might lead to excess returns from underpriced stocks. But in practice, when management sees their dividend is too high for their stock price, sometimes they will cut it and provide no other reason than that it is out of line with stock price[53].

Over long periods the returns from Philip Morris will be determined by the growth in its earnings, irrespective of risk or investor sentiment or the morality of its business. Its *intrinsic returns* may well depend on features of human nature stronger than economic forces. Investors can give many rational reasons for not bidding up the price high enough to equalize these returns. The surprising truth is that no price is high enough to do that. Shortly we will see why.

Irrational Exuberance?

The write up goes on to explain that Fama et. al. showed "*the amount of short-run predictability in stock markets is very limited*," and observes that it is strange that they should be more predictable in the long-term. My own view is that in the long run investors and citizens and politicians take action to damp out ill effects of short-run events and keep their economy and nation on track. We will see later a surprising reason for short-run volatility.

In 1996 Shiller suggested to Alan Greenspan, then chairman of the Federal Reserve, that the market might be overvalued, with prices driven mostly by enthusiasm. Greenspan incorporated an obscure reference to *irrational exuberance* in a speech on December 6th of that year[54]. A short market pullback caused the comment to be noticed and remembered, but then the market resumed its heady climb never to again fall below those levels, neither in the dotcom bust nor the housing crash. Any short sellers attempting to profit from that bubble are surely ruined by now. And apparently unpredictability extends to 17 year periods or longer. At least, one would have to conclude that the 5 years from 1996 to 2001 was a *short-run* spell of unpredictability. And for all the greedy mistakes investors and bankers made leading up to 2008, ignoring Shiller's warnings about housing is the most easily understood.

The CAPM

One more piece of the Nobel write up is interesting. It introduces terminology you may hear:

---

[53] e.g. Diana Container Shipping (DCIX) midyear 2013

[54] Quotation: "Clearly, sustained low inflation implies less uncertainty about the future, and lower risk premiums imply higher prices of stocks and other earning assets. We can see that in the inverse relationship exhibited by price/earnings ratios and the rate of inflation in the past. But how do we know when **irrational exuberance** has unduly escalated asset values, which then become subject to unexpected and prolonged contractions as they have in Japan over the past decade?" source: http://en.wikipedia.org/wiki/Irrational_exuberance

A related issue is how to understand differences in returns across assets. Here, the classical Capital Asset Pricing Model (CAPM) – for which the 1990 prize was given to William Sharpe – for a long time provided a basic framework. It asserts that assets that correlate more strongly with the market as a whole carry more risk and thus require a higher return in compensation.

In other words, reversing the logic "require a higher return," the CAPM holds that risk is the only thing correlated with higher returns. It is known as a "single factor model." The write up goes on to summarize some additions that attempt to improve the CAPM, that is, some additional factors, mostly value company factors.

To a large extent I do agree. In fact I have written a paper on corporate risk compensation that seeks to demonstrate that when higher returns are present, corporations will act to increase risk, giving rise to an inevitable correlation. Something similar to this is already well-known for individuals. For example, accident rates, costs and even fatalities increase over time in no-fault insurance states, resulting in the gradual elimination of this once popular strategy that was supposed to save money by eliminating excess litigation.

So I dove into the equity premium assuming I would find a better explanation for risk preferences. I had done other work proving from an entirely different angle that risk was associated with excess returns. And the whole economics profession thinks this. But for many years no one has been able to satisfactorily explain the equity premium.

Measuring and Accounting for Risk

Consider the accounting for bankruptcy losses we discussed earlier. The loss rate, or perhaps the maximum expected loss rate, can simply be subtracted from the yield of loans or bonds to get the effective return. If a large number of uncorrelated bonds or loans are held, this will be very close to the actual total return. There is not much risk here. It has all been accounted.

It would seem then, assuming I am rational, that a fair return for such a loan or bond would be the risk-free rate plus the bankruptcy loss rate. But this is not a risk premium. It merely brings the average total return back up to the risk-free rate. If an investor were going to hold only one bond or loan, of course this might not be so attractive. But hardly anyone holds just one of these. A small investor should enter the market by way of mutual funds. What then is the justification for a risk premium? We already noted that with junk bonds, essentially there is no risk premium, just a bankruptcy rate adjustment.

Consider the hypothetical game of roulette, with a 52.6% chance of winning on each spin, and therefore a 47.4% chance of losing. This investment-like game (because it is positive sum rather than zero sum) has a per spin return of 52.6 − 47.4 = 5.2%. Like the loans and bonds, if you only take a few spins it's pretty risky. Or if you bet too much of your net worth you might be forced to quit by your own bankruptcy, and again it's risky. But if you play a long time it's a reliable return of 5.2%. Is it as good as a risk-free return of 5.2%?

Hardly. I can be certain of the risk-free return on every spin. It's like all the numbers are red and I just bet on red. I cannot go bankrupt. I can bet *all* my capital and not hold any back, with no risk.

How much do I have to hold back when I am betting on the risky version of the game, to be nearly risk free? We need to pick a number, say a 0.1% chance of bankruptcy? That happens to be about the bankruptcy rate of investment grade bonds yielding in the neighborhood of 4%. It is a 1/1000 chance. In other words, the probability of accumulated losses exceeding my net worth (or credit) should not exceed .001.

The chance of losing on each spin is .474. The chance of losing twice in a row is $.474^2 = .225$. I have to increase that accounting for the number of spins (a bit more complicated than just multiplying unless the probabilities are small), because any spin could start a losing streak. Using the previous number of 30 spins, what series of losses can I tolerate with my $100k net worth? (Figuring is approximate.)

$$.474^n \times 30 \leq .001$$

$$.474^n \leq .000033$$

$$n \leq 10$$

So I can tolerate up to 10 losses with an acceptable probability. I divide my net worth by 10, and find I can bet $10,000 per spin. My average gain is $520 per spin. After 30 spins I expect to have about $15000 extra, or a net worth of $115,000. Now I can tolerate 31 losses, so I can play 30 more times with about half as much risk. I can either let my risk go down, or slightly increase the amount I bet. If I'm going to play very long I better let the risk go down. Otherwise I will eventually log 30,000 spins and my probability of bankruptcy becomes very high.

If I had a risk-free investment I could bet ten times as much. Using the 4% bond number, I could make on average 4% times $100k or $4000 on each spin, nearly 8 times as much. The rate of return on the game to match that would have to be 41.6% per spin! *That is a risk premium.*

But if I can find 1000 uncorrelated wheels to play, then the risk goes back down and I can bet $100 on each wheel and employ my entire amount. So it's not clear a large risk premium is justified unless there are really limited ways to diversify. Bonds are not wholly uncorrelated with stocks – they are issued by the same companies, and have similar interest rate risks. So Mehra and Prescott determined the risk of equities was worth about 1%. To verify that, you'd have to read their paper and employ statistical methods that would make this book very dry reading. Many smart people have looked over their work and I think we can accept it.

At least you now have some idea when a risk premium is appropriate and why. If you invest in such a way that you can't go bankrupt and don't need the money right away, it is mostly the average return you care about, and any risk premium would be small. If you are saving for expenses in the next couple of years, put that money in a bank which is FDIC insured.

Zheng's Problem with the CAPM

I ran across a paper by Liping Zheng[55] surveying various difficulties with the CAPM, and modifications to the CAPM, including difficulties fitting actual data for various models that in theory could exhibit the required effects. In particular she mentioned that the equity premium sometimes goes negative for extended periods, and asserted that this cannot be explained by any risk preference model.

A few months went by before it dawned on me what this meant. No one by any stretch of the imagination over any time period less than 20 years can claim the stock market is less risky than bonds. So no one can claim that any model requiring higher returns for risky assets can explain prolonged lower returns for stocks than bonds.

That is the bottom line. Sure risk is important. But no risk model can entirely explain the equity premium if Zheng's assertion is true.

Equity Premium Solutions & Estimation

About 80 to 90% of proposed solutions to the equity premium puzzle involve various mathematical models of risk, usually based on slightly varying assumptions about risk preference. All these models make predictions and therein lies the trouble with them. It amounts to predicting returns. Anyone who has ever invested knows no math model can do that. The efficient market theory holds that no human or model can do that – and the idea of making an exception for "risk" does not bear up if you

---

[55] Zheng, L., "A Survey of the Empirical Difficulties of the Consumption Capital Asset Pricing Models," J. Mod. Econ. Manag., vol. 2, no. 1 (2013)
http://scik.org/index.php/jmem/article/view/665

think about it. And most of all it makes these models very easy to disprove. Just compare them to actual data, like Zheng did.

I recently found a paper by Victor Modungo, an actuary, surveying studies of past equity premiums and methods of estimating future premiums.[56] The first point Modungo makes is that:

> *arithmetic mean of historical returns produced estimates that were consistently too high ...*
>
> *geometric mean was a better estimator*

This is the same problem we encountered in the first chapter with the lopsided money tree, for which the arithmetical average return failed to predict compounding losses due to volatility, as assets moved up and down in price failed to return to their starting points even when moving equal percentages. We saw it again affecting the return of ultra-funds.

"Geometric mean" is not a self-explanatory term, but sometimes "compounded" is not logically usable. "Compounded" works well to describe the returns of a particular asset growing or declining as a percentage through time. In the case of the lopsided money tree we had four assets which took different paths through the same two year time period, with cumulative returns of .64 (-36%), .96 (-4%), another at .96 (-4%), and .144 (+44%) respectively. We can multiply the four together .64×.96×.96×1.44 = .8493 and take the fourth root .8493^.25 = .96 to find the geometric mean.[57]

"Arithmetic mean" indicates the average, calculated as the sum divided by the number of items. Another useful term is "median" which means the value which divides the group in half. In the case of the money tree example this was also .96 but it would not have to be. You have a 50-50 chance of being either better or worse off than the median.

Non-risk solutions to the equity premium include the following:[58]

11

- Selection bias. The US market is the most successful in history. True, but there is at least a 4% world equity premium.
- Survivorship bias. Stock exchanges go bust, such as Shanghai and Russia during communist takeovers. True, but the corresponding and comparable bond markets are just as risky, which was the essence of Mehra and Prescott's argument. Pre-1949 Chinese

[56] Victor Modugno, "Equity Risk Premiums," Society of Actuaries, Pension Section News, no. 80, May 2013. http://www.soa.org/News-and-Publications/Newsletters/Pension-Section-News/2013/may/Equity-Risk-Premiums.aspx

[57] https://en.wikipedia.org/wiki/Geometric_mean

[58] https://en.wikipedia.org/wiki/Equity_premium_puzzle

bond obligations amount to $1 trillion by some estimates,[59] none of which has been paid. Russia has paid pre-1917 British bondholders.[60] Recently Greek bondholders were asked to take a "haircut" but most Greek stocks survived.

- Demands for liquidity, which Bansal and Coleman call a "monetary" model.[61] Bonds are no more liquid than stocks.
- Tax distortions, differences in rates on dividends and interest and capital gains, but these have varied over time.
- Borrowing constraints. Young people can't borrow.

I've summarized briefly, but that's all of them. Nowhere among 114,000 references is monetary *policy* mentioned, nor any kind of growth. From the title of this book and opening questions in the preface, obviously that's where I'm going to look.

---

[59] Jerry Gordon, "Why Does China Owe Americans $1 Trillion?" New English Review, June 2012, interview with Jonna Bianco of the Am. Bondholder Fd., http://www.newenglishreview.org/print.cfm?pg=custpage&frm=116983&sec_id=116983

[60] http://www.globalsecuritieswatch.org/060725EuroWeek.pdf

[61] Bansal, R., Coleman, W., "A Monetary Explanation of the Equity Premium, Term Premium, and Risk-Free Rate Puzzles," JPE, v. 104 n. 6, Dec. 1996 https://faculty.fuqua.duke.edu/~rb7/bio/Bansal_Coleman_JPE.pdf

PART TWO

INVESTING IN THE PREMIUM

PERPETUAL PORTFOLIO VALUATION
INVESTING STRATEGY & TECHNIQUE
HAZARDS & PITFALLS

Perpetual Portfolios

The Lifetime of Companies

In theory corporations have no lifetime limits. This has not always been assumed. After the Civil War railroads and other companies which began to assume national scope encountered thousands of separate jurisdictions across the country leading to regulatory problems. A number of lawsuits wound up at the Supreme Court, and cases in 1886 and 1888 held that corporations had equal protection of law under the 14th amendment, and may consist of *"a succession of members without dissolution."*[62]

Just over 450 US companies have lasted more than a century.[63] Banking and financial services account for about 1/3rd. Another 1/3rd are mostly familiar names, 26 oil or energy companies, 14 drug or medical, 16 retail, 24 consumer product, and smaller numbers of automotive related, chemical, mining and minerals, publishers, real estate, shipping or communication companies. The last 1/3rd are names most people have never heard of. Some of the less known companies are quite large, as I recall encountering them when studying the NASDAQ 100. Others are regional or specialty companies, such as The Madison Square Garden Company.

But legal ability does not automatically equate to market success. Most companies go out of business eventually. If they don't actually declare bankruptcy, they sell out when in decline. Their names and brands disappear, or acquire other corporate monikers, and their data is deleted from online financial databases because the shares are no longer for sale. It is as if they never existed.

Once one of the "four horsemen" of the NASDAQ, Dell is shortly going away. Compaq was absorbed by competitor HP, and HP has recently been dropped from the Dow Jones Industrial Average. Down Jones itself is now part of Standard and Poor's. Merrill Lynch is part of Bank of America and the name is hardly as visible as it was as an independent company. Circuit City and Pacific Stereo are gone along with many other appliance and electronics chains, and Best Buy is floundering. The old standard bearers J. C. Penney and Sears have questionable futures and have greatly retracted. Does anyone remember F. W. Woolworth? Actually it survived, but only the Footlocker division, and the name has been changed to that.

---

[62] Pembina Consolidated Silver Mining Co. v. Pennsylvania, 125 US 394 (1886). Via: https://en.wikipedia.org/wiki/Corporate_personhood

[63] S&P via USA Today, http://i.usatoday.net/money/_pdfs/11-0615-centurions.pdf

Most of the small bookstores were gobbled up by bigger chains, a trend made famous in the movie "You've Got Mail," and now all but one of the big chains has been undermined by Amazon. AT&T declined to a remnant and was bought by one of its offspring who was essentially just buying the name. Does anyone remember Digital Equipment Corporation? That was a new tech company, the Apple of the 1970s. IBM survives but no longer makes PCs or even laptops. TWA and Pan Am and Eastern flew away. Lockheed and Boeing absorbed once proud rivals, only to be challenged in spaceflight and rocketry by sideline businesses of internet billionaires. In fact in a century of Aerospace, no less than 79 well-known US companies have merged down to a remaining 5.[64] Motorola and Nokia were gobbled up to promote the agendas of their acquirers, not even as separate profit centers, and neither was making money when acquired.

Many of these were companies I owned. My lament is not theoretical. I had great confidence in Compaq's board. When the company would get in trouble, they would get interested and fix things. But then they hired a CEO who knew nothing about computers. Hewlett Packard, who bought them for a song, long ago spun off the trademark instrument business that built the HP brand, and decided giving away printers and selling ink cartridges was the way to the future of a Dow 30 company. But a lot of other large, competent competitors are also in that business and HP is no longer in the DJIA index. Just today the funds are finally coming into my account for Uranium One, a large formerly independent uranium producer. After the Fukushima meltdown, uranium stocks were depressed and ripe to rise again so I loaded up. But before they could rise, this Canadian company sold out to some Russians for what most shareholders felt was less than the business was worth. But the decision was not made by any market. It was made by CEOs who may have had other interests.

Oil companies make an interesting case. There were once Seven Sisters[65] which prior to 1973 controlled 85% of the world's oil reserve. This group was originally known as the "Consortium for Iran" as it was formed after the 1951 nationalization of oil by Iran, and included Amoco, Gulf, Shell, Chevron, Exxon, Mobil and Texaco, many known by different names at the time. The cartel was able to retain control of most third world oil until the rise of OPEC in the 1970s. After about 50 years only four of them remained, having acquired the others, sometimes under duress as in the case of Texaco, which lost a major lawsuit. Currently the future of one of the remaining four, BP, continues to be threatened by legal ramifications from a large oil spill in the Gulf of Mexico.

---

[64] http://dropby.com/ElGrande/spacehistory.html
[65] http://en.wikipedia.org/wiki/Seven_Sisters_(oil_companies)

The *Financial Times* has proposed a new list of seven, including China National Petroleum, Gazprom (Russia), National Iranian Oil Company, Petrobras, PDVSA (Venezuela), Petronas (Malaysia), and Saudi Aramco. As far as I can tell, currently only three can be purchased by investors in the US, Gazprom, Petrobras and Petronas. None follow strict US accounting and disclosure standards. So the leadership rotates. It may or may not be possible to invest in the new leadership. And it may or may not be a good idea.

Suppose your portfolio had consisted of the Nifty-Fifty in 1970. How many of those companies faded away? What would be the returns on that portfolio?[66] On any fixed selection of companies from 1960 or 1950 or 1940? Or any market index of any year, fixed and without change? Wait long enough and its value will be small. How then do researchers find an equity premium over a century or longer?

Composition and Turnover in Market Indices

A market, or an index intended to be representative of a market, is continuously changing. Companies are being added and dropped. Changes are made to the Dow 30 every couple of years and to the NASDAQ 100 every few months. The average tenure of a company on the S&P 500 index in the early days of the index, the middle of the 20th century, was 61 years. Today it is only 18 years.[67] Important companies come and go faster than your children grow up. Buy and hold of individual companies does not seem to be a winning strategy.

In other words, market indices are not a fixed list of companies. There is a lot of turnover, or rotation. The equity premium is based on historical data on large indices that hopefully represent the performance of whole markets.

One immediately wonders how companies are chosen for indices. In some cases it may be based mostly on size. But not entirely. For smaller indices like the Dow Jones Industrial Average (the Dow 30), a great deal of picking and choosing is done of companies that are thought to be representative and to also be representative of the future. Larger indices are intended to represent some part of a market, like "large cap" or a particular industry. While many indices do not go back further than

---

[66] According to http://en.wikipedia.org/wiki/Nifty_Fifty the 50 lagged for many years but by the late 1990's most of the companies returned to "correct valuations" - a period of greater than 20 years – but without the failed members

[67] Foster, R., "Creative Destruction Whips Through Corporate America," Strategy & Innovation, vol. 10, no. 1, Innosight, Lexington, MA, 2012
http://www.innosight.com/innovation-resources/strategy-innovation/creative-destruction-whips-through-corporate-america.cfm

about mid 20th century, the S&P 1500 Composite is a whole market index that can be mapped to earlier market averages, and is often used for equity premium studies. Certainly there are more than 1500 companies in the US market, as many as 15,000. The index just tries to be representative. The methodology of the index is described by S&P.[68] The basic family of market representative indices methodology, from the opening paragraph of the S&P document, is…

> *The S&P 500 focuses on the large-cap sector of the market; however,* **since it includes a significant portion of the total value of the market, it also represents the market.** *Companies in the S&P 500 are considered leading companies in leading industries. The S&P 500 is a member of the S&P Global 1200 family of indices. The S&P MidCap 400 represents the mid-cap range of companies, and the S&P SmallCap 600 represents small-cap companies.* **The three indices are combined and calculated together as the S&P Composite 1500;**

I have emphasized two portions. First, the S&P 500 is a reasonable representation of the whole market, because it accounts for most of the capitalization.[69] Second is the composition of the Composite 1500 which more closely represents the market, though it still does not include every public company.

Other eligibility criteria include minimum amounts of market capitalization (different for each index), liquidity including a minimum amount of recent trading activity, at least 50% of shares available to the public (which means in theory the public controls the company's board), domicile in the US with a plurality of assets and revenues in the US and listing on a US exchange and compliant with US securities regulations, a sector balance factor, financial viability as measured by four consecutive quarters of positive earnings, and the company is not a recent Initial Public Offering (IPO). It should have been on the market 6 to 12 months.

Real Estate Investment Trusts (REITs) and Business Development Companies (BDCs) *are* eligible for inclusion. Many other special types of companies *are not*, such as limited partnerships, master limited partnerships, royalty trusts, tracking stocks and ETFs, warrants, bonds, preferred shares, investment trusts, etc. This restriction omits some rather large companies and even industry segments. For example, many pipeline

---

[68] http://us.spindices.com/

[69] Capitalization, loosely, is just the number of outstanding shares times the share price, or what it would theoretically take to buy the company at today's market price.

companies are thus ineligible, as well as some natural gas and petroleum producers.

Problem Companies – Partnerships and Trusts

To learn of the exclusion of partnerships and trusts by the index builders was a strange coincidence because of what I had encountered in my own portfolio over the last decade. I owned numerous examples of all these types of companies, both the allowed REITs and BDCs, and the ineligible partnerships and trusts. Recently I purged the last of the partnerships and trusts. They are often highly touted by investment advisers. I recall a friend telling me about being told to buy limited partnerships thirty years ago, and that they caused her a great deal of headaches. I guess I was not listening, or not sure what she had bought was the same thing as the public companies I was buying. They had good dividends *and* growth in share price. But after a few years, each of them did something strange. Usually this was to declare some non-dividend distribution greatly in excess of what was actually deposited into my account.

Well of course my tax software did not know what to do with this, and frankly no accountant that I could find seemed to know much either. Generally the companies sent information packets which would take as much time to decipher as the entire rest of my taxes, or longer. I was going to have to pay tax on money that they made and kept, and if I were lucky and filled out a ton of paperwork – whose value at any reasonable hourly rate greatly reduced the yield on these companies – I might get back *some* of the tax I owed on money that didn't come into my account.

While I'm not licensed to give you financial advice, I *can* advise you on headaches and hassles, and I recommend staying away from partnerships and trusts. The management has license to transfer the company tax burden to you, because technically you are not a shareholder but a direct owner, but in reality you have not even as much voice as a shareholder due to the special way these companies are chartered.

Income from a Portfolio – BDCs and REITs

BDCs and REITs are fine, I believe, and I still own them. Some are better than others, and like any problem in efficient markets, it is hard to know which. The main point of this book is of course that the equity premium will be realized through index investing, and the why and the how of intrinsic growth and monetary policy that causes that to be advantageous. But what you will find is that if you require income, the index strategy will not produce enough of it.

Economists and some investment advisers will say that it doesn't make any difference. Just sell small amounts of your holdings to generate income. My research suggests that it does make a difference, that re-investment of dividends is a substantial part of the equity premium, and that increasing your total ownership share of the market is especially important in the long-term. If you are selling, you are decreasing your ownership share.

REITs and BDCs are very efficient at generating dividends. They are set up under special laws that permit them not to pay tax on money they pay as dividends, and require them to pay most of their income as dividends. REITs are usually pretty focused, on either residential or commercial, and a particular strategy within that segment, like either government backed (agency) or non-government backed (non-agency) mortgages.

BDCs sometimes are broader. They finance small or middle market companies. They may do so mostly by making loans, but they also may own shares. Some like Hercules Technology (HTGC) operate a little bit like venture capital companies, except that you don't have to be a qualified investor worth more than $1 million to buy shares. If you own three or four BDCs, you might indirectly own or finance 30 or 40 small and medium sized companies.

Arithmetic of the Parts and the Whole

For a portfolio of a fixed component list of stocks, the portfolio returns are the sum of the returns of the components. This is ordinary arithmetic like you learned in school.

For a portfolio in which assets rotate in and out, it can be more or less than that, depending on the circumstances. I assume the reader is familiar with the many efficient market studies that show that over long periods, mutual fund managers do not really do better than the market. They do 1% to 2% worse. But the index portfolios designed to *represent the market* even though they don't contain every possible company, are the benchmark that the professional managers have so much trouble beating.

How can a mechanically managed portfolio, like an index, have a long-term positive performance if most (eventually all) of its components go out of business or decline and are sold out at a loss?

The answer is that if the growth rate (combination of dividends and share price increase), for those companies actively growing, is greater than the loss rate for the companies that are declining, and new companies are coming into existence which can be mechanically selected much like S&P constructs their indices, then a portfolio can have a positive long-term growth rate *even though every one of its components will eventually be a total loss.*

As we saw earlier, some companies are still going after 100 years, and many companies are acquired when they are in decline, so most companies will not end in total loss. The mathematical minimum condition for the success of a perpetual portfolio is significantly exceeded by the actual market.

The portfolio growth in a single year will indeed still be exactly equal to the sum of the growth (or decline) of its individual components. Group the companies retrospectively for a particular year into healthy vs. declining and going out of business, categories. If we make the simplifying and worst-case assumption that the unhealthy companies go completely out of business at a final value of zero, then one can estimate the annual loss rate due to bankruptcy or going-out-of-business as $1/L$ where L is the average company lifetime. For example, if the average company lifetime is 20 years, then on average each year $1/20^{th}$ of the companies go out of business and the annualized loss rate is 5%. This is the same logic we used earlier to analyze how much to increase interest rates to cover bankruptcy losses.

If the average growth rate of the healthy companies is G_H, then it is easy to estimate the average growth rate of the portfolio which we'll call G_P.

$$G_P \approx G_H - \frac{1}{L}$$

Permanent Portfolio Simulator

I still had trouble visualizing how this would work, and believing the strange arithmetic. So I wrote a web script which I call the PERMANENT PORTFOLIO SIMULATOR, which you can find at the following URL:

http://mc1soft.com/papers/PerpetualPortfolio.htm

The webpage looks like this:

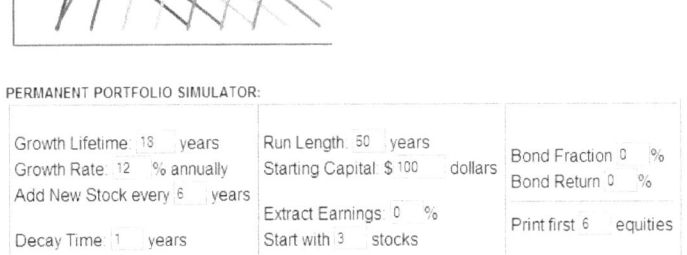

Simulator Webpage

The simulator is particularly mechanical and uses only average values. In other words, you cannot program different kinds of companies or random companies, etc. Every company grows for a few years and then goes out of business. The parameters control the rate of growth, rate of decline, and duration of each. A more sophisticated model could use randomized parameters and make multiple runs Monte-Carlo style, but as long as the simulator does not take any advantage of the fixed average nature of the identical securities, like knowing when to sell – it doesn't – then the outcome will be similar to a much more complex set of Monte-Carlo runs..

The simulator starts with equal amounts invested in the initial companies, which are pseudo-randomly distributed in their life-cycle phase. Some of them are young and some old. When a new company is to be added, the simulator mechanically sells the same percentage of each old company, so that the new company comes in equally weighted at $1/N^{th}$ of a portfolio of N companies.

In the simulation parameters on the form above, I have set up a test run with only 3 stocks. This is a ridiculously small number, but I wanted you to be able to see the mechanics of how it was working. I set the growth rate to 12%, just a guess at an average healthy company growth rate, and the company lifetime to 18 years, which is the current average tenure on the S&P 500 index, though of course companies don't exit that index with zero value as they do in this worst case simulator.

Given that lifetime, if I add a stock every 6 years, I will typically have 3 remaining in the portfolio. The script will make an appropriate recommendation if you change one of the parameters. There are provisions for extracting earnings or holding some bonds, but for this demonstration I didn't use any of that.

A run for 24 years is shown below, enough time for all the original 3 companies to have expired. After 6 years (in year 7) there is a big drop as the first company fails. A new company is added, *equity 4*. Of course a real market would not be so regular. We are just modeling *average* behavior.

Simulation of 3 companies, 18 year life, 12% growth

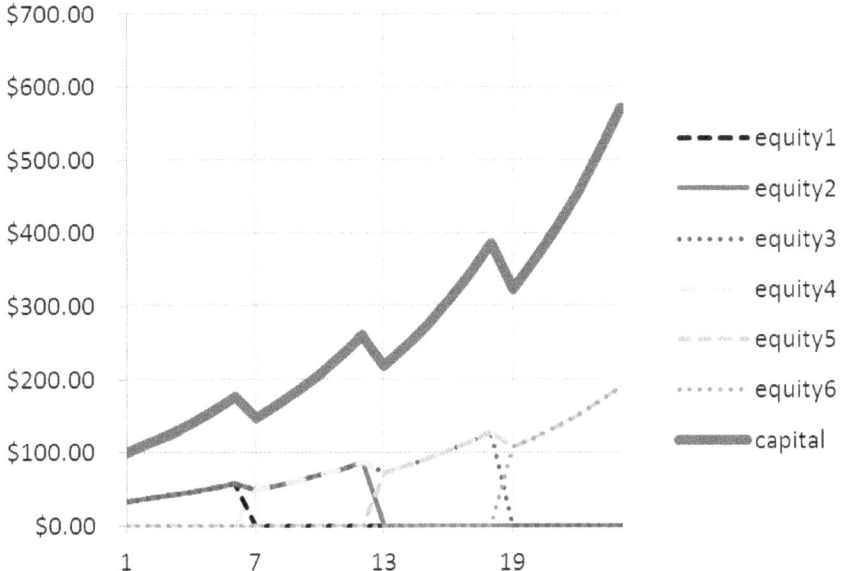

Below I have plotted as bar graphs the annual return, and the average annual return (darker lines) from the beginning, out to 50 years. It gets off to a bit of an artificially good start because it just happens that nothing goes out of business in the first 5 years. After that the annual return begins to average down toward the approximately 6.4% that it should be (healthy growth G_H of 12% minus $1/L = 1/18$ years which is approximately 5.6%).

Growth rate of 3 company, 18 year, 12% portfolio

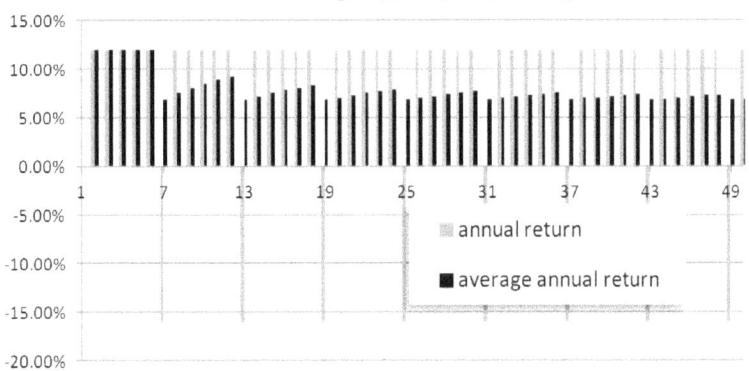

Any portfolio (i.e. investment account) operated on this principle should last indefinitely, barring complete collapse of the market it is in, or a major change of law regarding investments such as confiscation of shares, or confiscatory taxes. The simplest way to do it is to let the wizards at Standard and Poor's or other major market data firm do it for you and just buy an index, most of which now have corresponding ETFs which can be bought for miniscule broker fees and which have very low expense ratios.

However there are unexpected difficulties and surprises and temptations in such a strategy, and the impact of the implied time horizon is easy to underestimate or overestimate. We turn to these details for one chapter, as they will ultimately aid our understanding of the equity premium by providing a deeper understanding of the impact of choices on investors.

Pros & Cons of Perpetual Portfolios

One Strategy Does Not Fit All

Humans have complex and varied consumption needs – "consumption" being an economics term for the uses of money. As I am writing for two audiences, economists will interpret "pros & cons" as *preferences*, while to investors it is *when & how*.

We all need to be fed and housed today, and at the same time we need to know we will be fed and housed at various times in the future, and we need to educate ourselves and our children and beyond strict necessity we have self-actualization needs (a term invented by the psychologist Maslow) to realize our potential. This may range from a quiet hobby club to the grand exploration of space and other schemes which are the current ambitions of several billionaires.

Two investors who are presented with choices A and B with identical expected values but different time horizons, will often make different choices. While you might stretch the definition of risk to cover this, it's not exactly risk. For example, in the real world stocks are quite risky over one year periods. For the market as a whole there is a almost a 1/3 chance of a significant decline, roughly 14% or more in the next year. For bonds and savings accounts there is very little chance of that. From the table below, we see there is a 10% chance of major losses, of a bear market in the neighborhood of 20-40%.

It is interesting to note in passing that if we *assume* logarithmic intensity increase with decreasing frequency, as for floods and earthquakes, then at 200 year intervals we should see nearly total losses. Perhaps half the country may have been said to be a total loss in the Civil War, and for Russia the markets were lost in the Communist Revolution, so this is not out of line with experience. If we extrapolate this to 2000 years we might expect a connected series of many markets to fail, and indeed all large organized markets west of Constantinople took a long vacation following the Fall of Rome.

20 year S&P 500 gain/loss occurrences

year	gains	losses
1993	7.06%	
1994		-1.54%
1995	34.11%	
1996	20.26%	
1997	31.01%	
1998	26.67%	
1999	19.53%	
2000		-10.14%
2001		-13.04%
2002		-23.37%
2003	26.38%	
2004	8.99%	
2005	3.00%	
2006	13.62%	
2007	3.53%	
2008		-38.49%
2009	23.45%	
2010	12.78%	
2011		0.00%
2012	13.41%	
average:	17.41%	-14.43%
chances:	70%	30%

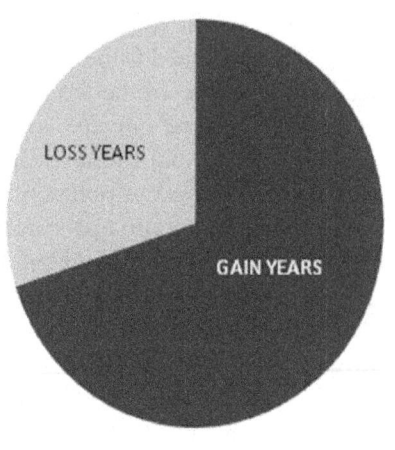

The period of 20-100 years is more interesting. We probably cannot estimate anything about the future beyond 100 years. But we have an idea at least of climate and political change within the next century, or at least we debate as if we do. And despite predictions of disaster which always abound, most of us think we will be galvanized into action. For example, prophets of doom have been preaching about the national debt for my entire life and worried what will happen if it exceeds GDP as in Greece. Here we are at 90% and the Tea Party arises, ready to halt the government rather than increase the debt one iota further. I do not mean to distract the reader with politics and will not endorse a particular party – though later we might see from historical trends that each party has strengths and weaknesses with respect to the economy – but just to observe that within American culture if a great problem arises, a great movement typically arises.

This is not true of every culture nor should it be. Variety in response may well be an adaptive trait that ensures all possible means of survival are tried. Some problems aren't real and ignoring them may work fine. Some problems can't be solved and it may be best to hide out until it is over. Some people have survived in poor or abusive economic conditions for centuries, later to emerge as among the most prominent.

Some humans need a lot of money next year, and some have all their immediate needs met and see the possibility of covering many decades of future needs with an investment that is irrelevant to the present. The latter may perhaps seek to capture the equity premium. The former will seek a job and a savings account. Different choices for different investors.

As for risk, it seems from the data of the last century that, at least when some inflation is present, in the 20-100 year time frame the equity approach has been *actually lower risk even though the return is higher.* To square this with economic theory, we only need observe that *in the near term equities are much more volatile, with a 30% probability of a lot less money next year (greater for individual companies).*

A large part of the problem of actually using index investing strategies is arranging to meet both near and far term needs within reasonable probabilities. We will discover in a later chapter that the standard-theory method of selling growth investments to meet immediate needs, thereby reducing share of ownership in the market, seriously erodes one's relative economic wealth in the long-term.

Recall our discussion of equilibrium and sustainability, and you will realize that constantly reducing one's share of the pie leads to *no pie*. Liquidation of working assets is in my view the number 1, 2 and 3 problem of the working classes. That is why they have to keep working instead of their assets working, and lose their voice as to what they are working toward. Instead of accumulating working assets, they accumulate non-working consumer debt. The equity premium will turn out to be closely connected to a different kind of debt, working or productive debt.

Comparison to Stocks

The comparison of a perpetual portfolio to holding individual stocks is … interesting. I suspect after you've been investing a few years, if it's not a major hobby interest you'll get tired of being ever vigilant and still getting surprised once or twice a year with really bad news on some company. Can you make the kind of gains that you can see in the market averages by looking at past data in the leading stocks? No. Not even close. Can you actually pick similar stocks in the future? I don't know anyone who has done so in the US market. I only know of a single person who was able to pick a small number of great stocks in foreign markets, all small cap companies which required specialized knowledge (he is from overseas) and the gains were still not anything like the historical gains shown in the chart below.

First note the title of the chart – *successful* tech stocks. There is selection bias. I didn't include the many, many stocks of the era that are bankrupt or were absorbed by others. Even stalwarts like Sun Microsystems are no more. It's product Java is used "on 3 billion devices" but that didn't keep it an independent company. Have you ever actually *paid* for Java to be installed on your computer?

Next note that most have not done well since 2001 and have not recovered their value as of that time. Recall back to 2001 if you can. It was well-known that Microsoft was in trouble from internet upstarts. Many stock pickers were selling it and putting the money into upstarts, most of whom are gone. What is the chance you'd have picked Amazon or Google? Facebook didn't exist yet. Yahoo was still thought to be a challenger for control of search and advertising.

S&P-Relative Performance of Successful Tech Stocks

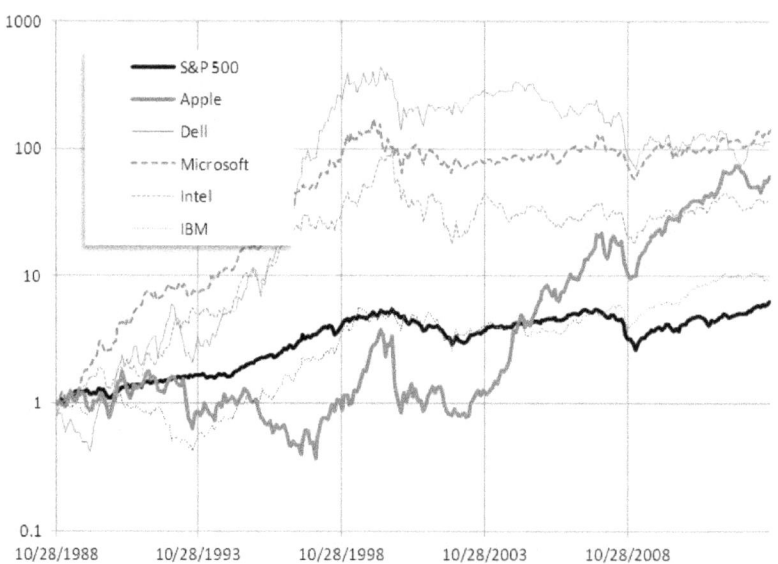

Notice poor Dell. It was the highest flyer of the bunch from a starting base of 1988, which happened to be its introduction point so of course it was up from a lower base. There were so many PC manufacturers it would be hard to pick Dell out in 1988, though it was clearly dominant later. But now it is down a factor of 6 from its high, steadily declining, and likely going private to lick its wounds.

I included older tech giant IBM just for reference. It was doing very poorly in 1993, down as badly as Dell is now, but the company stubbornly adapted and has done better than any of the PC tech giants since 2000 except Apple.

Apple is the only one that did well after 2000, and it did so by adopting a new product line under the guidance of a brilliant founder who is now departed. Being already one of the largest companies in the world in terms of stock value, it is unlikely to climb faster than the indices. By cap weight it greatly defines the indices and is more likely to be a drag on them.

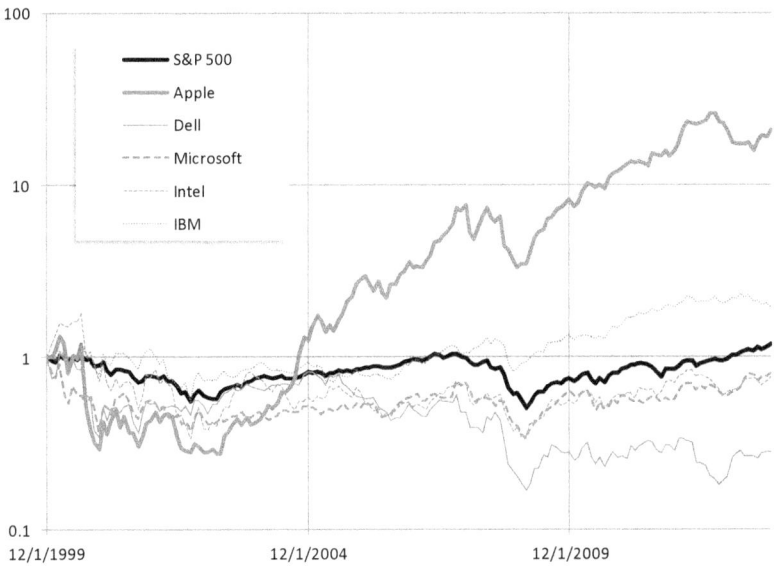

Relative Performance Since Peak in 2000

In the figure above, plotted from the market peak in March of 2000, notice that the index seems quite stable compared to the stocks. Apple takes off only after swooning downward about 80% (the chart scale is logarithmic). IBM dropped a similar amount, but also managed to climb back above the index. Of the other three one is slightly and two seriously behind. Now it looks more like a lottery. I personally had much more money to invest after 2000 than before, due to advances at work and inflow from other sources. In 1988 where the other chart started, I had a net worth of 6/10[ths] of a percent of what it is today and was not confident enough to bet it all on one of those stocks. What I did do was invest in a tech mutual fund, one of the Fidelity offerings, but by the early 90s it had not kept pace with anything and was losing money, so a typical tech mutual fund was not capturing the stellar gains you would think from these charts.

Later, in 2000, of course I had more to invest, but then I'd have had to be much more astute in picking one particular stock. Essentially during the 2000s I went for dividends in a sideways market, and in 2009 in about July I began to switch back toward some growth, a transition that is still continuing in my portfolio as I've added more index funds over the last two years.

Alas, if you like stock picking you will not be interested in an index fund. If you keep your wits you'll have a lot of fun and probably do OK. Like my one friend in the overseas markets you might do very well. It is kind of like the lottery, but there are better odds and more of your own effort is involved. If you are the sort of person who is able to easily pick the fastest moving queue in Wal-Mart or the Post Office, or the fastest lane of traffic, you should do very well. The problems are provably similar. Economists have rarely studied individual genius at analyzing just a few companies as far as I know, because it is hard to quantify and collect data, though if you recall the Ivkovic data from earlier, wealthy individual investors with portfolios concentrated in a few stocks did well. Studying fund managers does not count, because they have to invest huge sums on behalf of others, at times when others want it invested and which may not be their own preference.

Of more interest here, in the discussion of a perpetual portfolio where most companies go out of business eventually, is the observation that companies with high growth rates over 5 or 10 year periods do come along regularly, and have the growth rates to offset the losses inherent in a perpetual portfolio from dying companies.

I would like to have shown you a plot of all the companies that went out of business after the dotcom bust. But as I explained earlier, such data is not to be had. I also went looking for data on GM stock prices before bankruptcy. I found a lot of other people had been looking, as the data were needed to file for tax losses. On a blog I found that the bankrupt stock traded until 2011 under the symbol MTLQQ[70]. I was able to get data at one point, but later the data was not there.

Will Markets Still Be Efficient?

If we all invest in perpetual portfolios, or index funds, will markets still be efficient? No. There would be insufficient selection pressure on one company over another. But aside from brief euphoric

---

[70] http://www.freep.com/article/20120408/COL07/204080455/

bubbles like in 2001 there is little danger of this taking hold long-term. Short sellers will sense blood in weak overvalued companies.

Does Market Timing Matter?

Here is where we need to switch from the Fama mindset of efficient markets to the Shiller mindset of avoiding bubbles. According to Shiller, yes timing matters at least to the extent of avoiding bubbles. I already commented that I don't think Shiller did that quite well enough in 1996, calling a bubble at what turned out to be a floor of future prices.

Shiller's Floor – Dec. 1996

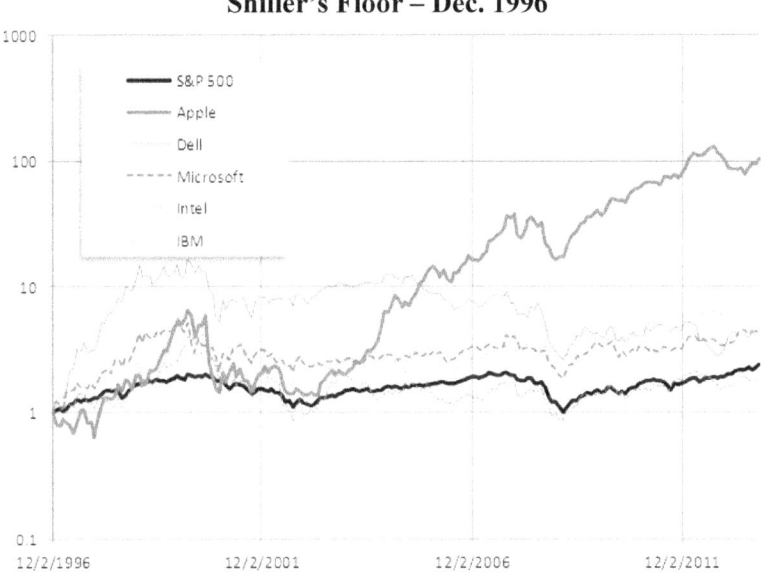

As you can see from the plot, Shiller actually called a floor quite well. If you had stayed out of the market you'd have missed any dividends, which for many stocks exceed bank interest and during much of this period enjoyed favorable tax status.

Had you purchased the Dow 30 at their 1929 peak of 381 and held until October of 2013, exactly 84 years, your share price return would have been an annual average 4.52%. That's actually not too unlikely, as there was high volume then and lots of buying fever. I won't compare that to buying at the bottom which most members of the public were doubtless avoiding. Who *was* buying at the bottom?

But suppose you bought after the first big leg of the recovery during Roosevelt's first year in 1933 at about 110 and held until 2013, for 80 years. Your annualized return would be 10.64%. The difference is 6.12%, nearly as large as the equity premium. In other words, the equity premium will not insure you against buying a bubble, even over most of a century. The cost over one or two decades is much higher, and many private retirement accounts are still paying the price of tech buying in the late 1990s.

Effect of market entry timing on 80-year returns

Purchase date	Price	Event	Sell date	Price	Annual yield
Oct 1929	381	Market top	Oct 2013	15626	4.52%
Oct 1933	110	Recovery 1st	Oct 2013	15626	10.64%

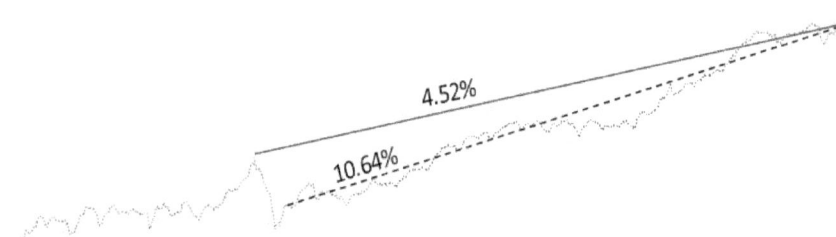

For all the luck I've had in my regular accounts, in which I almost completely avoided tech in that timeframe, my IRA fell victim and I've pretty much written it off as insignificant to my current financial picture. If I had bought an index fund instead of tech and tech mutual funds the IRA would be about three times higher than it is today, maybe four. In a similarly sized retirement account set up with my employer where I had only a choice between which of 3 index funds, it did well and contains about twice what I contributed, most of which was between 1995 and 2005.

Jeffery Hirsch has an interesting theory of long-term market cycles which he puts forward in *The Little Book of Stock Market Cycles*[71]. I am only referring to chapters 1-5 where he discusses long-term cycles, war, and the presidential election cycle. The seasonal and calendar cycles are elusive and transient as Rubinstein pointed out. You should only be concerned about avoiding really bad times to buy. If the market is going to be flat or choppy for a decade, just use the dividend income strategy I mentioned to supplement your index fund holdings Below is a repeat of the DOW chart from earlier, with the worst times to buy highlighted with gray shading.

---

[71] John Wiley & Sons, 2012

DJIA buying intervals resulting in 5+ year declines

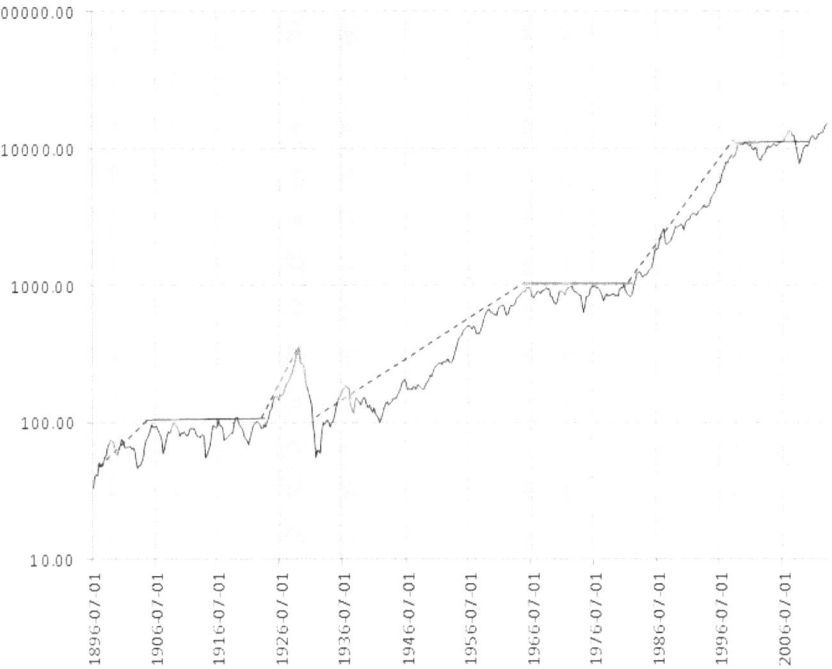

There are only 7 significant intervals since 1900 in which buying would result in a portfolio decline lasting 5 years or more. All but two of the intervals were only about 18 months in length, and those two were grouped about the depression era and together amount to less than 8 years. So you have roughly a 90% chance by blind luck of avoiding extended declines of 5 years or more. Only the Great Depression involved declines that were both serious and long lasting. The general market did not decline for long in 2001, and even though it declined steeply in 2008-9, by the end of 2010 indices had basically recovered, long before the economy itself recovered. If you owned a small business you might still be in trouble, and if you were laid off from a job you likely still are. Can we conclude market-representative index funds are not as risky as a job?

Comparing to Mutual Funds

As far as comparing to managed mutual funds, much has been written already. I would emphasize three things. The way mutual funds are traded annoys me. You get the closing price at the end of the day but you have to decide to sell before that. It seems like a small thing. Like I said, I'm just annoyed by it. Studies by economists do reveal that mutual funds on average have higher expenses and 1% to 2% worse performance than market indices. A fund might do well for 4 or 5 years, but we are talking about an investment strategy for 20 years to a century.

Another problem with mutual funds, the ones that are not based on an index, is that sometimes the fund will simply advertise an investment strategy, a market segment for example, like tech or energy, and they do not care whether that strategy does well or not. They expect their investors are making timed bets on that sector, or whatever the strategy happens to be. If it becomes a poor strategy, they are still bound by their charter. If it gets really bad, investors will withdraw from the fund and it will liquidate and close.

The perpetual portfolio does not liquidate and close unless the market, usually meaning the entire country, liquidates and closes, most likely due to war or revolution.

The third thing has to do with premature elimination of assets that have declined, discussed under bond funds below.

Comparison to Bonds

Bonds have the peculiar property that they are relatively safe, except when they are not. In other words, they can completely fail into default, and when they do many similar bonds are likely to also fail. This is true whether they are corporate bonds or government bonds.

Prior to 200 years ago, loaning money to governments was considered very risky. Usually higher interest rates were required, and often lenders were not paid back. Outside of the top ten or so countries in the world, it's still pretty risky. Some corporations are larger than many governments in terms of annual revenue, and are correspondingly less risky. With the establishment of central banks and the free floating of currencies, governments have been more able to guarantee payback, but the currency might have been devalued by inflation. At least that is the current fear, based largely on experiences between the world wars, and in the 1970s.

Many economies have experienced inflation, even runaway inflation, and most recover. Deflation probably is more risky and takes longer to recover from. The long market recoveries in the US after 1929 and more recently in Japan were both responses to deflation.

While stocks are short-term volatile, in the long run they have similar exposure to deflation, which can cause default of bonds and long periods of poor performance in stocks. This is the gist of why Mehra and Prescott concluded the risk levels of stocks and bonds were similar, at least for the long-term investor.

With the idea of the index fund, market based investing, or a perpetual portfolio, whatever you would like to call it, stocks in this form have an advantage over bonds that is quite striking. All bonds end, and all you get is what you contracted for. With stocks held in perpetual portfolios, you get future earnings that were not part of the original deal, that were not valued in the initial price. Fisher & Hoffman sum this up nicely in *The Little Book of Market Myths*, one of the best investing books I have read:

"Bonds are fine but they don't represent future earnings."[72]

We will be looking quantitatively at what that means in the next chapter. It is one of two key pieces that prevent bond and equity returns from being comparable and therefore equalize-able. Thus the equity premium is possible without a high risk and without undermining the idea of rationality in markets.

Individual bonds are tricky to buy. I thought bond mutual funds were cool in the 1980s because of the high interest, but in the end they declined in value. So I know firsthand about the long-term risk of bonds, at least when held in funds.

Another terrible thing about any mutual fund, which happened to me in another bond fund that held foreign bonds, is that the managers will sell losing assets rather than wait for the recovery. A fund that I held in the late 1990s dumped its Russian government bonds when it looked like Russia might default. Russia did not default. I had a terrible loss. What to do? I bought a Russian market index fund during the crisis to make up for the less-than-brilliant bond fund management. It worked.

Rents vs. Earnings

Sometimes economists use the word "rents" to refer to future returns from investments. There is a subtle difference in connotation. One buys a hotel or apartment complex, for example, and it has a certain number of rooms in a certain market, and a certain potential for future rents. It would *seem* like this might be equivalent to a bond with certain coupon payments. It would be if not for two things.

First, the bond is a contract with an expiration date. There are no rents or coupons beyond that date. The investor will have to buy a new bond which is tailored to the prevailing interest rate environment at the future time. The hotel price might have been comparable to bond prices for similar rents/coupons at the original date, but the owner of the hotel enjoys the hotel or apartment rents beyond the bond's termination, and irrespective of any interest rates or equalization pressures at the future time.

A second feature of the hotel or apartment vs. the bond is that, depending on management, and of course management is responsive to the owners, revenues from the property may be in part be used for improvements to get higher rents, and expansions to get simply more rents.

---

[72] Fisher, K., Hoffmans, L., *The Little Book of Market Myths*, Wiley & Sons, Hoboken NJ, p. 15 (2013).

These expenses may be deducted from revenue before rents are sent to the owners, or they may be financed through new capital issue. It is the former case where expansion is financed at least in part from revenues that fouls up the comparison to bonds. This is impossible with bonds.

If the net rents after improvement and expansion expenses are deducted from earnings, and earnings are compared to bond coupons, then it is an unfair comparison. A date should be chosen when the property would be no longer useful if unimproved, and that date treated like a bond expiration date. Expenses for improvement or expansion should be accounted as rents, making rents larger than they seem, for purposes of comparison to bonds.

This is easy to see for hotels and apartments. But what about tech companies like Apple? A large proportion of the people working at the company are developing new products, not collecting rents from the old ones. In fact, collecting rents for iPhones is largely outsourced to cell phone companies. Salaries are expenses deducted from earnings. So earnings today are one thing, but future earnings are intended to be much larger. This is the essence I think of Fisher & Hoffman's complaint about bonds not representing future earnings.

Comparison to other historical periods since 1871

Does investing in the equity premium via index portfolios always work? If not, how do you know what kind of era you are in? We will get more into the deep reasons for the equity premium shortly, but here is some data that, just by correlation with historical events, is revealing. This is a different kind of "timing." Above we asked if market timing was important and pointed out that investing a lump sum at the peak of a bubble could remove the equity premium for a long time. Here we look at various "eras" to see how the equity premium was doing in each of them.

Using the Shiller data[73] from 1871 to the present for all of the following, first I'll show an inverse relation between real interest (inflation adjusted) and the earnings growth premium (earnings growth in excess of interest rates, from which the equity premium might presumably arise). But the raw yearly data is virtually useless:

---

[73] http://www.econ.yale.edu/~shiller/data.htm

Earnings growth premium vs. real interest

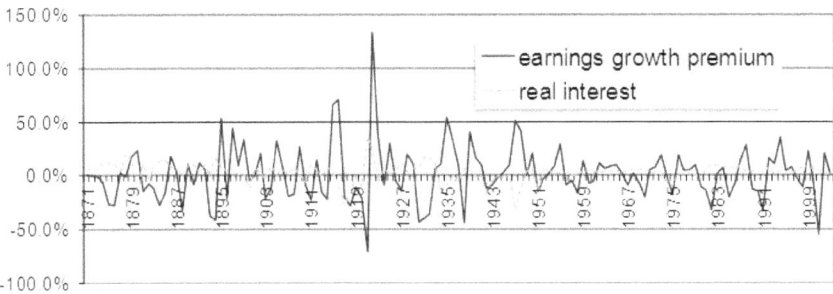

However, if we put this data through a 2-pole low-pass filter with a 75 year time constant (see appendix for method details), it is:

75-year filtered earnings premium vs. real interest

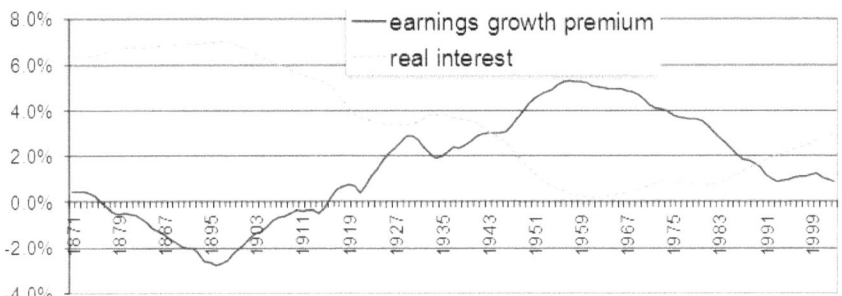

Interest was high in the late 1800s, trending down through the 1960s, and up slightly since. The earnings premium tipped into negative territory just after 1873 when the country went on the gold standard internally. This severely curtailed money supply growth and inflation was negative (i.e. there was deflation) from then until 1900. In 1900 various measures facilitated international trade, but the depression almost ended the party. Roosevelt ended the internal gold standard in 1933. From 1970 internal growth was hampered by energy costs and the rise of Japan. The turnaround occurs in 1991 after Japan's economy stalled.

Hazards in the Equity Premium

When Something Goes Wrong

There are two advantages to the perpetual portfolio strategy. One is not having to worry about something going wrong with individual assets. Either you or a large market data firm are just routinely identifying (usually mechanically) new assets.

The World on Your Side

The other is, if something goes wrong with the whole fund, i.e. the whole market, it means something has gone wrong with the whole country. That is usually not met with complacency. You have the government and all the companies and most of the citizens immediately working to correct it. If the government can't solve the problem the citizens will throw them out and get a new government, even if the country is not a democracy. If the market or markets you have selected are important to trading partners, you may get many other countries trying to solve the problem as well. *There is no other form of investment that can get action from the whole world when something goes wrong.*

This makes investment strategies possible that could cause big losses with individual companies. For example, when the index is way down in a crisis, you can buy more. You may not be able to time the bottom, but somehow it will survive. If you do this with a company or even a market segment, you better only do it once, and gently, because there is no guarantee. A list of bankrupt companies that I have doubled down on would fill a lot of paper (WestJet, Novastar Financial, and Luminent Mortgage just to name a few).

Markets declining or closing

In the last 200 years of good record keeping, the biggest markets that went out of business were the ones in communist countries that were confiscated in the first half of the 20th century. I am not sure if Islam can be said to have a consistent effect on markets. It has some opposition to interest rates as there was in Medieval Christianity. Of course war and disaster harm markets, but one only has to look at Germany and Japan to understand this is not permanent.

Investors who bought at the market top in the US in 1929 might have seen a 90% loss but had half their money back in 10 years and all of it in 28 years. Those who had funds in failed banks got pennies on the dollar and that was the end of it. Investors who entered the market in 1926 had all of their funds back within 10 years (though it continued to be volatile – that's what markets do).

Japan

The only major market that is not yet recovered from a long downturn is Japan. The supposed causes of this relate directly to our thesis (we will see later), and bear examination. A good short summary of six alternative views is found on a Wikipedia article about the Lost Decade, the Two Lost Decades, or the Lost 20 Years as it is variously called.[74] A 20 year timeframe is definitely relevant to the equity premium, especially since it is not clear it has ended yet.

First, I will summarily dismiss the point of view of Fingleton who asserts the lost decades are a myth which is disputed by proper accounting and which is kept because it benefits Japan's export-oriented industry, previously the target of much criticism in the West. It is not the substance of Fingleton's arguments that I reject, but the focus. Our focus in this book is on investment returns, and clearly any investors who bought during the prosperous times, the bubble, or whatever you call it – semantics are just a political game – have experienced a very real and unrecovered downturn and may well have been ruined. With all due respect to Fingleton, his point of view is irrelevant to us.

In Japan interest rates have hovered near zero for more than two decades, and long-term stock returns, with a basis before 1990, are negative. Any way you look at it, this is a negative equity premium. Stock returns are less than bond returns even when bond returns are non-existent. It is hard to find anything but a long-term downward trend in the Japan market (see Nikkei chart). It is hard to see a bubble bursting "crash" in this picture like the very clear one we have been looking at for 1929 in DJIA charts. All the Nikkei has been doing is bouncing between the two parallel limit lines shown, except for dipping below them in the dotcom and housing crises. And since Japanese stocks were (obviously) more risky than Japanese bonds during this 25 year period, there was no risk premium at all. It is an example of Zheng's point that relating a negative equity premium to risk is implausible.

---

[74] http://en.wikipedia.org/wiki/Lost_Decade_(Japan)

Japan's Lost 20 Years (going on 25?)

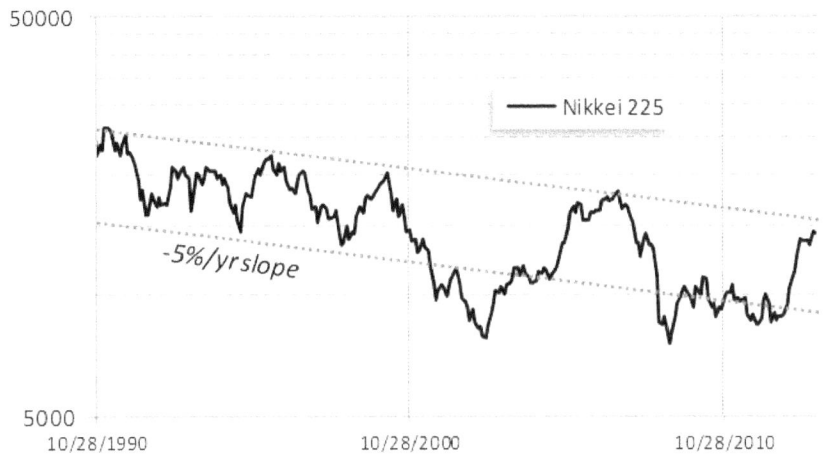

That leaves five points of view which *are* relevant to investors, and I will emphasize the aspects of each that will turn out to be interrelated by the mechanics of the equity premium.

Scott Sumner's argument that monetary policy was too tight during the Lost Decade is unconventional in view of near-zero interest rates, though we might revisit this later. However, one can take the view that Japan's monetary policy in 1989, raising interest rates sharply to attempt to deflate a bubble, was ill advised in view of the subsequent long decline. Bubble popping is not yet a science.

Paul Krugman suggests Japanese corporations relied more heavily on borrowing than on issuing equity (shares), because of the high personal savings rate of the Japanese and the cozy relationships between bankers and corporations and implicit guarantee of a government bailout. The US market is financed roughly 50-50 between debt and equity, with some variance, and this turns out to be a key parameter in the equity premium.

Richard Koo suggests the Japanese corporations *opted* to pay down their debts rather than to borrow and invest in new production, despite near-zero interest rates. This might be a cultural factor. However it represents economic contraction and there is no premium in that.

Finally, Fumio Hayashi and Edward Prescott (yes the same Prescott who co-discovered the equity premium) suggest that "*the anemic performance of the Japanese economy since the early 1990s is mainly due to the low growth rate of aggregate productivity.*" The thinking is that this is a different explanation than the asset bubble burst theory. Yes, but, if productivity, borrowing and the equity premium (i.e. stock returns) have an interrelation, then it would not be an *entirely* different explanation. We will see.

Switching Horses

I have spent so much time on Japan because it appears to be the one modern instance in which things have gone really wrong and our market index portfolio does not appear to have been safe. There may be times when you lose confidence in your portfolio, even if it is an index fund. In any case, whether you are investing in individual stocks or country indices or sector funds, there may come a time when you are just feeling doubtful about the long-term picture of an asset and need to be out of it.

So be it. Sell. But here is something to think about. Over the last 5000 years, for that matter over the last 4 billion, there has not yet been a time when the whole world went south and never recovered. And if the world does not recover, what good does it do you to hold worthless paper money? Better to own some group of companies helping to rebuild the world. In other words, if you must sell a major holding during a crisis at a low point, buy something else. Not something else that is in a bubble, but something in a similar crisis, but that you have confidence will recover. This way you are not losing your place in line and forfeiting the natural impetus of the market's tendency to "return to the mean" level of prosperity and growth.

Return to Mean

But by all means avoid using any technique similar to Martingale, i.e. literally doubling down, as the losses are unlimited. I would not even double the number of shares, which can be done for far less than the original investment after a serious decline. Some advocate dollar cost averaging, buying equal dollar amounts at intervals. The losses from a non-recovering market like Japan, if you happen to be that unlucky, can still be large. By buying equal numbers of shares, or less, good recovery potential is maintained and a profit may be made because of shares bought near the bottom even if there is no recovery to former levels. But when I've tried this with an individual company it works barely, poorly or not at all. So far, in over a dozen tries, it has not failed with country level or higher indices. I haven't tried it on segment indices and wouldn't, because a segment can cease to exist. Think of the horse and buggy industry.

Buying Bubbles

Averaging in as the market goes up is much more risky than as it goes down. On the way up, you may be buying a bubble and increasing losses in the long run. On the way up if I am under invested, I make a onetime investment which is maybe not as much as I'd like, but will not devastate me if I am buying a bubble. On the way down, wait with patience until a clear turn unless you have a very high degree of confidence and are using a very small percent of your portfolio. Of course if you are investing from your salary, you are sort of stuck with dollar cost averaging regardless of which direction the market is going.

These situations represent "preferences." At times when you are waiting for the next planned investment transaction, your money will be in a bank-like asset. It could be in bonds, but for small investors the cost of moving in and out of a bond fund is probably too great.

Oddly, corporations seem to know where the bubbles are. Baker and Wurgler report that corporations issue more equity shares than bonds just before periods of poor equity returns, and issue more bonds than equities just before periods of equity outperformance.[75] This is the supply side of the market. Not only do investors trade with other investors, but they trade new issues with the issuing companies, who are themselves market participants. An equity is sort of a bond without a fixed coupon and no maturity date. I have not seen a study of whether corporations prefer one or the other. There is a risk of loss of control with either, but for different reasons.

Leverage

Some of you might be asking, "If it's so certain, can I use leverage?" If you don't understand the word leverage, I'd prefer not to be responsible for introducing you to the casino. For those that already do this sort of thing, a few notes.

In the next couple of chapters we'll see how deeply everything is already leveraged, and you might change your mind, so hold on for that.

The first thing is to make sure that you have access to credit which is of sufficiently long duration (20-30 years) that the equity premium might show up, and you should be pretty sure you are not buying a bubble. If you've been investing less than 20 years, it's going to be hard to see the bubbles, because the hormones will be rushing and you'll be feeling left out. The start of a long bull run looks in charts much like a bubble, but the fundamentals are a bit different and the feeling is more skeptical.

The credit should be of sufficiently low rate that it is possible to imagine coming out ahead. Three percent is a good rate and 4% is tolerable. If you are buying a house and have the cash and can get a loan in that range, don't use the cash for the house. Preferably have a job that can pay off the house. If you lose the job, don't sell your investments to pay off the house. Just move enough into a variety of dividend stocks to

---

[75] Baker, M., Wurgler, J., "The Equity Share in New Issues and Aggregate Stock Returns," Journal of Finance, v. LV n. 5, Oct 2000.

cover your payments. If the situation persists, sell the house – assuming you are not in the middle of a new housing crisis, which I doubt.

Notice that this converts non-working consumer debt (the home loan) into productive working debt (a perpetual portfolio investment).

Caution for debt addicts – you can't do this with credit card debt. The interest rate is too high and most of those items are quickly gone and do not fill an enduring need. I doubt anyone reading this book is having trouble with consumer debt, but you never know. If so, read Suze Orman or Dave Ramsey.

Don't spend a lot of money on $80,000 cars or boats. These will depreciate too fast to be worth much as collateral, and the debt is pointless. While it's not as high interest as credit card debt, it can be much larger. That does not mean do not own a nice car. I have a Jag and a Mercedes. Neither was acquired new and both are nearing 20 years old, but no one who sees them realizes this. I have a friend at work who had a reputation for driving old beat up cars of the most mass-market brands because he didn't like to spend money on them. Another friend of his was always teasing him (in a very unfair but friendly way) about the dilapidated vehicles. I persuaded my friend to try buying a used upscale vehicle. He wound up with a BMW SUV which he keeps in good repair and looking great and says he would not go back.

Lastly, there are two options within your brokerage account – only one if it's a retirement account. These are trickier. Margin from your broker will come at too high a rate, likely around 8%. You can't be totally sure of an 8% return from anything, even over long periods. If you have over a million dollars and are willing to borrow half a million on margin, TradeKing offers 4% margin at the current time and other brokers will compete for your business if you ask them, and lower their rates. If you negotiate well, you can get 3%.

While this is in the range of the mortgage rates, it comes with strings. You can only borrow 50% of the value of what you are buying, and if it drops in value to where your equity is less than 30% you will get a margin call and be forced to sell at the worst possible time when you should be buying. Moreover, you won't be able to buy back as the market recovers until your equity rises to 50% again, which will lock in the loss. If you didn't understand what I just wrote, it goes without saying, don't try it! There is plenty of information on this subject on the web and in investing how-to books for the determined. All I'm giving you here is the implications of using it to try and leverage the equity premium over long periods.

For the broker margin arrangement, the interest you'll be paying is tax deductible. But since you don't know where share prices are going over periods less than 20 years, you *must* hold enough dividend stocks to cover the margin, even if half of them drop their dividend. In a crisis they probably will.

The other broker account arrangement is to buy the new class of 2x and 3x leveraged ETFs, sometimes called *ultra* funds. These manage the margin for you so you can use them in a retirement account, and generally will get lower rates on the borrowed money than you would personally. But they are incredibly dangerous. It is like motorcycle trick racing. I mention them because you might think of them for yourself and it wouldn't do for you not to be armed with information.

Most of these funds just decline and decline throughout their history. They are meant for day traders, not for long-term holding. For example, if the index goes down 10% and up 10%, you lose 1%, but your 3x fund goes down 30% and up 30% to arrive at 91% of initial value and you lose 9%. That could happen in a few weeks time. So it is not a true perpetual portfolio strategy. It is contaminated by trading ideas. At least pick one that has a very low volatility underlying index. Plot it against its underlying index during a choppy market and see if it comes back level with the index when the index goes down and up. If not, simply do not touch.

You cannot really combine margin and ultra funds, because brokers wisely won't let you borrow much against ultra funds. And you also lose all dividends, except in one case (currently) which is MORL. However, MORL has declined often in share value. Dividend companies often do, and leverage makes any bad thing worse.

Some of my friends love to trade options. You might think this is a form of leverage, but it comes with a short expiration date and a high cost. The worst thing that ever happened to my investing life was a year of success with options in the early 1980s. I kept trying to repeat it, and missed most of the 80s bull market. Options are completely incompatible with a 20+ year time frame. You might think you could sell out-of-the money put options on an index, but it would tie up capital you could have invested.

Country Diversification

Can you capture an equity premium from other countries, or world markets? Certainly. Should you? Maybe. It is difficult to know if the high growth emerging or recently emerged markets are honest, or government engineered bubbles. Often foreign ownership is restricted, which violates two of S&Ps guidelines. Liquidity might be threatened in a crisis, in which local buyers disappear, and if not fully publically owned without restriction the companies are not public-controlled and therefore not responsive to public investor needs. They may even be a scam, and many have been exposed in the last few years. But there are also scams in the US, like Bernie Madoff. The big clue so many people missed was that Madoff's fund was not short-term volatile, and it should have been.

For established markets, there is an excellent paper available, "Equity Premiums around the World," by Dimon, Marsh and Staunton.[76] Their figure 2 – which unfortunately I cannot reproduce here but the paper can be freely downloaded and I suggest you look at it while you read this – shows equity, bond and bill returns for 20 established economies from 1900 to 2010. The rates are adjusted for inflation, so-called "real" rates of return.

A note about use of inflation in analyzing the equity premium: adjustment is necessary when comparing countries, because inflation might be different between the countries. But within a country it doesn't matter. If there is a certain difference between bond returns and equity returns, inflation affects both.

Some observations from Dimon et. al.'s figure 2:

- Annualized equity return is highest for Australia, and their bond rate is very low. Real equity return about 7.5%.
- South Africa almost ties Australia with a slightly higher bond rate.
- Sweden has about a 6.2% real return, with a still higher bond return of around 2.5%.
- Next is the US, similar to Sweden in equity return but a lower real bond yield, around 2%, giving a 4.2% equity premium, somewhat lower than Mehra and Prescott found in their methodology.
- Canada, New Zealand and the World aggregate follow with nearly identical numbers.
- Finland has a similar equity return, but slightly negative real bond return. Bond returns go up for the U.K. and up to the highest of all for Denmark, so Denmark's equity *premium* is actually the smallest of all, though Switzerland is very similar.
- Europe as an aggregate is next, and Norway has similar stats.
- Japan has an equity return a little over 4% and a strongly negative real bond return and almost a -2% bill return, giving it a fair sized

---

[76] Research Foundation Publications, vol. 2011 no. 4 (2011),
http://www.cfainstitute.org/learning/products/publications/rf/Pages/rf.v2011.n4.5.
aspx or full text PDF at
https://www.commonfund.org/ei/2012%20EI%20Level%20I%20Prereading%20
Material/Required%20Readings%20for%20Day%201%20-
%20Monday,%20July%209th/Session%203%20-
%20Long%20Term%20Global%20Equity%20Returns%20and%20the%20Equity
%20Risk%20Premium/Rethinking%20the%20Equity%20Risk%20Premium%202
011%20-%20CHAPTER%204.pdf

equity premium, higher than the US (note this period from 1900 includes Japan's great growth in the 70's and 80's and isn't comparable with our post 1990 discussion earlier)

- At the bottom of the list are the countries that have been having problems in Europe: Ireland, Spain, France, Germany, Belgium and finally Italy with a tiny 2% equity return and a -1.7% bond return.

Checking on the market performance of the top contender, Australia, via the iShares ETF with ticker EWA, data is only available from 1996. Over that time it is dead even with the S&P 500. You can pull this sort of data up easily on Yahoo Finance.[77]

Checking next on South Africa, since 2004 it has more than doubled the S&P's performance, but looking at any time frame less than 5 years the S&P is going up while South Africa is mostly declining until the last 6 months.   Except for the financial crisis, it is not particularly correlated with the US market. However, I know nothing about South African business. The index appears to be consumer, banking, telecom, energy. I guess I was expecting diamond mines. The South Africa data probably includes a dramatic revaluation. South Africa investments were heavily discouraged by many governments during apartheid.

The situation you may run into with overseas diversification is that you may have no feel for the country itself. However, if you regularly travel to or are from one of these places, you may have a better feel than for the US I do own a Russian index fund, which I bought after the big decline following Putin's re-election. I am very unsure of it, though I do have a substantial amount in it and it is doing well at the moment. But I have traveled to Russia 6 times in 2 years and spent over two months there, and am married to a Russian. In the past I have owned for long periods EEM (emerging markets), GUR (Eastern Europe), and for shorter periods HAO (China small cap), FXI (China large cap), and MAKOX (Korea), but own none of them now. Five years ago the China small cap and Korea bounced out of the recession quickly and over that period more than doubled while the S&P is up only 50%. But looking at the last 2 years the S&P is steadily rising while the others went through a 20% down, 20-30% up maneuver. The China small cap and Korea still look the strongest.

Jumping from country to country is not a perpetual portfolio strategy. It is simple trading and without expertise it will result in losses. There are many indices vying to become regional or global equivalents of

---

[77] http://finance.yahoo.com

the respected S&P family, but as far as I can tell there is not enough data history to make any country diversification strategy more than ad hoc.

The Euro and Gold

The grouping of the troubled southern Euro zone countries at the bottom, together with the previous observation that countries became more able to pay back their debt when currencies became free floating, i.e. when the gold standard was revoked, suggests an analogy between the Euro and gold. Effectively the weaker Euro countries have regressed in monetary policy.

They have *regressed* to a currency based on a scarce gold-like commodity – the Euro – over which they have no control. There is a fixed quantity of Euros as far as these countries are concerned. From when the US became totally committed to the gold standard in 1900, to the total meltdown of US markets in 1929, was 29 years. Euro currency and banknotes entered circulation in early 2002[78]. The European sovereign debt crisis began in late 2009, after less than 8 years.

Greece, Spain, Portugal, Italy, Ireland and so forth have almost no control over the European Central Bank policies. The central bank caters mostly to the Germans who are inflation-phobic for traumatic and understandable historical reasons. The European Central Bank, unlike the Fed, has no charter to maximize employment. In retrospect, what were they thinking? Maybe the weaker countries will remain in the Euro. But personally, I do not believe I will invest in any European country, weak or strong, until the Euro is dissolved and valuations have re-adjusted. It does not matter how strong a currency is if an economy is not growing. With a free floating currency, a poorly run economy suffers inflation and is spontaneously devalued and their goods and services become cheaper for export while their debts become easier to pay. Lenders had better consider this possibility when they make loans, and be glad they are getting paid something and the country has not defaulted.

Bonds actually become less risky with a floating currency. The risk of outright default is replaced by currency valuation risk. But over the long-term the better export position allows the country to recover and the currency become strong again, without the stressful machinations of deflation and actually cutting wages formally. They are cut de facto. So the bonds may recover.

War and Monetary Policy

Pre WWII Germany is not a similar situation to the modern debt of weaker European nations, and the German paranoia about inflation is harmful in the current context. Technically it was unemployment, not

---

[78] http://en.wikipedia.org/wiki/Euro

inflation, that caused extreme hardship in Germany, and it is unemployment in the weaker European nations that is being fostered by German monetary policy.

German debt was war reparations debt, not voluntary bonds, and was due in *gold* upon which the inflation of its internal currency had no effect. Foreign trade at the time was based on gold, not on floating currencies. The feedback self-correction mechanism I described above could not operate, so domestic inflation went unchecked and had no benefit for the economy. According to Mehra and Prescott in a 2003 retrospective:

> *There was a marked increase in the US equity premium after 1933 when the US abandoned the gold standard.*[79]

That is the particular comment that put me on the track to solving the equity premium puzzle.

In 1929 a committee headed by Owen Young and including the likes of J. P. Morgan, Jr. proposed a new plan allowing Germany to postpone $2/3^{rd}$ of its payment each year. Over Britain's objection the plan was adopted in 1930, but due to the onset of depression American banks recalled credits that made the plan possible.[80]

Given hard economic times, opposition to the repayment of any war debt was growing in Germany, even the reduced amount of the Young plan. Hitler's party joined a coalition which brought about a referendum to enact a Liberty Law repudiating the debt and admission of war guilt, and re-claiming territory. The referendum was defeated but Hitler's National Socialists had used the occasion to establish political legitimacy.

Unemployment in Germany reached 33.7% in 1931 and 40% in 1932. In 1933, the same year that Roosevelt took office and confiscated American's gold, repudiating the gold standard internal to the US, world trade fell to $1/3^{rd}$ of its former value and Hitler came to power and repudiated the reparations. Germany quickly reversed its economic fortunes and became a major industrial power. But the political damage was already done, and it used its power to wage global war.

The blind following of emotional attachments rather than the true historical meaning of money rooted in mutual exchange leads to mistakes in monetary policy – mistakes that have serious consequences.

---

[79] Mehra, R. and Prescott E., "The equity premium in retrospect," in: G.M. Constantinides & M. Harris & R. M. Stulz (ed.), Handbook of the Economics of Finance, edition 1, volume 1, chapter 14, pages 889-938, Elsevier (2003).
[80] http://en.wikipedia.org/wiki/Young_Plan

Pitfalls of Windfalls

The Likely Timing of Windfalls

Whether it is a large gift, winning the lottery, or the rare case where one of your investments goes up by a factor of ten (very rare, trust me), a sudden influx of more money than one is accustomed to handling can stress the financial decision making process and lead to poor investments or unlucky timing. In particular in the case of a gift from a relative or a large bonus from a business deal or from your employer, consider that the timing of this in relation to market valuations is likely not coincidental. Market bubbles form when people are generally feeling confident about making money, feeling like they have enough money to do business deals and share with relatives, and take more chances.

This is probably why you got the money at that time, instead of some other time. I received a series of small windfalls in the late 90s just before the dotcom bust, and a larger one in 2006 which I had just got up enough courage to move fully into the market by 2008 as the financial crisis began. By March of 2009 as the market declined 40% (i.e. nearly in half) my newly doubled net worth was almost back to what it had been before the windfall.

What really happens to lottery winners

STATISTIC BRAIN reports that *44% of lottery winners had spent their entire winnings within 5 years.*[81] On the bright side, those hundreds of stories on the web about the disasters that befall lottery winners – losing all their friends, their spouse, and their health in many cases – may not be representative. SB reports 95% stay married to the same person, and of the unmarried ones 100% stay in the same relationship. But the financial risk is there. The *Review of Economics and Statistics* reports 1900 Florida lottery winners go bankrupt each year, *twice the normal per capita bankruptcy rate.*[82] There is something about a sudden influx of money that increases the probability of an out flux of even more money. And there is nothing about an influx of money that changes poor financial habits.

Whether you have a windfall, or create your own windfall over a lifetime of work and investing, you will be in a different place in life and will probably wonder how much to change and how much to keep of your old self, how much to help others or whether you are just encouraging dependency, and whether to trust any of this money to a volatile market.

---

[81] http://www.statisticbrain.com/lottery-winner-statistics/
[82] http://www.marketwatch.com/story/why-lottery-winners-go-bankrupt-1301002181742

What to do with $80 million

I don't know of a systematic study of *successful* lottery winners, but Brad Duke, who won $220 million in 2005, was recently giving interviews and still has his life and his money. Eight years is well beyond the infant mortality period for windfalls, so let's look at what he did. He says:

> *"I stayed in my house, I drove a used car for up to three years afterwards, The more I started to fantasize about what I could do with the money, the more I felt like I should try to keep my feet on the ground and change as little as I could."*[83]

It sounds like he took a page out of Warren Buffett's playbook. Buffett famously lives in the same house he bought in 1958 for $31,000.[84] (Less sensational and less often reported is that Buffett owns a home in Laguna Beach valued at $4 million,[85] still insignificant compared to his fortune, and still small potatoes compared to the homes of many billionaires.) Here is what Duke did with his windfall, again from SB[86]:

Brad Duke's disposition of $220 million in 2005

item	thousands
low risk (e.g. muni-bonds)	$45,000
high risk (oil, real estate)	$35,000
family foundation	$1,300
trip to Tahiti with 17 friends	$63
pay off mortgage on 1400 sq. ft. home	$125
pay off student loan	$18
new bicycles	$65
used VW Jetta	$14.50
annual gift to each family member	$12
TOTAL:	$81,598

Probably Brad went for the lump sum settlement which is much less than the total annuity if paid over many years, and then there are taxes. While the annuity sounds like a plan for avoiding loss, it will greatly

[83] http://www.npr.org/2013/08/11/211019737/lottery-winner-stays-grounded-after-220-million-jackpot

[84] http://thestir.cafemom.com/home_garden/149934/Billionaire_Warren_Buffetts_Home_Is

[85] http://www.huffingtonpost.com/2013/01/18/warren-buffett-home_n_2507179.html

[86] http://www.statisticbrain.com/lottery-winner-statistics/

increase the temptation to use credit to accelerate a part of the lump sum forward.

However, not only do you need to think about your own financial health, but of the other people you care about or are responsible for. I think Brad's annual gift to family members is an insightful choice. If he makes a commitment, they can begin to plan on this amount. It is enough to help them toward their goals, but it is not so much as to eclipse their own efforts at a career or education, which might result in their feeling both ineffective and dependent. And Brad need not worry too much that he has purchased their affection. Brad also seems to agree with my advice about cars, though I understand he has moved up from the Jetta recently.

What of the investments? Looks like Brad slightly favored bonds. In all he invested $80 million, and immediately spent only about $300k, two thirds of which went to pay off productive debts (which I recommended against, but the amount for Brad was so insignificant it was worth it to clear his paper clutter each month).

Of course Brad's current financial picture is not public. Let's consider two alternatives. The first is an approximation to Brad's strategy using ETFs with similar stated objectives. Since ETFs are a new and growing investment tool, the particular ones needed weren't available until a year or two later and probably Brad used a private investment management company. One could have used mutual funds. But for an example in this book let's pick ETFs as they are the most relevant modern investment structure, with easy access and low costs and lacking proprietary formulas. The results will all be annualized so the comparison is fair. We just have to be careful to avoid ETFs that were created near the bottom of the housing crash in 2008-9 in order to be timing neutral.

The strategy uses a muni-bond ETF that I owned for about a year, which avoids selection bias (looking at survivors and picking one with good performance, i.e. I picked it in the late 2000's). This is Market Vectors Long Municipal Index, symbol MLN. It is interesting to note in retrospect that this was originally a Lehman security, acquired by Market Vectors after Lehman went bankrupt. This should not affect the performance of MLN since its assets were not cross linked to any Lehman strategies, but were a public list of municipal bonds. It starts in January of 2008.

The second ETF, for the oil and gas part, was arbitrarily chosen to be iShares US Oil & Gas Exploration & Production, symbol IEO, with a start date in January 2007. I assumed capital gains would be left to accumulate, and dividends and interest would be withdrawn as annual income, with no tax on the munis and the 15% qualified dividend rate on oil and gas dividends. If an investment went down in value (one did) I assumed part of the yield was used to replenish capital, reducing annual income but not working capital. This affects only the dollar annual income figures. The annualized capital gains, average yield, and after tax income are given below.

For an alternative comparable to a perpetual portfolio strategy, I assumed the entire amount was invested in the S&P 500 via the SPDR S&P 500 ETF, symbol SPY, in October of 2007. End date on both data sets is October 31, 2013.

Bond + Aggressive Strategy vs. Perpetual Portfolio

Investment	Initial amount	Total gain/loss	Annualized gain/loss	Typical yield	After-tax income
Brad's Strategy:					
Muni-bonds	$45 M	-9.91%	-1.91%	4.23%	$1 M
Oil & gas	$35 M	30.64%	4.55%	1.23%	$.4 M
Total	$80 M	7.83%	.92%	2.92%	$1.4 M
Perpetual PF:					
S&P 500	$80 M	14%	2.2%	2.02%	$1.5 M

The end value of the perpetual portfolio was $91.2 million, and the end value of Brad's strategy approximation was $90.7 million. The income from Brad's strategy should have been higher, but as I took about 2% of yield to replenish loss of working capital (which increased the final value), Brad has an after tax income of only $1.4 million vs. $1.5 million for the perpetual strategy. The oil and gas strategy may require adjustment over the next century, and it must have been nerve-wracking to hold $45 million in municipal bonds during the crisis when many thought there would be wholesale bankruptcy of municipalities due to declining revenue from residential taxes.

The overall performance of the two approaches is similar over a 6 year period. Mr. Duke actually did extremely well.

The S&P is doing enough better on an annualized basis that the difference might grow over time. Equity premium studies have shown that to be the case. Notice that either portfolio did OK even during a financial crisis. Bank interest is fully taxable at rates up to 38% and has dropped into the 1-2% range. The numbers are a bit theoretical because MLN is not liquid enough to absorb $45 million. The size of the muni-bond market is not unlimited. The muni transaction would probably have to be handled by an expert broker with a high commission, and still the munis would not be liquid.

If you look at just muni-bonds the results were terrible, but were compensated by good performance in oil and gas. The oil and gas did very well by itself in capital gains, but did not produce much annual income.

This fund is volatile and dropped 30% in the first quarter of 2012, recovering only in early 2013.

Which portfolio would you rather have?

Full Disclosure

Ah, you are wondering what happened to me, your author, who lost all of a huge windfall during that period? I sold my munis and bought REITs and BDCs while they were down, and three months after the market bottomed I took my broker up on an offer of 3% interest on a large amount of margin. The loss was recovered and I am up 28.6% over the 6 year period, for an annualized gain of 4.3%.

This is not directly comparable because I am not retired yet and have withdrawn funds only once, to pay taxes.[87] If you take the S&P strategy and re-invest the dividends, it comes out to a 27.94% gain. So all my time and energy strategizing and moving money around only gave me a .66% advantage over the perpetual portfolio strategy.

If you scale Duke's winnings down to something reasonable, you see that to retire only on your investments at the current time with an income of $150,000 a year after taxes, you need to have working capital of $8 million. I do not have nearly that much. That is why I have BDCs and REITs, with dividend yields in the 6 to 15% range. These can possibly have the same problem as the munis and erode in value over time. The BDCs have only been around about a decade and no one is yet sure over time what they will do. It is possible to hold index ETFs of either BDCs or REITs, or a combination but the yields are on the lower side of the range (e.g. KBWD has lost 2.64% in the 9 months I've owned it and only yields around 7% annually). In addition to the Russia fund I mentioned, doing well at the moment, and recent acquisition of an S&P 500 fund, I have things like shipping stocks which are extremely volatile and risky, but if the world economy improves they should have both capital gains and dividends.

What not to do with a small amount of money

My problem with how to generate future retirement income from a smaller portfolio, without sabotaging long-term gains, brings up the question of what do you do with a small amount of money? It is sort of the opposite of a windfall. I have always been more successful with larger amounts for some reason. For one thing there is more diversification, and often my 2nd and 3rd choices outperform my 1st choices. I have normally been successful only with accounts around $100k or greater. Below that it is a savings program more than investing.

---

[87] I have not added funds either, making the computation straightforward.

I tried a training-wheels account with my wife and watched $5k decline to $4.3k in a year in which the overall market did fairly well. It was almost entirely income oriented. Not such a good idea, apparently, and we guess that Brad is probably looking over his munis and thinking the same thing. Notice I did not say *dividends* were not a good idea. An all growth approach fails when the leading company fails without ever having paid investors a dime. The perpetual portfolio captures some of everything.

Recap

A portfolio with unlimited growth life can be crafted from companies that themselves have limited life expectancy and ultimately zero return on share price.

So far, this is only known to be reliable with selections of companies that represent entire markets, generally known as index funds. Citizens and governments will act to protect and restore markets giving them a high probability of long life, but they will not always rally around individual companies.

Using such a portfolio for investing purposes presents many challenges, chief among them patience, as in the short-term many alternatives will appear better.

Whether generally the time preferences of investors result in substantial equalization pressure from the long-term values either of long lived companies (which do exist) or long-lived portfolios has not been studied as far as I know. However, in the next chapter I will show that widely different intrinsic returns without an end date *cannot* be equalized.

This will mean that all equalization would have to come through assets that do not have intrinsic returns, such as bonds which have contractual returns that can take any value. That will lead *eventually* to the final piece of the puzzle, which is whether a central banker can set such rates lower than average intrinsic equity returns without evoking an unacceptable market reaction such as inflation. But several factors that bear will need to be explored.

PART THREE

Solving the Puzzle

Equalization vs. Intrinsic Growth
Monetary Policy & Productivity

Intrinsic Returns

Perpetual vs. Maximal

The only claim made about perpetual portfolios has been that with a bit of luck, no nuclear winter or asteroids or alien invasions, one should last indefinitely. As we saw in the previous examples, they are clearly configurable to produce varying amounts of income. If all of the funds are retained in the portfolio, then it produces its maximum return, and I call it a *maximal portfolio*.

This does not mean maximum in an absolute sense. One country may do better than another or a lucky investor may produce a higher return some other way. Just that for a particular set of stocks with a particular rotation through time, all of the earnings are retained and re-invested.

There are a number of limits on the maximal strategy. Tax will have to be paid on the dividends. If the holding is personal and large, some estate tax will be due when it is passed on. A corporation might escape the estate tax, but owners of the corporation would not. But for purposes of an illustration we'll ignore those details.

Let us take rates of return similar to the Brad Duke example. Suppose a bond return of 4%, and an equity index fund with a dividend yield of 2% and earnings growth of 2% for a total return of 4%, same as the bond (actually much worse than historical averages). We assume the earnings growth is reflected in the stock prices and P/E ratios remain fairly constant.

It should be clear without my drawing a bunch of graphs that the future returns of the two strategies are identical, and the returns are equal and equalized. If such were not the case initially as it is here, economists would expect it to come about by adjustments to the price of bonds or stocks or both.

Investor Rank

One further word about limits on the maximal strategy. The bond version is limited by the availability of bond issues. That is not of much interest. It is just some limit. But the equity version, assuming the index fund properly represents the whole market, has a more clearly known upper limit, which is the size of the market.

Financial media are fond of publishing lists of the 500 largest companies, the 400 richest people, etc. Since few people hold their wealth in cash or gold, this amounts to a list ranking people by ownership of the world's economy, i.e. businesses and resources.

If one buys a certain amount of an index fund representing a capital market, the percentage of ownership represented by that purchase will remain unchanged until that investor buys or sells more shares –

provided of course the index fund functions as it is supposed to. This is not true if the investor buys some other type of fund, one that is not constantly adjusted to be representative. This percentage effectively establishes that investor's rank.

Forbes Top 10 Ranking for 2013[88]

rank	investor	worth $B	source	Δ 2012	%Δ
1	Bill Gates	$72	Microsoft	$6	8.3%
2	Warren Buffett	$58.50	Berkshire	$12.50	21.4%
3	Larry Ellison	$41	Oracle	0	0.0%
4	Charles Koch	$36	Diversified	$5	13.9%
4	David Koch	$36	Diversified	$5	13.9%
6	C. Walton fam.	$35.40	Wal-Mart	$7.50	21.2%
7	Jim Walton	$33.80	Wal-Mart	$6.70	19.8%
8	Alice Walton	$33.50	Wal-Mart	$7.20	21.5%
9	S. Robson Walton	$33.30	Wal-Mart	$7.20	21.6%
10	M. Bloomberg	$31	Bloomberg	$6	19.4%

Money is after all relative. About 90% of a stock's price movement is typically due to general market movement. If the market goes up, almost all investors get richer and few get relatively richer than they were. The price of yachts and exotic islands will just go up with the market, as the same pool of investors are bidding for them and only their relative wealth matters. It's a little more complicated of course. Often the people at the very top seem to be able to acquire wealth faster, and the rank spacing may change. But when times turn bad they can lose it faster too. At times when the middle class is rising, rank spacing tends to contract.

Notice on the chart from Forbes that Bill Gates, retired and concerned with distributing his wealth for philanthropic purposes, is far ahead but likely to drop in rank eventually. Warren Buffett, who seems to accumulate wealth habitually for no particular purpose, is rising at an astonishing rate, as are the Waltons who dominate the list, occupying 4 out of 10 slots with a net worth that if combined would easily out-class Gates, and whose rates of increase eclipse all but the aging Mr. Buffett. The Waltons are not even first generation wealth. Apparently, someone has clued them in. If your ambition is to use the method I have suggested to create a family dynasty over the next 100 years, it would appear these will be your company at the top of the list.

---

[88] http://www.forbes.com/sites/forbespr/2013/09/16/forbes-announces-its-32nd-annual-forbes-400-ranking-of-the-richest-americans/

The Effect of Dividends

Bonds convey no investor rank whatever. They only convey cash payments. A bond investor might have a theoretical rank based on converting bonds and cash to equity at a particular time, but there is no mechanism to preserve rank as with equities.

The returns from equities are of two distinctly different types. The price growth portion of the return of a market representative index maintains investor rank. The dividends are *extra*.

So-called growth companies are companies that have declared their intent to outgrow other companies and increase their rank. Since many such companies compete with one another, and a lot of capital is lost and wasted in the inevitable failures – it's not unusual for 100's of companies to compete for a new market where 1 or 2 or 3 will be successful – a growth strategy is in my opinion a bit risky. As I said earlier, if you find you can always pick the shortest queue, the fastest lane, this is your talent. Go for it.

An alternate strategy to increase rank is to use the index fund, which is mechanically adjusted to represent the market and preserve rank, and use the dividends to acquire more shares. Re-invested dividends increase an investor's share of the economy.

Selling shares to meet cash needs decreases an investor's share of the economy. Of course, if you have no children and only wish to fund your retirement activities, this is quite reasonable. Earlier I asserted 8 million dollars was a reasonable retirement nest egg. But that was assuming the nest egg should remain intact, for heirs or for some noble endowment upon the investor's death.

If the next egg can be depleted, a couple million should do nicely. Unless of course someone invents an anti-aging serum. Then liquidation may not appear to have been a great strategy. But such a consideration is a bit beyond our scope in this book. The normal advice given by financial counselors is to plan a depletion approach to retirement. But in this book we are going to be talking about 100 year analyses of the equity premium, and thus 100 year returns by necessity, as they are evidenced in data, and we cannot be concerned by the limited lifespan of investors. If human investors will not buy stocks and hold for the long-term, then presumably corporations will.

Before you get carried away with your plans, a little dose of reality. The market capitalization of the S&P 500 is $5.14 trillion[89]. Not so large when you compare it to the US debt, so I would not worry about running out of bonds to buy. I also would not put too much stock in the

---

[89] http://us.spindices.com/indices/equity/sp-500

idea of taxing $5.14 trillion to pay off the US national debt of $17 trillion, increasing at $2.59 billion per day.[90] And with reference to the equity premium, if the $5.14 trillion in assets earns a little more than the $17 trillion, it is a drop in the bucket.

But the market cap is large compared to most private wealth. The Waltons collectively own 2.56% of the S&P 500 market cap, and they had to replace practically every store in small town America to reach that level. The Forbes top ten have the equivalent of 7.99%. If you *started* with $1 billion and attempted to make it onto this list by investing in the 500 index and re-investing 2% each year, it would take 153 years to reach the $20 billion entry point (assuming the cap value remained 5.14 trillion). Presumably better investment alternatives are available to these people on this list. Or maybe they just got there by luck. However in Warren's case, I don't really think it was entirely luck, nor in the case of the Walton's forebear Sam Walton.

If you attempt to take over all of the S&P 500 by this method, it will take 432 years. I would prefer corporations pay more dividends. I already stated what I think of the wastefulness of the competitive growth no-dividend strategy because of the large number of failures, and the possibility of never getting any return at all from an investment. However, in the next section we will learn a potentially powerful method for utilizing growth that can go beyond the 2%. Some variation of this is undoubtedly used by the people on the Forbes list.

Intrinsic Returns

If an equity return has been equalized by price action in a market setting, then the return on the market price is the supposed equalized return. But the business activity has a return on the private capital that was used for actual costs – to buy material and equipment and pay people to operate the business in the first place before it was sold to the public. The return on these actual costs is the intrinsic return. This continues to be relevant after the business is sold to the public, because as money is deployed within the business, it continues to earn this intrinsic return which may be lower or higher than the public return.

We presume that if the intrinsic return is lower than public market returns, the business is declining and liquidating and will presently cease. Or that management will not deploy capital in expanding the business, since a greater return is available in public markets or elsewhere. This seems to have been, for example, exactly the reasoning of Warren Buffett after he bought Berkshire-Hathaway, a textile mill. Instead of deploying capital to expand a business with lower returns than available elsewhere,

---

[90] http://www.brillig.com/debt_clock/

he terminated textile operations and used Berkshire as a holding company to acquire higher return businesses.

While sometimes Mr. Buffett has acquired shares of companies in public markets, it was usually when in his opinion they were less than fair value. More often he has acquired entire companies. This has two benefits for him:

1. Expansion capital may be deployed within the acquired companies at the intrinsic (or private) return rate rather than the public capital market rate.
2. Earnings capital from a company in excess of what is needed for expansion can be re-directed to other companies in Berkshire's portfolio and a return realized at their intrinsic rates.

The success of Berkshire's methodology is evident in a Berkshire share price exceeding what most consider to be the fair market value of its components (net asset value). Usually, in the case of a closed-end fund, the fund value will be less than NAV. In a closed-end fund, or any kind of mutual fund or ETF for that matter, ownership and management of the companies is not controlled and the companies are free to hoard cash or ineffectively deploy capital. Moreover in a closed-end fund only the fund management can re-deploy the publicly available capital, not shareholders, thus the depressed valuations of closed-end funds is probably linked to their position on the low end of a spectrum of capital re-deployment flexibility.

Public companies or funds convertible into cash at the underlying NAV of public companies occupy a place in the middle of the spectrum. And a company such as Berkshire has much greater flexibility than public investors in capital re-deployment.

At the time of the current writing, Apple has one of the largest cash piles ever seen at a corporation and refuses to re-deploy it, probably because they perceive their expansion limited only by the market and their innovation pace, not by capital. Re-deployment of this capital could actually hurt Apple by cannibalizing its business from within. Certainly distributing it to shareholders will allow them to re-invest it, and some of those funds would go to Apple competitors. While Apple is in an enviable position at the top of its industry, expanding by re-defining what industry it is in and creating new industries, it has dug somewhat of a hole by its success in amassing such a cash pile and admitting it does not know how to re-deploy it. This un-deployed capital dilutes the effective intrinsic return at Apple. I have no advice for Apple. I only wish I had their "problems." But I use the situation to illustrate basic points about capital deployment and intrinsic vs. public market returns (which might be called extrinsic, I suppose).

Estimating Intrinsic Returns

We can estimate *typical* intrinsic returns of US corporations by at least two different methods, and thankfully they yield answers that are at least similar.

Perhaps the simplest is to examine the known returns of investors who have great access to intrinsic returns through direct ownership and/or control of companies, such as the members of the Forbes top ten list above. We would expect them to have a return perhaps on the high end because of selection bias. Their cap-weighted return for the year 2013 over a 2012 base is 15.4%.

But we should not estimate *typical* intrinsic returns that high. We might plausibly only estimate that this return is typical of an active business in its growth phase. Indeed, the fortunes of the two list members which seem to be based on mature businesses from which they are not branching out, Gates and Ellison, average more like the 4-5%, typical of bond returns. And there are no businesses on the list that are in full decline (yet, anyway). Dell or J.C. Penney would be examples of businesses in decline with negative returns over an extended period.

Based on the permanent portfolio simulation model that was developed in an earlier chapter, we can now identify that the healthy growth rate G_H of 12% in that model is analogous to the 15.4% Forbes top ten growth rate above identified above. The 6.4% average growth rate G_P of the model after accounting for the 18 year average tenure on the S&P 500 is the average intrinsic growth rate we are looking for. This was arrived at either by simulation or by subtracting a 5.6% penalty for the 18 year lifetime. If we subtract the 5.6 from 15.4 we arrive at a (probably high) estimate of average intrinsic growth for billionaire-owned companies of 9.8%.

A second way of estimating the intrinsic growth rate is to look at very long time periods. We will see below why it cannot be hidden over long time periods, and shows up in market returns. Market returns over the long period are equal to bond returns plus the equity premium, if there is any premium, by definition of the terms. Since the equity premium is in the range of 6% to 8% in most studies, a few as low as 4%, we can pick a middle value and add our base assumption of 4% bond returns and we find an estimate of average intrinsic return of $6 + 4 = 10\%$.

Oddly, and I didn't plan it, the 10% estimate is within .2% of the 9.8% estimate based on the Forbes list. This is probably due to the use of similar business methods with similar productivity and competitive profit margin. It is probably not an accident that the rate is similar. To use a favorite argument of economists which underlies rational efficient markets, why would any competent billionaire deploy capital for returns lower than commonly available? Well, of course for altruistic-humanitarian reasons as in the case of Bill Gates, and possibly in the case of some sports team owners. But otherwise the private capital market is probably efficient.

Using this higher return of 10%, repeating our earlier questions of how long starting with $1 billion to join the Forbes list, or to own the S&P 500, we find much accelerated times of 32 years and 90 years respectively. This is *much* more practical. If the child of one of these rich people were endowed with $1 billion at birth, presumably they would own 80% of the US economy if they chose to do so by age 90. Alas we have not factored in taxes, but they would still do quite well. Even a modest endowment of $100 million and taking out 25% dividend tax each year would result in membership in the Forbes top 10 list by age 74 without any other business activity or above average success.

To scale this down to our size, if you can accumulate $1 million to endow to your child at birth in this fashion, they would have $200 million at age 74. By then they could endow a grandchild, your great grandchild, as estate tax should only take half the 200 million, who would become a member of the Forbes top 10 at age 43 after taxes. Repeating this two more times reaches the range of owning something like 1/3rd of the S&P 500. It would seem that the very rich are not as greedy as we assume, because none of them have done this. Gates and Buffett both made only modest provisions for their offspring by comparison. Buffett is not using his money for very much, apparently, and Gates is giving his away. Even those making political contributions or entering politics would probably tell you they have the interests of the country in mind, and probably they are sincere even if you or I might disagree with their values and opinions.

Equalizing Intrinsic Returns

Now suppose you are the successful entrepreneur with an intrinsic return of 10%, and you offer shares in your company to the public. Being altruistic, you offer them at the intrinsic return rate. Shares valued at $10 will have a claim to $1 of earnings or growth in the current year.

Assuming a P/E ratio of 25 is the going public rate in your industry, pretty typical for growth businesses that are already profitable, the lucky people who scoop up your IPO will immediately offer the shares for sale at $25. The earnings return for these shares will be $1/$25 = 4%. How about that. Over the first year at least, the shares are equalized with 4% bonds. Market efficiency is upheld, and your altruistic action only benefitted a few favored clients of the brokers handling the IPO.

However, you made no promises about dividends. Your business is young. You keep all the earnings and re-deploy this capital at 10%. In the 2nd year, your earnings are $1.10.

The lucky holder of a 4% bond acquired for $25 finds earnings in the first year of $1. If this bondholder re-invests *all* of the earnings in additional bonds at the same 4% bond rate, then earnings (interest payments really) in the second year will be $1.04. In the 2nd year, rational investors find to their surprise that your shares have more earnings than the bond they *equalized* them with last year. They immediately bid up the share price to $27.50 to maintain the P/E of 25 and 4% earnings, even though of course they haven't got their hands on a dime of the earnings yet as you continue to keep them all for re-deployment.

Discovered Growth

Now comes phase two of the equalization game. A savvy analyst notices that your real growth was the earnings growth, reflected in the share price increase of 10% from $25 to $27.50. This analyst boldly predicts you will keep up this growth rate for ten years before dropping back to market average. She issues a target price of $30.25 for year three, and of $64.84 for the tenth year, based on this 10% growth.

Financial types are not slow with numbers. The bond analyst figures out that at the 4% bond rate, he'd have to buy $45.55 worth of bonds in year one to match your target value of $64.84 in year ten. Immediately analysts fall to arguing about the confidence of the original equity analyst's prediction of a growth rate of 10% for ten years. This is at best somewhat more risky than a bond. A risk premium should be applied.

At first they assume your business has average risk, and they apply the 1% risk premium that Mehra and Prescott suggested, so the discount rate for your company is to be 5% rather than 4%. Investors listen and heed and the share price becomes $41.79. There might be some oscillations because momentum traders will see the jump and think there is some insider information driving it, but it will eventually settle back to $41.79.

Below is a table of the original analysts forecast price trend (the 10% column) and 10 year discounted price tables at 4% and 5%.

Below that is a *chart* of the original analysts 10 year price forecast, and of the 5% discounted price curve investors settled on in year 1.

10-year discount pricing at 5% or 10% growth

P/E in year 1 with earnings of $1.10:

	25	41	38
year	10%	4%	5%
0	$25	$25	$25.00
1	$27.50	$45.55	$41.79
2	$30.25	$47.37	$43.88
3	$33.28	$49.27	$46.07
4	$36.60	$51.24	$48.38
5	$40.26	$53.29	$50.80
6	$44.29	$55.42	$53.34
7	$48.72	$57.64	$56.00
8	$53.59	$59.94	$58.80
9	$58.95	$62.34	$61.74
10	$64.84	$64.83	$64.83

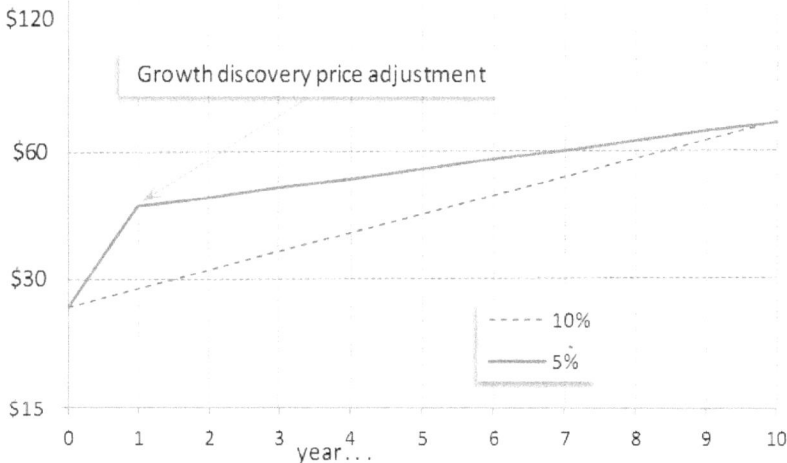

Anyone who bought the stock before the equity analyst discovered the growth in year 1 experienced a windfall, as the year one price jumped from $27.50 on publication of the article, finally settling at $41.79 after a risk rate of 5% was agreed on by way of averaging analyst estimates and investor sentiment. There might be a few who think the risk rate should be much higher, that the company is even doomed. But no one thinks the risk rate should be set equal to the growth rate of 10%. What connection would there be? No, the risk rate is a separate proposition, a reflection of risk in the business plan. The growth rate is a reflection of mechanics of the business plan, the ability to field a bug-free product, ramp up manufacturing, handle distribution and marketing and maintain margins in the face of competition. Risks are things like consumer enthusiasm or lack thereof, unexpected glitches, and unexpected competition.

Notice that after the stock is "equalized" to the 5% risk rate, there is no longer any advantage to buying it. It has the same return as any other similarly priced stock, and accounting for the risk factor most investors consider it an even proposition with a nice safe 4% bond. Apparently these are not the muni-bond ETFs which our Brad Duke simulated portfolio found so disappointing. A good deal of the share price value is dependent upon the future 9 years distant, and small fluctuations in investor feelings about that distant future can swing the current price of your shares easily plus or minus 50% without any change in current earnings.

What you see a lot of in investing is people and fund managers trying to *guess* where growth will be discovered next, to catch those big jumps of re-valuation. If there were some systematic way of doing this, then the growth would have already been discovered.

Notice also that if you are late to the party and buy the stock at $41.79, you get a paltry 5% return. If you had instead bought a dividend company with an intrinsic return of 10%, like a BDC, then you'd really be getting a 10% return. At least this is the theory behind BDCs and the special law that *requires* them to pay out most of their earnings as dividends. BDCs have not been around long enough to assess whether they are a long-term alternative to the more complex scenario with the equity premium and periodic discovery of growth.

It's not equalized yet

You the entrepreneur, unless you were planning on retiring in ten years, have no intention of following this analyst's plan. You will keep deploying capital at the best available rate, which for a long time has been around 10% and will continue to be. If this business fizzles out, then like Jobs or Buffett you will simply go into another one. IBM went into consulting. Dell tried some other things but just wasn't able to execute well. GE has been in so many businesses no one remembers them all.[91]

The P/E jumped to 38 after the discovered growth in year 1, and will gradually decline to 25 again in year 10 if you keep your plans secret and the equity analyst cannot guess them. Indeed it will look like the business is maturing. In year 11 you announce a new product line and

---

[91] Figuratively speaking. I'm sure records are available. However, note that "conglomerates" are not as favored as they once were and corporations may somewhat serialize their ventures, or start entirely separate companies like for example Jobs' Pixar.

your earnings again jump 10% from $2.59 to $2.85, rather than the expected 4%. Everyone realizes you have another ten years left in you, and instead of 4% growth you will continue to deliver 10%. At that point your share price again jumps just like it did in year 1. It jumps 60% to over $110. Sound familiar? Successful companies do this all the time.

If you run all the numbers and continue this to infinity, and take the long running average of the returns of this company, they will always be 10%, or whatever the real intrinsic return rate is. They will never be anything else except temporarily for a few years at a time. They cannot be. It is a mathematical impossibility.

This means that equity and bond prices in the long time frames in which the equity premium is observed *cannot* be equalized through equity prices. There are a number of other ways in which they might be equalized, and we'll discuss each in turn. But the most common one cited in economics literature is equity price adjustment, and it is a fiction. Or an oversight perhaps would be the more accurate phrase. But a really big oversight, because this is not rocket science yet. We'll get there later on the monetary policy end of things.

Proof

The loose almost anecdotal arguments above are meant to entertain and enlighten the casual reader. If that describes you, please skip this section so that you will not give me a bad review. For a complete exposition of course the serious reader can see the formal paper. But here is a quick summary of the proof of the proposition that equalization cannot occur through equity pricing.

The proof proceeds by introducing a standard economic concept called a time preference. It is the time horizon in which an investor is interested. The subject has informally come up many times in this book. Some investors are saving for tomorrow, or later this year. Some are investing for retirement or their children's education. Nothing matters beyond this time preference value N years. However, we assume investors are constantly leaving and entering the pool of investors, so every year the whole question of valuation and time preferences is re-visited.

We value future returns using the appropriate risk adjusted rate R_1 to discount a future payment P_N after N years to a net present value in year 1:

$$NPV_{PN,1} = P_N/(1+R_1)^N$$

If an investment is a business activity, it has some intrinsic return on equity which we designate as R_E. We may suppose that the business activity is originally financed at some cost C_0 and the cash value at year N

can be estimated by $P_N=C_0(1+R_E)^N$. At the formation stage, R_E is a function of costs C_0 and bears no definite relation to risk rate R_1 at which the investment may be resold.

Consider a large pool of investors, with new ones entering and old ones retiring, so that the average time preference N for the pool can be presumed to be relatively constant. After a year goes by, the future cash value P_N appears closer and the value should be: $NPV_{PN,2} = P_N/(1+R_1)^{N-1} = NPV_{PN,1}(1+R_1)$.

If this were a debt instrument either terminating in year N, or continuing to earn income at the risk discount rate R_1, that would be the end of the story. But it does neither. The investors collectively see a new interval of N years ranging from 2 to $N+1$, and a new final value $P_{N+1}=C_0(1+R_E)^{N+1}=P_N(1+R_E)$. The investors dutifully compute the net present value of this new "final payment," and discover:

$$NPV_{PN+1,2} = P_{N+1}/(1+R_1)^N = P_N(1+R_E)/(1+R_1)^N = NPV_{PN,1}(1+R_E)$$

Thus equalization measures have been ineffective regardless of the size of N, and the annual returns are over long-term equilibrium equal to the intrinsic returns.

In the paper I go on to discuss how an investor who is aware of this difficulty might try to equalize the price by making further adjustments, and so forth. This results in P/E's in the thousands or tens of thousands, which we know investors do not pay. It also results in extreme sensitivity to events in the far future. For example, I discuss a case where an equity with a life of 100 years has a net present value of $1653, but if growth is just ½ % higher it is worth $2581, but if growth stops after 90 years it is worth $788.

To some extent it is a matter of semantics. Perhaps you might say this volatility based on the far future requires a rather high risk premium. But in fact bond risk premia increase very little between 20 and 30 years, though certainly this opens up the bond to unforeseen events, so we don't have any evidence that investors are attaching huge risk premia for reasons of the far future. The explanation that investors are simply not able to equalize the intrinsic rate is much simpler and matches what we observe in markets.

Bonds also have sensitivity to the far future. No one knows what interest rates will be in 100 years, and they have varied immensely over time, perhaps more than intrinsic returns. Bond and debt return are, after all, merely artifacts of a contract and can be anything. They have no intrinsic return.

Volatility & Competition

Risk as a Function of Valuation & Time Preference
Notice that there is minimal *absolute* risk in the hypothetical company that you are operating in the preceding chapter. We have not specified that it is in any business of particular note, and it has a perfectly average return chosen to be that way, and coincidentally equal to the return of the risk-averse DJIA over the last 80 years (see chart in previous discussion of market timing).

But there is plenty of risk and volatility once the analysts and efficient market equalizers get hold of it. Your offer price of $10 jumped to $25 by which you lost $15 a share. Anyone selling at $25 lost another bundle when the price moved to $41. So there is risk in an inaccurately low P/E.

We didn't go into missed earnings, but the farther out in time investors project the earnings, the more compound discounting in the price, and the bigger the share price correction when future estimates are revised downward. There is not only risk in too high a P/E, but in a long time preference interval N. If an earnings miss results in future earnings revisions downward in, for example, year 3, the compound discounted price would be affected as follows:

Missing projected 10% earnings growth in year 3

Year 3 earnings growth	Year 3 price loss
8%	-14%
6%	-26%
4%	-36%
2%	-45%
0%	-53%

Notice that if earnings in year 3 simply remain the same as year 2, nevertheless the stock price declines 53%. That qualifies as risk. This corresponds to a time preference and forecasting window of $N=7$ in the year of impact. If instead investors were using a three year window, pricing in only earnings growth out to year 6, then flat earnings in year 3 would still result in only a 43% decline in year 3. If investors were forecasting and considering only the current year, the earnings miss by 10 percentage points would make a corresponding 10% dent in the share price. The very important takeaway point is that:

Equalizing future returns amounts to extreme leverage

If we use the conventional nomenclature of ultra-ETFs, 2x, 3x, etc., and the base deviation as the -10% from this example, then discounting future returns at 5% over 7 years amounts to *5.3x leverage*. Even a modest 3 years was equivalent to *4.3x leverage*. The leverage comes from two parts: (1) the number of years over which the deviation extends, and (2) the difference between the original projected growth rate and the discounting rate. If the discount rate were always assumed to be the growth rate, then NPV would be independent of growth entirely and there would be no volatility beyond the present year deviation. So there is a corollary takeaway:

A low discount rate increases earnings-driven volatility

So there are a couple of ways risk can vary given a constant behavior of the fundamental parameters of the equity (in this case, a particular earnings miss in year 3). The investor time preference and consequent P/E is one influence on risk, and the discount rate is another. These risks are not actually inherent in the equity, but come from how it is coupled to the environment. Indeed, if earnings growth resumes in year 4 with expectations it will continue, the share price will largely recover and the volatility has been a big to do about very little. This will not comfort those who needed to raise cash in year 3 and sold unfavorably.

If equalization were taken to 100 year extremes, while there was a substantial difference between interest rates and intrinsic returns, then volatility would be extreme and markets might not function.

Portfolio vs. Individual Equity Valuation

Now we introduce another catch 22. You probably have seen where this is headed. There is a conflict between what the buyer of an individual equity thinks it is worth, and what the buyer of that equity inside a perpetual portfolio thinks it is worth, even if the two investors have the same time preferences!

How? As long as the time preferences are long enough to encompass the fact that companies decline or go out of business, the individual stock buyer will see a very limited total return unless a particular company is likely to have a very long life. If it is a growth company paying no dividends, then a buy-and-hold investor may think it quite worthless if there is a prospect it will decline. The perpetual portfolio investor views the company as a source of short-term growth which will produce capital that will be siphoned off to buy still other companies that don't even exist yet.

The longer the time preferences (of both investors), the greater the difference of opinion about value will be. If the portfolio investors get control of the market, the individual equity buyer will cry that a bubble has formed. When the individual stock buyers have control, the index fund investors will think the market undervalued and protest the lack of foresight into true long-term value.

Volatility decreases time preferences and ... volatility

Two of the three sources of volatility – excessive length of time preferences and conflict between portfolio and individual valuations – can be mitigated by reducing time preferences. This is also a natural response to volatility. When the market behaves erratically the future of business activity is in doubt, and investors can hardly consider what might happen in 20+ years. This results in a more near term focus, which amounts to a reduction in time preferences. In turn this reduction eases the tension over valuations.

Eventually one would expect the volatility to decrease, as a result of shortening time preferences (N) and investors would again begin to look farther into the future – just another of many factors that keep markets guessing and efficient. Well, at least guessing. An interesting corollary of the relation between interest rates, volatility and time preferences could be summed up this way:

Low interest rates may shorten investor time preferences

However, equity premium researchers *always* look at 20+ year intervals of time and usually much longer, far beyond investor time horizons. When investors try to tiptoe into such heady territory, the resulting volatility quickly scares them away. To cast this in terms of investors adjusting the price of risk is a possible way of looking at it, but does not seem to match well with the actual dynamics we have uncovered. What's actually going on is more like investors with natural time preferences sometimes adjusting their time preferences according to market conditions.

When the markets are volatile and the time preferences shorter, they include less of the future's earnings and prices are correspondingly lower. Then the forward looking long-term equity premium (which will have those earnings) will be higher. Conversely when markets are stable (or interest rates higher?) and the future is more predictable, the forward looking long-term equity premium should be lower.

The backward looking equity premium, i.e. the last 20+ years, will be just the opposite. When prices are depressed due to volatility it looks lower.

Equalization by Competition

We have considered re-pricing equities and found many obstacles to bond-equity equalization by that route. We have considered volatility and adjustment of investor time horizon as a corollary and found little to support equalization there. However equities might be equalized by directly affecting returns.

At the current time we are assuming intrinsic returns are, well, intrinsic. Later we will get some more insight into them. But there is another factor in our equation for the growth rate of a portfolio, or a market in the case of an index portfolio:

$$G_P \approx G_H - \frac{1}{L}$$

The aggregate growth rate will be reduced by $1/L$, the inverse of the lifetime of companies (or their lifetime in our index). While a company could fail through incompetence or fraud, we more often think of them declining because of competition. Competition is heightened by the lure of superior returns, as in the case where new productive technologies are created.

It can take a while for competition to develop. Perhaps engineers and designers must be recruited and trained, and investors must be persuaded that they have some advantage in costs or ingenuity over established companies. The established companies will try to maintain their advantage through intellectual property if available, and through contracts and temporary pricing tactics. History shows that effective monopolies do often hold off competition.

Recall that since 1958 the average tenure of a firm on the S&P 500 dropped from 61 years to 18 years in 2012.[92] When a corporation ceases to maintain growth, generally its value drops. It often faces bankruptcy or buyout at a low price compared to former high growth values. Most of its value is lost. To derive our simple factor of $1/L$ we just assumed all of its value was lost. If a company has declined 80% as is often the case when it exits, this is a pretty good assumption. Below is a plot of loss from lifetime limitations with the 18 year mark highlighted.

---

[92] Foster, R., "Creative Destruction Whips Through Corporate America," Strategy & Innovation, vol. 10, no. 1, Innosight, Lexington, MA, 2012
http://www.innosight.com/innovation-resources/strategy-innovation/creative-destruction-whips-through-corporate-america.cfm

Loss Rate from Corporate End of Growth Lifetime

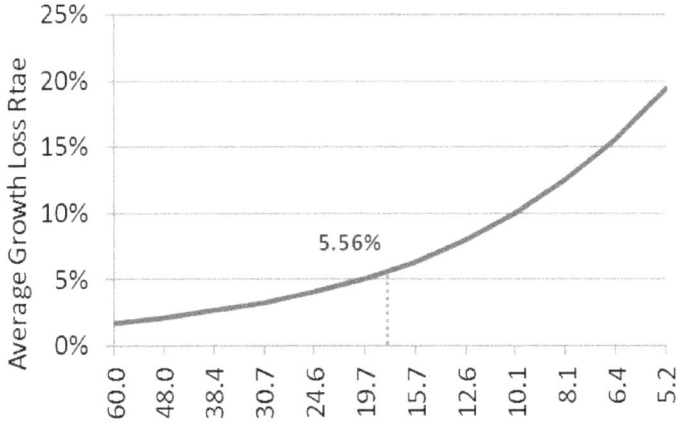

Growth Phase Life in Years

More than half of the lifetime decrease, to an average of 25 years, occurred by 1980, which under our assumptions of zero value at the end of life would be a 4% penalty to growth. The equity premium (EP) declined 1.5% during that time (see figure below), but the earlier value includes the entire period to 2012. The EP is not a reliable measure for the short periods necessary to make a definite correlation with company lifetimes, but there is no doubt it was on average higher in the earlier part of the period of the figure. Shorter corporate lifetimes, which we suppose to be due to competition, could well be eroding the EP.

S&P 500 vs. 3-mo. T-bill Equity Premium

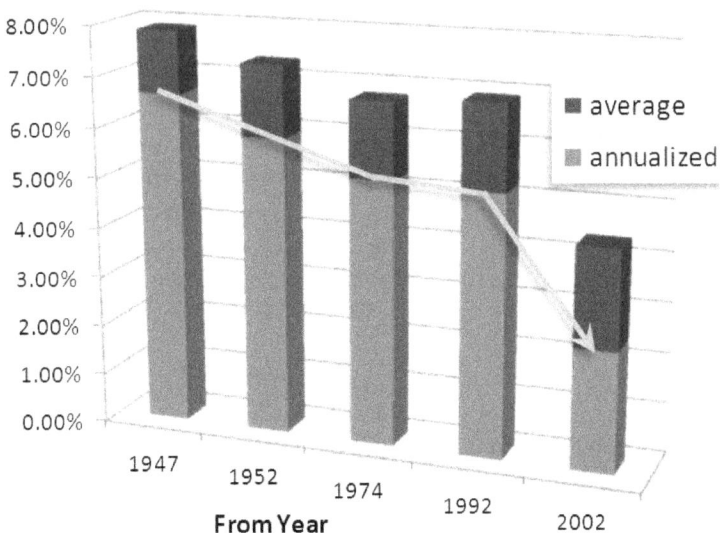

This chart is a summary of my own look at equity premium data. I thought I should look to make sure I could get similar results. The study was modest, using 1947 as a starting point because consistent data for one type of debt security, a T-bill, was available for that interval, and the S&P index we have been using is available, or a ready equivalent.

You will see both average and annualized data plotted. Why are they different, you might wonder? Average is computed by taking the data for each year and averaging it over the interval. Annualized values are computed by taking the total performance of the T-Bill and the S&P over the interval, and computing an annual rate that if held constant would yield that total performance. The difference you see is the effect of volatility on the annual rates. Since the actual annual rates are volatile, they are not as effective in compounding as a constant rate would be. The equivalent annualized rate implicitly has no volatility and will usually be lower. Both views are useful. In comparing equity premium data from various researchers it is obviously important to check and see which kind of data you are dealing with, and if you are comparing apples to apples.

Each interval is from the named year to 2012. So the earlier intervals include the later ones. The last interval is only ten years (from 2002 to 2012), and from our previous discussion we would not expect an interval less than 20 years to really match the long-term equity premium, but it is an interesting data point for other reasons. It includes two market crashes, and a lot of volatility. It shows the equity premium to be low during that time as we would expect.

Buy Signal

If the conjecture in the previous section holds up, then the equity premium will be larger in the future, and now (roughly speaking, plus or minus a couple of years) is a good time to buy. While I can't give you investment advice, I can propose this as a test of the theory developed in this book. Not all market watchers are predicting a bull market. There are always bears about. But I am inclined to agree with Jeffery Hirsch whom I cited earlier, and for similar reasons. After ten or fifteen years of volatility and sideways chop, and the winding down of major wars and a renewed interest in domestic policy, the US market typically begins a ten or fifteen year move up. See limit lines on the DJIA chart in the market timing section.

Jeffery might say it is the change in the policy environment that causes the different phases. I would add that the volatility causes the near term focus on economic factors that result in the moves up, and the moves up encourage confidence and heady excursions into policy misadventures, and the cycle repeats. So the policy and the market cause each other.

This cycle may extend to actors outside the country as well. We already encountered Fingleton's theory that Japan's bureaucrats *like* the downturn because it softens Japan's image abroad with economic competitors. And after a record 28 year run up in US markets, in 2001 Al Qaeda chose an economic target, the World Trade Center, as the preferred symbol to attack, dedicating two teams to it out of four, not to mention the earlier attack in 1993.

Understanding Corporate Lifetime Pressures

More recent drops in corporate tenure on indices are easier to understand because our memory of context is fresh. Companies of the appliance, food, electronics and media boom of the 1950s through 1980s dropped out of the index, replaced by Internet businesses in many cases, with a few specialty retailers and some genetics and health, and also super-discount chains. One might suspect that global trade had a role, but that is beyond our scope.

The point is that the existence of an equity premium attracts capital to new issues. The shorter corporate lifetime becomes, the greater the incentive to rotate fresh companies into a portfolio. Since companies exiting the index do not typically have zero value as in the computer simulation, the 5.56% estimate for end of lifetime loss is high. The 4.2% loss in equity premium between the 1947 to 2012 period and the 2002 to 2012 period is similar in magnitude. The lifetime loss rate is real, and the equity premium would have had to have pressures to increase from other sources to compensate for the lifetime losses. The lifetime losses may well be a component of equity premium loss, and may well represent rate equalization pressure, driving equity rates down toward bond rates.

The implication of this, if true, is that the objectives of the Fed, specifically employment objectives, are being circumvented in a hidden way. Lifetime employment is no longer an option if companies don't last that long. Workers experience income losses (lower returns on education) by the same formula. With student loan debt increasing, they face unfavorable economic prospects compared to earlier generations of workers.

In summary, equalization by competition probably is occurring but could not have removed more than half the equity premium. Recent trends indicate corporate lifetime is stabilizing at its current level. So a significant puzzle remains, and we move on to consider the bond price or debt interest path.

The following charts comparing 1900 and 2000 (using data compiled by Modugno[93]) show entire industries appearing and disappearing as significant fractions of the total US stock market. It may

---

[93] Victor Modugno, "Equity Risk Premiums," Society of Actuaries, Pension Section News, no. 80, May 2013

be hard to see the shading variations. Railroads, over half at 1900, are invisible (0.2%) in 2000. Information technology and pharmaceuticals are zero in 1900.

1900

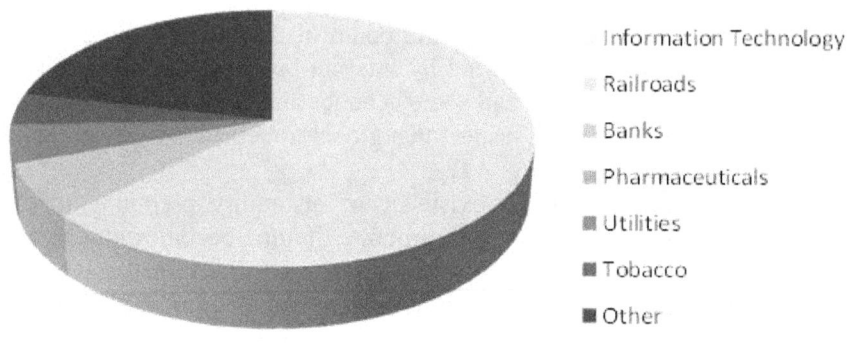

2000

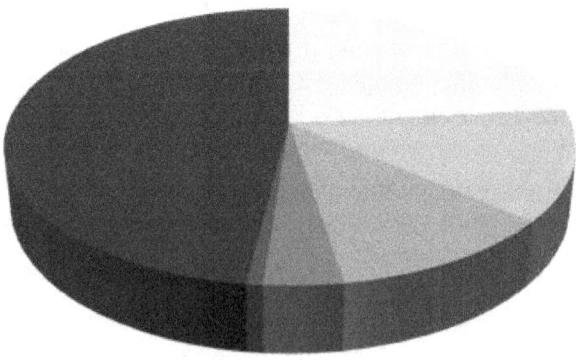

Monetary Policy

Now we begin to explore the bond or interest rate side of things, to determine what might prevent equalization of bonds and equities by acting on bond prices or interest rates, two sides of the same coin. We will be looking for an explanation of factors that determine, increase or decrease the equity premium, and since inflation is connected with interest rates we may have to understand that as well. It would seem to be a bit more involved, less mathematically precise, and dependent upon a larger range of human behavior than the equity valuation side of markets. It also involves a new type of market participant, one who is not rational in the sense of being a profit seeker.

Monetary Agents

The Federal Open Market Committee (FOMC) meets every 5 to 8 weeks, votes on future policy, and makes an announcement – carefully worded and cryptic by tradition. Fed Chairmen and Chairwomen experiment with clarity at their peril. The policy consists of three tools:[94]

1. *Open market operations* – the purchase and sale of securities by central banks on the open market.
2. *The discount rate* – interest rate charged on loans from the Fed to commercial banks.
3. *Reserve requirements* – the percent of deposits a bank must hold in reserve and not lend.

Ask an economist what determines interest rates, and he or she will probably say that rational market participants (i.e. making logical decisions to maximize profit) make offers to buy or sell and transactions are made at mutually agreed prices. A bond which pays a certain amount each month or quarter will be sold at a price, and the ratio of its payments to the selling price is the interest rate.

If we look carefully at the function of the FOMC, we see that the central banks act as market participants. They purchase or sell anything they decide by vote at their regular meetings. At the present time, for example, they are purchasing 90% of US Government newly issued debt, and have acted similarly a few times in the past. The Bank of Japan purchases ETF's on the open market! Central banks around the world occasionally cooperate to buy or sell currency, gold and other securities, usually with the express purpose of manipulating and influencing markets.

---

[94] http://www.federalreserve.gov/monetarypolicy/fomc.htm

If private companies or individuals cooperated to influence markets, they would be breaking the law. But this is the chartered purpose of central banks. Moreover when central banks need money for such transactions, most of them have the power to just hit a button on a computer screen and create it.[95] There is no printing involved. I am intending only to remind you of what you already know, for the purpose of pointing out that:

- A central banker is a market participant.
- A central banker creates money and has no profit motive.[96]

It hardly seems reasonable to call such an entity a "rational investor." I will call them *monetary agents*.

And it is unsurprising that monetary agents are almost universally hated. First of all they are a kind of banker, and bankers are hated because they can decline our dreams, or confiscate them when we miss a few payments. Most of us spend our lives desperately working for money and doing without. Even the main branches of government can't get money without taking it from someone by taxes or fees. What monetary agents do seems like theft to conservatives and cronyism to liberals. Two attempts to do without them have been made in our history but the results were disastrous.

Monetary agents are the creation of social and political forces, not of rational investors or efficient markets. I will take two approaches to understanding and quantifying their goals, powers and effects. One is theoretical, to use a simple model economy to understand the effect of interest rates on business returns using a one-industry one-rate economy. Then we'll look at the on-again off-again central banking and monetary standards of the US which make practically an ideal experiment for studying the effects of monetary policy.

The Yellow Brick Road

The US fully adopted the single-metal gold standard in 1900. Few people seem to know this, and I believe most people assume as I once did that we were perhaps always on a gold standard, but it is not so. That was the same year that Frank Baum published *The Wonderful Wizard of Oz*.

Many people have speculated that Baum may have intended political symbolism and satire.[97] [98] [99] The yellow brick road represents the

---

[95] When buying dollars, the Fed must use some other currency, which it cannot create. The dollars purchased are effectively destroyed, decreasing the money supply and thus raising or as the term is often used "defending" its value.

[96] The Fed usually does make a profit, but incoming funds are for all practical purposes destroyed since newly created dollars could as easily be created.

gold standard, the Emerald City greenback paper money, the scarecrow the American farmer, and Dorothy the American people. Many different interpretations are given and Baum can't have meant all of them, for example the Cowardly Lion may be interpreted as the American military in the Spanish-American War, or William Jennings Bryan. Oz has the requisite isolation to be used as a simple model economy, but too much is already known about the economy of Oz and it is much too complicated.

Almost every sophomore economics student has tried to create an "island economy" to understand prices, usually about the time the laws of supply and demand are introduced, and has come away discouraged about ever being able to understand money. I have had famous economists express this frustration to me, and I endured it myself. But several simple mistakes cause this frustration.

The first mistake is that more than one product or commodity is considered, and students try to understand the relative market values of the products, and the transient price movement of prices and their causes. Markets compare and set values well, but individuals generally do not (there are rare exceptions, usually making their living as buyers or sellers in markets). Certainly economists do not, or they would have studied business instead! In macroeconomics mostly what we care about is the total value or price of the whole market. One commodity will suffice for that.

A second mistake is to be obsessed with dynamic relationships, perhaps even dragging differential equations into the model. Mehra cured me of this, stating flatly that for equity premium analysis I should use equilibrium models. Suddenly I didn't need differential equations and the models were much simpler.

The third thing is you must have lenders, or nothing but barter will occur.

And finally, almost every student modeler discovers there is no way to determine what money is worth or what the inflation or deflation rate is. A model must have a monetary agent to stabilize prices. Neither the world nor a model works without one.

97
http://en.wikipedia.org/wiki/Political_interpretations_of_The_Wonderful_Wizard_of_Oz
98 http://voices.yahoo.com/political-symbolism-the-wizard-oz-book-movie-561662.html
99 http://www.themoneymasters.com/mm/the-wonderful-wizard-of-oz/

A Pre-Equity Economy

To keep things simple let's examine a hypothetical agrarian economy with:

- farmers,
- lenders,
- a monetary agent who creates and manages money.

We will call it the Land of Zo, since it's more backward than Oz.

In its pre-equity state of development, Zo's farmers must borrow the money to buy seed and pay for labor to produce crops. Zo's lenders demand a return of 6%. Each year the farmers price their harvest so as to cover expenses, including repayment of the loans. There is only one commodity in Zo, food, and the farmers keep back whatever they need out of their harvest, and this is their consumption. I purposely ignore seasonal or annual variations in production since only an equilibrium model is required to address the equity premium.

It is easy to see a couple of scenarios depending on the relative power of labor and lenders. In the year to year chaos of a real economy, the clarity of a particular circumstance is lost. Here we will assume that a circumstance is static, that it continues indefinitely. Then we will see what builds up as a result.

Full re-circulation of money

If the lenders spend their 6% return consuming the farm products, then there will be no inflation, and they will get the real return they desire, but they will not increase their wealth (unless they are hoarding food).

This situation is not only static, it is in equilibrium. It produces the same situation next year that we have this year, the same relative wealth, the same land ownership, the same production capacity, etc.

It may appear at first that lenders are getting a free ride. To understand their function we must recall our discussion of the history and evolution of money. Originally the temple and later the government stored seed, gave it out for food during hard times, and loaned it out for planting in the following season. Storehouses had to be built and the grain guarded from theft and protected from pests and weather. This could be a considerable amount of work as well as risky. It could, for example, entail fighting a war.

The simple economy of Zo is already quite sophisticated, then. It has replaced grain with the abstraction of money. Money in that context can be thought of as a piece of technology, in fact a highly productive piece. Imagine having to carry bags of grain with you to the mall to fund your shopping.

The lenders could directly build storehouses and pay guards. But this requires many special talents such as designing storehouses, managing construction projects, and training and managing guard forces. The abstraction of money in Zo allows the lenders to build up expertise in predicting future conditions and managing money.

Specialized companies can perform the actual storage functions, and according to Adam Smith[100] may do so more efficiently if left to their own devices than if centrally planned by the lenders. So someone now narrowly specialized as a lender gives money to farmers to buy grain from these other unnamed parties, the Zoian equivalent of Archer-Daniels-Midland or Monsanto, and after the crop is sold the farmer repays the lender and the Zoian grain industry stores some of the crop and saves it for next year. We won't need any of the details of the storage process for our allegory.

Modern necessity & functions of lenders

Why, you might ask, do not the farmers just save their profits and buy their own grain, or indeed save their grain. One question at a time. Zo's farmers are free to do either at this stage. Perhaps some do and perhaps many did in the past. One year a few farmers were robbed, and the other farmers felt sorry for them and set up a lending consortium to bail them out. Since the bailout recipients had to pay back the loan, they continued needing new loans every year. So the consortium became an independent entity, now known as *the lenders*, because the farmers were busy farming and didn't want to fool with it every year.

With lending available other farmers experienced the pressure of *risk compensation*.[101] One man's wife was sick one year and she needed an operation. Another's daughter needed to go to college. These expenses were required for the family's survival in both cases. Had lending not been available, the farmer would have had to weigh his family's future against the future of the entire Land of Zo, which might wind up with un-fed citizens. But with lending available, the choice is simple.

The hard choices between family and country are thus outsourced to lenders. If a farmer has problems several years in a row, he does not

---

[100] Smith, A., *An Inquiry into the Nature and Causes of the Wealth of Nations*, first published in 1776, coincidentally the date of the Declaration of Independence. See http://en.wikipedia.org/wiki/The_Wealth_of_Nations

[101] Popular online discussions are superficial and confuse risk compensation with risk homeostasis, e.g. http://en.wikipedia.org/wiki/Risk_compensation . For a good list of references and a mathematical analysis of the inevitability of corporate risk compensation, see the author's paper "A Quantitative Model of Corporate Risk Compensation," currently under review at a leading journal but also available at the author's website http://mc1soft.com/papers/

have to tell his wife that he won't pay for her surgery. He can just say that the bank won't because he has delinquent loans. Then they can both hate the banker instead of each other. In return for absorbing so much of society's frustration and negative energy, the banker demands a reasonable return.

Such is the origin of lenders and the explanation of their function in society. People don't want to make unpleasant decisions, exercise strict self control or incur the animosity of their close relatives, so these tasks are outsourced. And that is why it is a good rule never to lend money to friends or relatives.

Excess returns accumulated by lenders

If the farms are very productive, *or* if there are a small number of wealthy lenders, then the lenders may not need to spend 6% in consumption. Wealth will transfer to the lenders until, one year, there is not enough money owned by others in Zo to pay the 6% return. Some farmers will default. If the lenders do not change their expectations, they will add the default rate to the 6% and demand a higher rate so as to obtain a 6% rate after losses. What happens next depends on relative power.

Labor has more power

If the farmers or labor have more power, they will organize and collectively raise prices and limit supply, producing inflation.

Lenders have more power

There might be situations in which farmers and labor do not have such power. Perhaps they are not trustful of one another, or some of them live very far away, or some food is imported from other countries. Then power shifts to the lenders and they gradually confiscate farm assets and reduce farmers and laborers alike to subsistence wages. Some of them may simply remain unemployed and become beggars or live on welfare, if there is any.

Monetary action triggers

The monetary agent, charged with stabilizing prices and ensuring full employment, is compelled to act in either scenario. Lenders will argue for tight money so that debts are not relieved by inflation. Farmers and labor will advocate for loose money with which to repay their debts and to finance production.

A historical similarity

It is interesting to note that this "hypothetical" scenario dominated American politics in the 2nd half of the 19th century. The US was on a bimetallic standard, silver and gold. Discoveries of large new silver deposits were inflating silver currency. In 1873 the US effectively went on a gold standard inside the country.

Farm interests lobbied for the re-introduction of silver currency for the reasons attributed to the farmers and laborers of Zo. Eastern banking interests lobbied for gold, and wished to extend the standard to cover foreign transactions, making trade simpler with England which had adopted a gold standard.

Lending resource being depleted

Farmers in this simple economy do not store anything from year to year. That function is for the lenders (and the implicit businesses which store the grain that the saved money represents). The lending function can be out of balance in only two ways, excess hoarding, or depletion of funds. We have covered the cases of balance, and of hoarding. The depletion case does not happen. If it did, we would simply be back to the conditions from which lending arose in the first place. In a cooperative society the farmers would form an emergency consortium and make contributions to a lending fund, reversing the depletion. In a non-cooperative society the farmers who happened to be better off would either buy out the unfortunate farmers, or become lenders and lend to them.

One thing the financial crisis of 2008-9 proved is that societies are dependent on their banks and will bail them out no matter how much they hate them. However we are now engaged in a game of mutual suffering, levying fines and penalties on the banks year by year (their suffering), and postponing economic recovery (our suffering).

Summary of monetary issues in pre-equity Zo

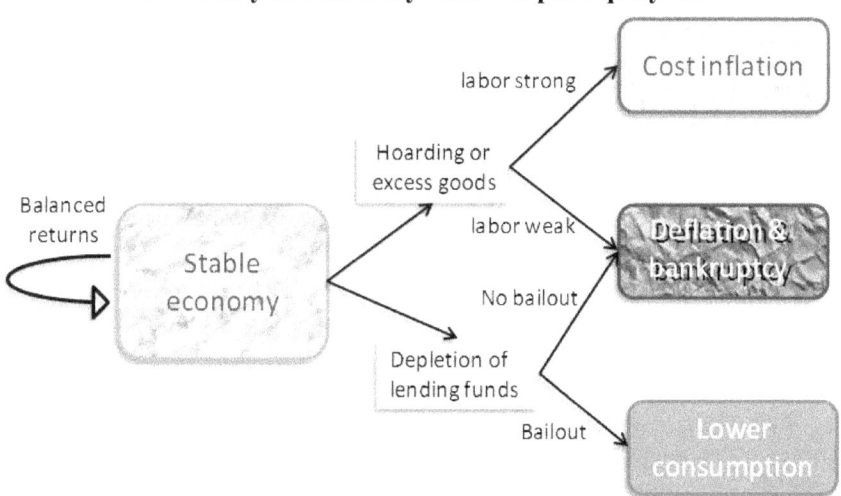

Policy actions in pre-equity Zo

We can draw several conclusions regarding pre-equity Zo. First is the counter-intuitive observation that in the case of hoarding lenders, if the monetary agent printed enough money to cover the 6% returns demanded by the lenders there would be no inflation. The monetary agent could print money at a rate matching the rate at which lenders were removing and hoarding money. Without a net change of money in circulation there would be no change in prices and no crisis. If the lenders quit hoarding, that is a new problem. Recall we are only considering *static* conditions one at a time, not the one thing after another situation that clouds real economies (or student models).

Hoarding is presumably possible only because there were excess goods being produced, i.e. it is a problem of excess productivity. We do not necessarily care about the cost of goods in a particular year as long as all the money is spent and all the goods are consumed. If the harvest is double what it is normally, the cost per bushel will be half of normal of course. And everyone will just have to eat a second helping. Perhaps this will lead to hoarding around the waistline, but that is not a monetary concern. The food is perishable unless stored in a granary. The granaries have a fixed maximum capacity and excess is disposed. *But,* if the politics of Zo are such that citizens want stable prices, then even if the lenders are not hoarding the excess, money will have to be printed to cover the excess. All the money, less any hoarded, divided by all the grain is the price of food.

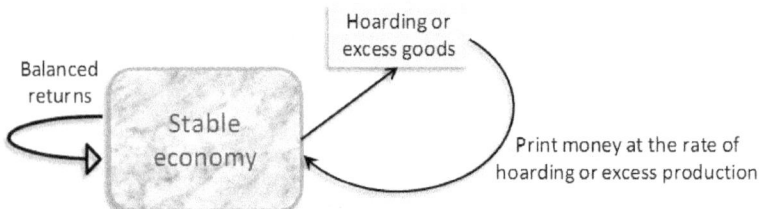

In the case where lenders are hoarding and farmers and labor have some power, if the monetary agent does not increase the money supply there are likely to be shortages of goods and cost-driven inflation despite ample production capacity, unless there are foreign suppliers or other factors weakening farmers and labor.

It is also possible for the monetary agent to print but not unconditionally distribute new money, instead lending it at low rates to the farmers. Technically, this money would return to the monetary agent and not add to the money supply. However, unless the monetary agent sets a rate of zero interest, more is returned than is loaned, and the monetary agent finds itself in the same situation as the lender, and must spend the interest it receives or watch the impoverishment of the population. The prospects for Zo are rather sad, but roughly correspond to the feudal systems that developed in much of the pre-industrial world.

Here are some possible policy actions and consequences:

If the monetary agent lends at a low rate while the lenders are hoarding, the economy and jobs are saved, but the lenders seeing their returns drop are not likely to be persuaded to quit hoarding.

If the monetary agent mistakenly lends at a low rate while the lenders are spending all their returns, then demand-driven inflation would be the likely outcome.

If the monetary agent does not act while the lenders are hoarding, and labor does not have the power to demand sustainable wages, then the shortage of money produces deflation, default, and unemployment.

If anti-hoarding is occurring and the lenders are spending more than their returns, this is the same as depletion already discussed. But what if anything should the monetary agent do? If the lenders are not making high enough returns to cover expenses, and the monetary agent has done something to lower interest rates, it can stop doing that and allow rates to rise.

If the monetary agent is not currently doing anything, there is really no action available at this time to combat depletion. When the lenders run sufficiently low on funds, market demand for loans should drive returns up again. But if the monetary agent has lowered interest rates this market mechanism will be disabled. When the lenders are broke, they will be either bailed out or re-started as described above.

If the lenders are simply spending money that they previously hoarded, again the monetary agent needs to look at its own past role. If the lenders were able to hoard because the monetary agent increased the money supply, then the monetary agent can simply destroy the excess money being spent. If the money supply was increased through loans, this is particularly convenient. If the monetary agent had just printed and distributed money, then a tax could be used to recall it, but it will be unpopular. That is why monetary agents prefer to lend rather than actually "drop money from helicopters."[102] Buying government bonds is one way

---

[102] In a 2002 speech, following concerns in the financial press about deflation, Ben Bernanke referred to a statement made by Milton Friedman about using a

to lend, buying mortgage backed securities is another, and making loans to banks through the discount window is still another.

If the previous hoarding was not due to monetary agent action, then possibly it could just wait until the hoard is liquidated, and the economy will return to normal after temporary inflation. This depends on the depth of the hoard and the rate of spending. Spending the hoard can create a serious bubble, an artificial inflation of the values of some assets in the economy relative to others, i.e. the values of whatever the hoarders are buying. When the bubble breaks, non-hoarders who bought the assets out of necessity would be harmed by falling prices. Or the excess spending could inflate all assets rendering inadequate the value of smaller hoards kept by the farmers for emergencies.

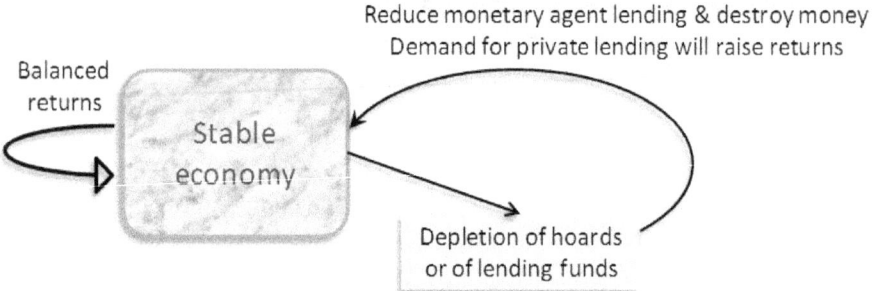

In either case, the monetary agent might choose to remove money from the economy while the bubble was in progress and quickly replace money in the economy as the bubble begins to burst. Not *after* it has burst. Monetary agents are almost always either too slow or unaware they need to intervene until the damage is irreparable.

It probably appears counter-intuitive that the monetary agent should reduce its own lending just when lending funds are scarce. The kind of straightforward response most voters and politicians can understand is that if we need more of it, set up an agency to produce more of it. But the scarcity of lending funds is due to a long history of money being too easy to get and returns on loans being too low. The solution is to make money even more scarce so that the profit from lending it will replenish stockpiles.

Another common problem the reader will recognize is that money to be lent may be scarce because lenders perceive risk. In this case the

---

"helicopter drop" of printed money to fight deflation. This earned him the nickname of "Helicopter Ben." But the Fed's response to 2008-9 deflation was to buy up risky debt and to buy new debt (i.e. to make loans) at low rates. See http://en.wikipedia.org/wiki/Ben_Bernanke

government often offers a guarantee. Sometimes this is necessary to avoid catastrophe. All we are trying to do here is understand the mechanics of the alternatives. We can judge their merits later.

The guarantee makes the monetary agent (or other agency) a party to the lending, and is basically just another way of lending which will in the long run make government-independent capital less available. This is exactly the problem that occurred with the 2008-9 financial crisis. With government guarantees we avoided oblivion, but it is taking some time for private capital to gain confidence, and it cannot compete with the low interest rates on government loans.

It is easy to see that monetary agents are essential if a society is not to be whipped about by the whims of a few of its citizens. Like other aspects of civilization, it becomes necessary after a while as people give up the expensive and time consuming traditions of self-reliance because food is always available at a reasonable price at the corner grocery. Living in a city where stores are open late at night and are located on my way home from work has left me so lax that I often fail to keep even one day's supply of food at home. Imagine what my ancestors would think who had to work all summer to store up food for the winter? But on the other hand, none of them had time to write a book. Without preservation of their knowledge and experiences, I would imagine they like most other Americans bounced around in the political winds voting for and against the same misguided economic policies over and over again.

Even in the simple economy of pre-equity Zo, with only farming and lending, the essential features and causes of action of a modern monetary agent are apparent. Notice that inflation is of two different kinds – demand driven or cost driven – and whether the response to a certain set of conditions is inflation or deflation depends on the relative political power of labor and lenders.

Now we make it more complicated. To understand the equity premium we must of course have *equity*.

Equity & Productivity

EQ·UI·TY – NOUN :

- FAIRNESS OR JUSTICE IN THE WAY PEOPLE ARE TREATED
- A SHARE IN A COMPANY
- A RISK INTEREST OR OWNERSHIP IN PROPERTY[103]
- OWNERSHIP AFTER ALL DEBTS ARE PAID OFF[104]

Which of these definitions do you think is applicable, or helpful, in understanding the equity premium?

Starting from the bottom, we see that equity is defined in relation to debt. Without debt, there is no need for the term equity. So there is some relation between equity and debt. The reciprocal is not true for debt. We managed to have an extensive discussion of debt without any notion of equity.

It should be obvious to anyone who lived through the financial crisis that equity is a protection against the bankruptcy of debt. It is the headroom or margin, the pad that buffers against default. So it stands to reason it should be more at risk if it protects the debt. Thus economists logically reasoned it should yield higher returns, but we have seen that the long-term risk is with the debt, which attempts to give up ownership for security.

Moving up to the idea of a share in a company, a business activity providing needed goods and services, this is what gives equity its tremendous growth potential.

And finally, we see that equity is fairness. The lenders will take all they can get (equalization pressure), but it is not fair. In fact it would seriously damage parts of society that have nothing to do with equity. What we will explore now, quantitatively, is the mechanism of fairness.

Effects of Industrialization and Equity

Referring to the Land of Zo, suppose there are some engineers who begin to develop technology that reduces labor and increases yield in agricultural production. Based on the usefulness of their equipment and seeds to farmers, and thus the price farmers will pay for the improvements, these innovators find that they can make an 8% return on the money they must pay for materials and labor, even after also hiring an executive and a marketing agent. They quickly realize they could make much more money if not limited to their own funds. There is money available from lenders at

---

103 http://www.merriam-webster.com/dictionary/equity
104 http://www.investopedia.com/terms/e/equity.asp

6%. Note that it is not necessary for the new business return to be higher, but there would no business motivation if it were lower!

Origin & meaning of equity

The lenders are not sure what they would wind up owning if the engineers defaulted. Unlike farmers, the engineers have no land. And the engineers, having seen the plight of the farmers, are leery of being in a position where they might default. An accommodation is reached in which lenders will only match the funds the engineers already have. In other words, the engineers must come up with 50% *equity*. This equity is fundamentally different than debt. It cannot result in default. And it constitutes a buffer which prevents default.

If, for example, there is a 5% loss rate in this new industry, due to bad luck, factory problems, bad designs and so forth, then figured as a ratio to equity rather than total capital, this doubles to a 10% loss rate, which we might well call "risk." But unless the loss happens all in one firm, it is possible the debt may not be touched, and there will be no default.

This is intended to be a simple numerical example, but nonetheless realistic. 6% was a typical bond rate during the early part of the 19th century when there was no equity premium. Railroad bonds were sold as 6% bonds for the transcontinental railroad. As of 2011, 45% of the capital of American companies was debt,[105] 1/3rd of which was short-term less than one year or money market,[106] and the rest longer term, so the 50% equity assumption is also reasonably realistic.

Return on equity

What is the total return on equity for this new industry? There is an 8% return on total capital (by hypothesis) and equity is part of that, so there is a direct 8% return on the equity. On the debt capital 6% has to be paid to the lenders leaving an excess return of 2%. Since there were (conveniently) equal amounts of debt and equity capital, this 2% of the debt is also 2% of the equity amount, and is pocketed by the equity owners so it is also a return on equity. Therefore the total return on equity is 8% plus 2% giving of 10%.

The equity partners have used leverage to increase their return from 8% to 10%, and to grow the business to twice the size it would have been using only their own funds.

---

[105] Crook, M., Brian, N., "Bear markets in bonds: separating fact from fantasy," Wealth Management Research, UBS AG, NY-Zurich, Feb. 25, 2013
[106] Easterling, E. "The 60/50 Rule," Crestmont Research, Dec. 28, 2012, http://www.crestmontresearch.com/interest-rates/

It works just like the leverage we discussed in the chapter on investing, multiplying returns and volatility. If you use 50% leverage when investing in corporations that use 50% leverage, the total leverage is 75% representing 4x or four times the volatility of basic earnings, and four times the growth.

If the returns on equity and bonds were the same, there would be nothing left over after paying debt interest to increase the earnings of the equity partners. Why would the equity partners put themselves at double the loss risk in order to gain nothing? The answer is they wouldn't.

Equalizing the equity returns

What is the effect of these high returns on the economy of Zo? According to the assumptions of rational investing the returns must equalize. We have already seen that the structural 8% return cannot equalize downward. Therefore lenders will demand more. They will not be able to get 10%, however. Every 1% additional they demand lowers the return on equity 1% in this example. The most they can get is 8% because that is the breakeven point for the engineers, and they are not willing borrow at that rate as we have seen, because they gain nothing for their *doubled* risk. We might suppose, hypothetically, that about 1% is the least margin for which the engineers will go to the trouble of borrowing. This would imply they might borrow at 7.5%, giving equity owners a return of 8.5%.

However, that could leave the farmers paying 7.5%. And it could leave the lenders hoarding even more since they now enjoy a higher return. The farmers would have to raise prices, and there would be inflation, or if they do not have pricing power there would be default and deflation and unemployment. In one case or another, it is soon necessary for the monetary agent to intervene.

Equalization triggers monetary intervention

We have traced down, in a hypothetical economy, the original impact of equity returns and attempts to equalize them. We find that equalization occurs through interest rates as we expected after our long exploration of intrinsic returns of equities. And we find that the new conditions in the economy pass the already long established conditions for monetary intervention. So *the very presence of equity and high intrinsic returns necessitates monetary policy*.

We do not know that things happened in this order in actual history (the introduction of equity and high return businesses followed by innovation in monetary policy). But banking changed a lot at about the time of the industrial revolution, and it's likely much of modern monetary policy was invented as a result of necessity to deal with equity-derived disruptions.

To find the optimal intervention, we must make some assumptions about the relative size of the new industry. Suppose it is ¼ of the economy. Suppose the monetary agent decides to simply force the average return on capital back to the former 6% level. If the monetary agent lends at 4% (which it might do through bank intermediaries by offering them a slightly lower "prime" rate), then the leveraged industrial return on equity will be 12% (1/4 of the economy), and the debt return will be 4% by definition (3/4 of the economy), for an average capital return of ¼ (12%) + ¾ (4%) = 6%.

If lenders become diversified investors, cap-weighted in debt and equity, they can have the same return as before, and if they consume as much as before there is no inflation pressure. There is some loss of farm jobs, but if the new industry markets and prices effectively, it captures the job revenue and uses it to pay its own employees. There is an equity premium of 12% - 4% = 8%. And if the monetary agent returns its 4% gains into circulation there is no net change in the money supply.

We can formalize the relationships in this example as follows. Let D be the fraction of capital which is debt, and R_B the intrinsic return of the new business. Then we have the adjusted return on equity, using D leverage, as

$$R_E = R_B + (R_B - R_1) D / (1 - D)$$

If the default risk is expressed as an annualized loss rate R_L, then as long as the loss upon default does not exceed equity we have the new leveraged loss rate R_L' as

$$R_L' = R_L / (1 - D)$$

Inflation-Deflation Consequences

What is the effect on inflation of the new high-return business? The new high returns are being extracted from the economy and given to the business owners. If they spend it, then it should be inflation neutral. If they do not, it should be deflationary because of the effective money supply contraction.

We assume that in a competitive market, the new high-return business is making products of superior or new quality or quantity, or making the old products at lower prices. In the latter case, it is clearly deflationary. In the case of simply higher quantity, the laws of supply and demand assure that they cannot sell more products at the same price, so the middle case reduces to the last one and is deflationary.

Note that the new business can generate deflationary pressure even if not a higher return business. In that case, monetary intervention will be triggered by deflation, interest rates will be lowered, and the new business will *become* high return compared with lending because of productivity changes. This produces an equity premium even where it wasn't intrinsic.

In the case of superior or new products, these compete with the old products for consumer dollars. While there is no explicit basis for inflation comparison on the superior or new products, their market success implies less money available for pre-existing products. By the laws of supply and demand, then prices for pre-existing products must decline. Therefore, it seems fair to suppose that in a general sense the new high-return business, provided it is not based on a monopoly, will tend to be deflationary.

We have certainly seen this in agriculture and manufacturing as technology increases harvests or production and decreases labor. It is called productivity growth.

Let us suppose for the sake of relative comparison that we have an economy in equilibrium, absent either inflation or an equity premium. The lending risk rate associated with no inflation is R_1. We represent the inflation characteristics[107] of this economy qualitatively in the figure below.

prior economy

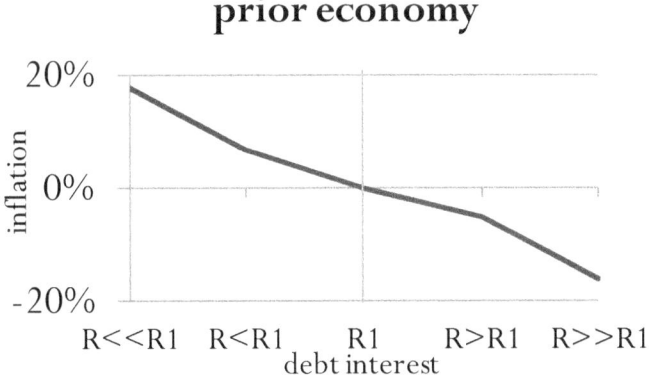

$R_1 = non\text{-}inflationary\ rate\ in\ EP{=}0\ economy$

---

[107] Prior to 1960 the relation between inflation and interest rates was not as clear as it was after that time. See http://www.crestmontresearch.com/docs/i-rate-relationship.pdf Crestmont Research, "INTEREST RATES & INFLATION: 1900 – 2012"

Now introduce a new high-productivity business with intrinsic return $R_B > R_1$. Without monetary intervention, by our above assumptions and analysis, there will be deflation.

Further assume that investors, still without monetary intervention, are able to equalize the market lending interest rate to a new value $R_2 = R_B$. Assuming inflation-deflation behaves as it has since 1960, there will be even greater deflation. The monetary agent is prompted to act.

However, to restore an inflation-neutral equilibrium, the interest rate will have to be driven to a new value $R_2' < R_1$.

premium economy

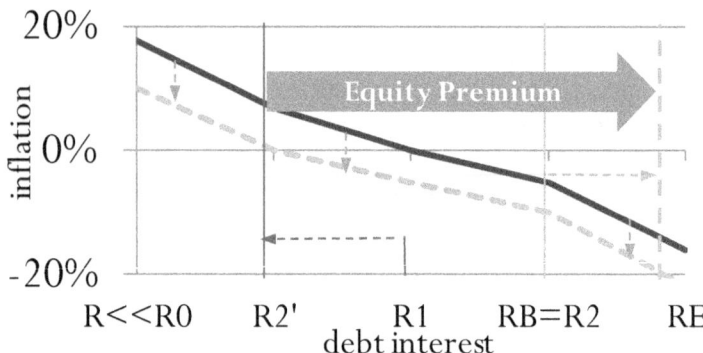

In the figure above we see an illustration of a restored inflation-neutral equilibrium. The inflation curve has been pushed down (to the dashed line). The lending interest rate had to be lowered to R_2' to prevent deflation. The expected equity returns were increased first by the intrinsic return superiority of the new business to R_B, and again by leverage using the lower cost capital at the new lending rate to R_E.

The EP & monetary policy are maintained

We seem to be able to conclude from this that the effect of "progress" in business may be to enable the monetary agent to *maintain a low interest rate and a high equity premium.*

Indeed, it appears that progress might be "bad" for an economy if investors were allowed to equalize rates, causing deflation which in turn might decrease economic activity and lower business returns from both less activity and the collapse of leverage. The apparent threats to this economy are twofold: if the monetary agent is unwilling to *keep rates low* and thus causes deflation, or intrinsic business *productivity declines* causing inflation.

Prescription for Japan

With our newfound insights, let's try to analyze one of the world's most perplexing economies – Japan.

Since inflation did not prevail in Japan, was Prescott not correct about a decline in aggregate productivity there? From the end of WWII Japan "caught up" with the US in productivity, then stopped in 1990.[108] This brings up an interesting point about productivity and inflation/deflation. The effect of productivity integrates over time, so there is a considerable lag. Japan was sufficiently productive during the 1980s to run a steady $40+ billion annual trade surplus.[109] Japan was producing a lot more than it was consuming.

Agreements were reached to re-align the two currencies, resulting in the yen/dollar dropping from 250 in mid 1985 to 125 in mid 1988. This amounts to 50% deflation over three years on the cost of not only overseas goods but also real estate or travel or anything else appealing to the Japanese. However, internal consumption of all they had been exporting was surely not an option. Japan was not isolated like the Land of Zo, and sudden currency changes can masquerade as productivity increases. Conversely, the cost of anything Japanese should have doubled in three years when measured in US dollars. Except that it didn't. Japan aggressively invested in overseas manufacturing plants, and is still doing so. Japanese cars were simply built in the US for the US market. So Japan is facing de facto productivity increases at a time when its jobs are being sent overseas.

The price of real estate and of Japanese companies *should* have gone down almost immediately by about half. But factory workers do not buy expensive real estate, executives and bankers do, and they had not yet felt the pinch. They still had profits from overseas operations. The newfound power of their yen must have been heady, and a bubble formed. A bubble is by definition psychological, not based on real values, which measured in yen should have been deflating, due to the increased international value of the yen.

The lesson of gold and of the tumult of the early 20th century should have been that currencies should not be manipulated, but with Japan's bureaucratic resistance to US imports, and its culture of saving rather than consuming, it had excess production and the result was bound to eventually be deflation, and it was. The intervening bubble just

---

[108] Gilbert Cette, Yusuf Kocoglu, and Jacques Mairesse, "Productivity Growth and Levels in France, Japan, the United Kingdom and the United States in the Twentieth Century," NBER Working Paper No. 15577, Dec. 2009
http://www.nber.org/papers/w15577
[109] http://en.wikipedia.org/wiki/Japan%E2%80%93United_States_relations

confused the issue and threw policymakers off the track, leading to a tightening of monetary policy in the late 1980s because of the supposed bubble. Japan's money supply could rise up to 100%, since a 100% up move is required to cancel a 50% down move, in order to restore the economic growth conditions of 1985.

Japan's real estate values declined at over 20% for four years running in the early 1990s eventually to 1/3rd of their peak bubble value, as the yen continued to rise.[110] Given pre-bubble rises of 30-40% per year in real estate for four years, the decline had only been enough to correct the bubble, and prices continued to fall, albeit at a lower rate, to catch up with the yen. Fortunately, the yen began to fall somewhat after 1995, but not much in comparison to how much it had risen (and it has since risen again). Stocks meanwhile exhibited the volatility we've learned to expect from threats to long-term growth, with P/E ratios falling. By 2000 the S&P 500 had accumulated a 700% relative valuation change with respect to the Nikkei, and this relative valuation has more or less remained the same since.

With such dismal equity returns, it is no wonder Japan has not matched investment in other parts of Asia and the US since 1990, and has lost its edge in consumer electronics. Fortunately for Japan it is still competitive in such fields as automobile manufacturing, but the factories aren't in Japan.

Suppose we were asked to advise the Bank of Japan what to do to restore a reasonable equity premium to attract capital so Japan could at least match the economic growth of other developed countries? Can it even be done? Of course things must change, but the idea is to produce financial motivation for changes.

The return on equity estimated from the limit lines on the earlier Nikkei chart was -5%. The lending interest rate will have to get underneath that before anything starts to happen. Negative lending interest in the absence of inflation is difficult to engineer. Are you going to take money from people's savings accounts? That is just a tax, and you know how popular taxes are during an economic downturn.

Indeed, how does one stimulate inflation without being able to lower interest rates? Currently the Bank of Japan is buying equity via the open market purchase of ETF shares. How does that help? Apparently the BOJ does not know about intrinsic returns. Driving up equity prices, for a given intrinsic return and amount of debt capital, will lower the return on equity in the near term even if the capital can be effectively deployed. The

---

[110] Okina, K., Shirakawa, M., Shiratsuka, S., "The Asset Price Bubble and Monetary Policy: Japan's Experience in the Late 1980s and the Lessons," Monetary and Economic Studies (Special Edition), Feb., 2001. Online: http://www.quartetfest.ca/documents/4743/jap_bubble.pdf

example of Apple's cash stash suggests it is not that easy to deploy capital right now. I imagine it would be especially difficult in Japan if there is lackluster consumer demand there. Japan is also a small country which is out of space, limiting the consumption of many items. There is no place to store them! In America, closet sizes have increased dramatically over the years, and self-storage facilities have sprung up near even the best neighborhoods with the largest houses.

The BOJ actually needs to destroy equity (valuations, not shares). This would be politically hard to do. A short-term way to destroy equity is to suddenly dump all the ETF shares it has accumulated, driving the price down. I don't know if that would be enough, not to mention that the bureaucrats would all lose their jobs. All along many commentators have noticed that Japan with its face-saving culture has been unwilling to clear assets off the books at bankruptcy values, and so equity and asset values did not fall fast enough. Though one never welcomes disaster, the earthquake could have provided useful economic stimulus by destroying equity. Let's look at the interest rate side of things.

To drive interest rates down to -5% in principle one would have to lend at -5% or less. This means giving someone a loan, and when they pay it back you give them a 5% bonus. Per year.

One course of one action to consider is to simply print money rather than make loans. In fact Japan could increase its money supply 5% a year and just barely achieve the required -5% interest rate (through the inflationary evaporation of value in savings accounts). The BOJ's target of 2% inflation is nowhere near enough, and their methods of getting there aren't even producing 2%.

The yen has been noticeably too strong for many years. It should be pretty simple to debase a currency. Lots of countries do it without even thinking. Perhaps Greek consultants should be brought in? The world has the talent to solve most any problem if it can just be moved where it is needed. With a lower yen, Japanese exports would be more attractive. Instead of investing in plants in cheaper Asian economies as they have been doing, Japanese investors would begin to consider the advantages of quality and innovation from having their researchers and factories at home. This would boost Japanese consumer confidence. They might not be able to buy so many items from abroad, because of exchange rates, but they would have extra impetus to buy the production of domestic businesses.

There is the solution. Finding the political means to implement it? You will have opposition from savers at home and competitors abroad. Perhaps if Japan indexed government payments to inflation and placed large new contracts with both domestic and foreign suppliers, some of the opposition would be reduced.

Equalizing a Declining Currency

By looking at what might happen if, hypothetically, the Bank of Japan announced it would devalue the yen by 5% a year, we can gain further insight into the general issue of equalization. Today the yen is selling at ¥98.24 to the dollar. What would it equalize to? There is a chicken and egg problem. The currency is nominally still worth what it is now, because presumably the issuance of new yen will occur smoothly over the year. But by next year there will be 5% more and so on. If you are holding yen you have to decide when you are going to spend them, how many years from now. That is exactly the time preference value N which we used earlier. Yen held for 100 years are worth little if devaluation continues. But if you offer $1 for ¥260, the presumed exchange rate after 20 years of 5% devaluation, my guess is you won't get any takers.

Notice that the earlier 3 year decline from ¥250/$1 to ¥125/$1 amounted to about 15 years of 5% changes. It was done much too fast.

In fact the 5% devaluation is not as far off from what Japan is trying to do as you might think. Over the last 12 years Japan's industrial production growth rate averages just over 1%.[111] It takes an annual 1% money supply increase just to stay even and not have deflation. A 3% monetary expansion (currency devaluation) is required for the 2% inflation target.

The yen fell 20% in value last fall during election season as it began to be clear monetary reformers would come to power, and long before any announcements were made. But from December to May 2013 the Nikkei rose 55%.

Assuming the 20% drop in currency value was in response to a credible 2% shift in monetary policy, currency traders have a time preference $N = 9$ years. Assuming my 5% per year suggestion amounts to a 2% shift from the current baseline (the original being 1% matching industrial production growth), then there would be another 20% currency decline and the Nikkei would be up another 55% to 27,000, a level not seen since 1990. We would have a tolerable yen value of ¥120/$1. The curse would be broken.

---

[111] http://www.indexmundi.com/g/g.aspx?c=ja&v=78

Lending Friction & Supply

Practical & Impractical Equalization Dynamics

Let us consider an investor determined to profit from the equity premium to a degree that might bring about equalization. In classical theory, this investor simply sells debt (i.e. borrows) and buys equity. To guarantee equalization there must be no limit on the amounts. Notice this method is inelegant compared to rational investors simply agreeing one morning on new rates and prices. That is why there must be no limit on the amount of arbitrage. We will consider methods, the performance of those methods, obstacles, theoretical performance if the obstacles were removed, and techniques for reducing the obstacles based on newer products offered by the investment industry.

The first obstacle is efficient market theory itself. The investor must either believe the market is inefficient, or that it will take a long time to reach efficient prices (leaving the equity premium in place – this is not a case where the profit is made by equalization occurring as in arbitrage, but only if equalization doesn't).

Then the investor will encounter the following legal and tax difficulties:

1. Legal borrowing for investment purposes is limited to 50% of assets in the best cases, often less, and is forbidden entirely in most retirement accounts.
2. Interest expense may only be counted against dividend income for tax purposes, not against capital gains.
3. Forced selling during market drops will cause capital losses which above $3000 a year are not deductible from other income.
4. Due to bid-ask spreads and quick or overnight movements (gaps), the investor will not be able to exactly restore positions that have been forced sales as the market rises again. Foreign securities may exhibit most of their price movement as gaps if traded through a US broker on US exchanges. Obtaining accounts in other countries is expensive and may involve additional tax liability.

The investor who attempts to utilize the maximum available margin could encounter forced selling (margin calls), and definitely will be unable to restore any forced sell positions as the market rises due to being under the purchase margin limit of 50% (hold margin limits are lower than 50%). The sensible solution is to limit use of margin so that expected market volatility will not create forced selling. In practice this means only about 30% use of borrowed funds, a far cry from "unlimited" borrowing.

The investor might borrow for other purposes and re-direct the funds to equities, but risks committing fraud or encountering unsecured rates as high as 15%.

If we waive the borrowing constraints, we find that the expenses of forced selling become more frequent and severe. As much as 90% borrowing was permitted prior to the Great Depression, and was viewed as contributing to the rapid decline (though margin requirements were already increasing in 1928 so it was not the only cause).

With the advent of computers, it became possible to offer Exchange Traded Funds (ETFs) with exotic properties. The "2x" or "ultra" fund type mentioned earlier is roughly equivalent to 50% borrowing, but it is the ETF which does the borrowing, making it possible to use this kind of leverage in a retirement account. Usually such an ETF is subject to higher margin requirements by one's broker so that the leverage cannot quite be doubled.

More recently "3x" ETFs are being offered, which is similar to being allowed use of 67% borrowed funds. Such an ETF reduces borrowing as the market declines, and increases it as the market rises, to try to keep a constant leverage. The most frequent re-balancing currently promised is "daily." Even the S&P 500 has had 4 changes per year since 2008 above 4.6%, which means more than 13.8% in the 3x ETF UPRO. When movements are so large, tracking of the underlying securities breaks down due to compounding on the re-balanced positions, which we discussed earlier.

An examination of results shows that the best of these ultra funds, while doing a pretty good job on a daily basis which is all they advertise, are unable to return 2x or 3x since their inception, usually in the late 2000s. UPRO is an exception, luckily conceived in 2009 at a market bottom, but it is untested by a major decline. Because they are recent, ultra ETFs cannot have affected the past equity premiums. We might suppose they could contribute to equalization going forward if they were not limited to 3x. Due to our arguments about equalizing through equity prices, we assume most of the pressure would be on interest rates to rise. This would require short-term rates reach the 8% range, which they have attained only for one period in the last century.

Perhaps the most germane finding from this section is that the levels of volatility encountered by an investor employing the strategy that might accomplish equalization are *not* the levels analyzed by Mehra and Prescott, but some large multiple of those levels. Further, it is not merely a matter of "tolerance" of this volatility and postponement of consumption. Many of the high leverage funds are set up such that if values drop below some threshold, the ETF automatically liquidates (e.g. MORL). So effectively a large loss becomes permanent.

It is possible to diversify against large losses in individual companies. Indeed, corporate expected lifetime as we saw earlier has dropped by a factor of 3 since modern portfolio theory was developed, possibly because of it. But an S&P 500 based 3x ETF is already diversified, and an investor has no option to use portfolio tricks to reduce exposure to this loss, only to reduce leverage and thereby reduce equalization pressure.

Equalization need not be accomplished directly by individual investors. Banks, of course, are prevented from using deposits to buy equities, and from 1933 to 1999 normal banks were not allowed to buy equities at all. (Outside the US this distinction is not necessarily followed, even in other G8 countries.) In the last decade or so a number of "financial" companies have been formed, often favored by legislation, such as Real-Estate Investment Trusts and Business Development Companies. BDCs can issue debt (i.e. borrow money) and use the funds to buy equity. Of course they also issue equity, which they use in combination with other assets as collateral, in the same way other corporations depend on equity to secure low cost debt financing.

Equity & Debt Ownership Patterns

An examination of the leading equity and debt ownership[112] shows some interesting patterns. See pie charts on page opposite.

- Households, mutual funds and private pension funds are the top two and 4th largest holders of equity.
  - Each holds about half as much in bonds as equity.
  - Are they using a similar theory of allocation?

- Foreign holders have the 3rd largest equity position.
  - But they hold twice as much debt as equity.
  - Probably for safety & currency diversification.[113]

---

[112] U. S. Census Bureau, "2012 Statistical Abstract - 1201 - Equities, Corporate Bonds, and Treasury Securities--Holdings and Net Purchases, by Type of Investor," The National Data Book, Washington, DC (2012). http://www.census.gov/compendia/statab/cats/banking_finance_insurance/stocks_and_bonds_equity_ownership.html

[113] The information on the motivations of foreign accountholders while not the result of systematic study was provided by a colleague at an international bank based on his experiences with clients, and those of his own colleagues.

○ If they are invested outside the US, their portfolio allocations may not be as different as the US numbers suggest.

These top holders, plus life insurance companies, state and local retirement, and miscellaneous small holdings by federal and local governments, savings institutions and similar non-speculative parties account for approximately 90% of equity holdings. It does not seem that much of this capital could be attempting to arbitrage the difference between bond and stock returns. However the larger allocations to equities suggest they are taking some advantage of it.

2010 Equity Ownership

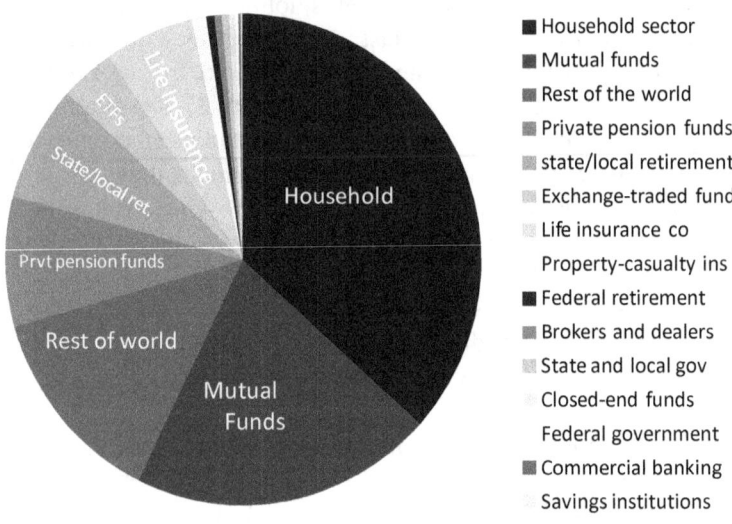

- Household sector
- Mutual funds
- Rest of the world
- Private pension funds
- state/local retirement
- Exchange-traded funds
- Life insurance co
- Property-casualty ins
- Federal retirement
- Brokers and dealers
- State and local gov
- Closed-end funds
- Federal government
- Commercial banking
- Savings institutions

2010 Bond Ownership

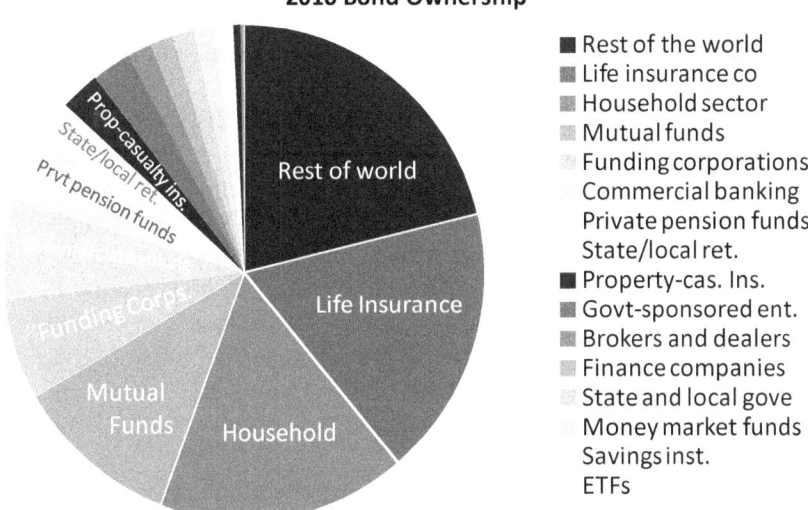

- Rest of the world
- Life insurance co
- Household sector
- Mutual funds
- Funding corporations
- Commercial banking
- Private pension funds
- State/local ret.
- Property-cas. Ins.
- Govt-sponsored ent.
- Brokers and dealers
- Finance companies
- State and local gove
- Money market funds
- Savings inst.
- ETFs

There is a lot more debt than equity as we saw when comparing the US $17 trillion debt to the $5.14 trillion S&P 500 capitalization. Much of that has to be foreign as it is the only major segment which holds more debt than equity. But much of it is also the Fed itself, conditionally expanding the money supply.

Of the remaining, 6% is ETFs. It seems reasonable to assume that the 6% in ETFs is about the maximum amount of capital that could be attempting to arbitrage the difference between bond and stock returns.

Even if *all* of the ETF capital were deployed for the purpose of equity premium arbitrage (which it assuredly is not) then the maximum impact would be a small increase in equity prices. With daily gains and losses often 1-2%, average yearly changes of 7% to 8%, and yearly changes of 30% common, the impact of rational investors would seem to be in the noise. (A turnabout on "noise traders"?) If the ETF capital were all deployed at 2x leverage (which again it is not) then 50% of it (3% of market cap) would be borrowed, accounting for some demand for debt, but small compared to Fed supply of, and Treasury demand for debt.

Rational Banking

The monetary agent may in fact need to lend very little money to keep interest rates down, if other lenders believe it has unlimited power to do so. There is a natural market mechanism that may be willing to assist the monetary agent, and strong reason for it to do so, and that is banking.

In ancient times deposits were made in temples, and later with governments, for safe keeping. Amounts as much as $1/6^{th}$ were charged for security. Deposits of grain were loaned to farmers as seed. Some deposits were to facilitate trade. Modern banking origins are traced to the Renaissance, when the banks of the Medici transitioned to private banks. For trade, notes against bank deposits could be moved without the fear of robbery associated with moving gold or similar assets.

Bankers, already heavily involved in trade, discovered they could use deposits to buy and sell goods (via loans) and cover the cost of storage and security, and even provide interest to depositors. While this might attract more depositors, such deposits could hardly be compared to investment capital. A merchant who personally engaged in trade would expect a much higher return (the "fairness" principle, he is risking his own equity). The practice of issuing "discounted" notes arose to avoid the term "interest." Private loans from ancient times had carried rather high rates of interest, for example 12% in Athens, and religious and moral objections developed.

Fractional banking – other people's money

A rational banker would seek, presumably, to maximize *his* returns. But the money he uses is *not* his, and may come to him almost without cost, or he may be paid to keep it. If he can offer a low rate to a business which will employ workers who will open consumer accounts at the bank increasing the total deposits, and who will eventually incur consumer debt at 15% or higher, the banker finds returns increased two ways. There are more returns from larger deposits, with returns being computed only on the bank's fixed costs not the deposits. And there are returns from related transactions at higher rates, which the bank is able to capture.

Even if the bank is completely solvent, there are not enough funds to cover all deposits, and at some point a run on the bank will develop. At that time, the economy has become dependent on banking, and the government must step in and guarantee the assets that have been "banked," i.e. any capital that has been used in a bank-like manner with respect to risk management. Banks typically reserve only a tiny fraction of deposits (e.g. 3%) when compared with the equity of private companies. In the case of the US Federal Reserve, solvent banks have access to very low interest loans at the Fed discount window to cover demand withdrawals, or for other purposes. Even depositors of insolvent banks receive some guarantee, but the insolvent banks are closed and their investors face losses.

A case of overnight debt-equity equalization

Anyone who loans money to a bank with expectation of something more tangible than just to share in future bank profits is in effect a depositor. When Lehman went bankrupt in 2008, there was a small loss in money market funds that held Lehman notes, and this caused a run on money market funds that froze the market for short-term commercial paper, overnight driving up interest rates from a bank-like 2% to an equity-like 8%. With 45% of corporate capital coming from debt, and 30% of the debt short-term (less than one year), a change from 2% to 8% in the cost of this capital would have a dramatic effect on business returns. Almost immediately, government insurance was offered for money market deposits because they had become a banking function.

Bank-like assets

It is our argument that this is an inevitable and repeating course as technology and banking evolve. Whatever seeks to avoid risk and is deposited mainly for security will be used as low-interest capital and the economy will become dependent on it. A "bank run" will trigger government insurance, and then it officially becomes bank-like. Its uses will be regulated, and it will not be freely used as investment capital.

By contrast, while a "run" on a stock is unfortunate for investors who are late to sell, the companies themselves usually continue to operate, sometimes for years after becoming "penny stocks," and occasionally even recover from this situation.

Central banks evolved from ordinary banks. One of the two or three earliest was the Bank of England, organized mainly to help finance war with France. From central banks evolved monetary agents, quasi-independent (depending on country) bankers with public responsibilities. It would be natural to assume in our allegory of Zo that the monetary agent would work through bankers to implement its policies.

Earnings equalization is common

The economy of Zo as we left it after industrialization appears to be in equilibrium and to be rational, at least until some new factor emerges, or preferences change. A lender will find no agricultural demand for debt above 4%. And while industrial returns cannot equalize through price to other than their 12% return, the price to earnings ratio of their shares will rise to whatever level begins to make investors uncomfortable. The author's guess is that might be somewhere around 25, which corresponds to industrial earnings of 4%, and then *in regard to earnings equity is equalized with debt*. But because of the surprising math of discount pricing of long life returns, there is still an 8% equity premium when price appreciation is added to earnings.

Credit card rates are not a risk premium

And of course, if banks are utilized by Zo's monetary agent, they may offer consumers unsecured loans at credit card rates. This is not a risk premium. Credit card defaults are in the 3 to 4% range, and even at

2009 peaks rarely exceeded 6% (Bank of America the exception), indicating that around 9 to 11% was essentially risk free. Credit card rates are simply discriminatory pricing. It is difficult to enter the business of providing credit cards. It is after all a "business" with complex networks and procedures, and it has a business return. An investor wishing to capture this return buys stock in a bank, or starts a bank.

While not a derivation of any particular equity premium, the example of Zo demonstrates that *an* equity premium exceeding the expected risk premium *can* exist in equilibrium without irrationality, and without exhausting the means or will of the monetary agent.

Rational monetary agents

The monetary agent has latitude to choose its intervention rate. The value chosen in the above example was arbitrarily selected to make the economies before and after the change easy to compare, having the same total average return. But a rational monetary agent seeking to maximize employment and willing to tolerate some inflation might choose a lower rate, creating a larger equity premium and faster growth.

Answer to efficient market questions

When the author discusses these concepts with economists versed in the equity premium, sometimes there is the question, "But what about markets? There is a borrower and a lender. How do they agree on price or rate?" There are two key things to keep in mind. First, efficient market theory only holds that market participants will not be able to profit from widely available information. It does not hold that all market participants agree, either on price or risk. The question asked with the article "a" implies homogeneous participants, which is not the case. Money has not disappeared from banks as interest rates have dropped toward zero and fees are even required in some cases. But money did disappear from overnight lending after a 3% default due to Lehman.

While this does not challenge efficient market theory, perhaps the reader will argue it challenges rational investor theory. This thorny and legitimate question is fortunately avoided because low interest *market* capital is not necessary if the *monetary agent* is willing to lend, as for example in the massive Quantitative Easing program of the Federal Reserve, and prevents the money it has lent from being invested in equities, and if bankers are rational, passing on the monetary agent's rate for reasons described above.

Next we should look at a bit of history to see if our theory is empirical as well as rational.

The Era of Free Banking

In the 2003 article cited earlier, Mehra and Prescott observe that the equity premium was zero from 1802 to 1862. During this period the charter of the Bank of the United States was allowed to expire in 1811. There was no central banker. The United States experienced great difficulty financing the War of 1812 due to severe inflation, with the result that the credit and borrowing status of the US was at its lowest level since the country's founding. A charter for a Second Bank of the US was granted in 1816, and the bank opened in 1817, but became entangled in partisan politics and was closed by Andrew Jackson. Again no central banker. All banking business was done by state chartered banks until 1863, when the confusion of banknote values and instability of banks was judged to be an intolerable problem and Congress passed the National Bank Acts of 1863 and 1864, again during wartime.

This period of "Free Banking" as it was called (was it "free market banking" we wonder?) is notably coincident with the period of a zero equity premium. A passerby not otherwise burdened by politics (of that time or ours) might think it at least pardonable to look in the direction of banking and monetary policy for an explanation of the lack of equity premium. When banking was relatively unregulated, it seems the returns equalized as economists would expect. However, this alone does not explain *why* they do not equalize *otherwise*. It merely indicates a direction in which to look.

Just the fact that banks were risky does not by itself argue for an effect on the lending interest rates. While most investigators have focused on the risk premium, we have seen the effect of interest rates (a quantity essentially controlled by monetary policy) on business returns. Business returns, not prices, must determine the long-term equity return, because investors with limited time preferences who are also confounded by the friction between individual and aggregate (index) returns and limited time preferences will not be able to equalize 100 year aggregated market returns.

Banking was not the only focus of the federal government during the 1860s. The nation was at war yet again, and became the first nation to spend more than a billion dollars in a year. Two thirds of the North's costs were financed with bond sales. 12% was financed with the printing of "greenbacks" which could *not* be converted to gold. The remainder was raised through tariffs and taxes. The South was not in a good position to sell bonds to its population, or to raise tariffs, and induced severe inflation by relying on printing currency. General Lee became unable to purchase supplies.[114]

---

[114] Gordon, J.S., "The High Cost of War," Barron's, NY, April 9, 2011.
http://online.barrons.com/article/SB500014240529702039901045761910612 0778 6514.html

Evolution & Sustainability of Productivity

If you want growth you have to pay for it. Specifically, you have to grow everything to get growth in some things. A potted plant outgrows its pot, if it grows at all, and eventually dies or must be moved to the garden. If you grow population, production, trade and most of all productivity, you must grow money as well.

Once one understands the combination of growth and money, the idea of tying money's value to a non-growing substance seems as perverse as fiat money did to policy makers of 1929 who let the country slide into depression. The next section is about men of the late 19th and early 20th centuries who were the star CEOs of their day, and who firmly understood they had invented something that would forever change the world and especially money. They invented productivity, especially the idea of continually increasing it.

The Industrialists

The basis of modern corporations was laid with the tracks of the transcontinental railroad, initiated by legislation in 1862 and 1864. Disputes over the route were more easily settled without the South's presence in Congress. Construction was financed by the sale of bonds at 6%. The bonds were guaranteed by the sale of land grants in addition to operating revenues. Further, the government guaranteed a market for the railroads by land grants to homesteaders, prompting a significant population increase. We will come back to the role of population growth in business returns in a moment.

Previously we mentioned that the 1880s established an *unlimited lifetime* for corporations, making financing by equity issues significantly more attractive, enhancing the ability of the corporations to generate returns, and reducing risk.[115]

These legal developments had the opposite effect on risk vs. returns from the economic forces of investor choices and demands. The government was pushing interest rates down to finance wars and railroads, and pushing the possible business returns up in order to create a national infrastructure. While few corporations from that era realized the potential of unlimited life, and few do today, several such as Union Pacific and General Electric are still with us.

Indeed, the early shareholders of GE and Standard Oil would have been justified in paying nearly any price for their shares, provided only

---

[115] Hartman, Thom, *Unequal Protection – The Rise of Corporate Dominance and the Theft of Human Rights*, Rodale, Emmaus PA, 2004, ISBN-10 1579549551

that their time preferences for consumption included a preference for the success of their descendents. When Jay Rockefeller retires in 2014, the United States will be without a Rockefeller in high office for the first time in four decades and only the second time since the 1950s.

Silver had been demonetized in 1873 as new deposits had undermined its value. Bimetallism or "free silver" would have allowed farmers to pay their debts more easily. The Panic of 1893 intensified debates. In a famous speech at the Democratic Convention of 1896, William Jennings Bryan said, "You shall not crucify mankind upon a cross of gold."[116] [117] But Bryan lost the main election and in 1900 McKinley reinforced the single metal standard, which restricted the money supply available to fuel growth while facilitating trade with other gold standard nations such as England.

Debate continued as farmers were joined by successful businessmen who also opposed banking and trade views on money. A 1921 New York Times article[118] describes the efforts of Henry Ford and Thomas Edison to promote commodity based money instead of debt based money. Both men were famous for setting up mass production assembly lines, and could not visualize other than catastrophe if a limited quantity of gold money were divided by all they could produce. Edison is quoted as saying, *"Gold is a relic of Julius Cesar, and interest is an invention of Satan."*

So the strongest form of the gold standard had only lasted 29 years when in 1929 a worldwide depression and severe deflation reversed political fortunes and the winds of global trade.

Growth and Free Trade

Without doubt structural differences in the means of generating returns between bonds and equities were introduced by legislation and court rulings. There arose a new class of businesses engaged in innovation and mass production, whose interests were more aligned with miners and farmers than with lenders and landholders. They did not get "commodity money" in 1921, but they got rid of gold completely by 1971 and with free floating currencies the nation which produces the most sees its currency rise in value. Isn't that commodity based money? For all practical purposes, Edison and Ford won in the end.

---

[116] http://historymatters.gmu.edu/d/5354/
[117] http://en.wikipedia.org/wiki/Cross_of_Gold_speech
[118] "FORD SEES WEALTH IN MUSCLE SHOALS," The New York Times, December 6, 1921. Retrieved February 24, 2013.
http://query.nytimes.com/mem/archive-free/pdf?_r=1&res=9C04E0D7103EEE3ABC4E53DFB467838A639EDE via: http://en.wikipedia.org/wiki/Thomas_Edison

The rhetoric of the debates has changed little. It appears the tide may have turned merely because with a higher growth rate, the industrialists and their successors came to control most of the capital and jobs.

The charter of The Federal Reserve pre-dates this adaptation, and does not mandate "growth." However, the relation between growth and employment is well-known, and a monetary agent is a political entity which cannot remain immune to the dominant thinking of its context. If for no other reason, the dominant thinking mode controls how markets will react to the monetary agent. Interest rates are not set in stone. What markets think the central bank can or will do on average over time is more important than today's rate, because the equalization pressure of the discount pricing model from very-long returns makes future growth very important in today's prices.

So we argue that a *rational monetary agent* will *adopt* a goal of maximizing growth, in addition to anything that may be written in its charter. The success of the experimental new policies of central banks today will determine which policies are adaptively carried forward and become the goals of future monetary agents. The Bank of Japan, for example, has gone beyond interest rates and buys equity (using Exchanged Traded Funds). In our model this does not appear to increase growth, but Japan is desperate to experiment after decades of stagnation.

The European Union at this writing appears to be coming under older influences. Even their monetary charter is different, not addressing employment. In our simplified analysis we supposed central bank lending to be used for production, but many European governments have used credit for less-than-productive spending.

China has possibly the most aggressively managed economy in history, having evolved a kind of capitalism from its communist central planning roots. This is culturally supported in China more than some other countries because of a very long history of coordinated action and preservation of social good. Favorable capital rates are made available to business not only through monetary and banking means, but also government direct ownership of businesses. Time will ultimately decide if this system is well adapted. If it is, then countries with low production growth rates will become poorer in the de-facto era of commodity based money. Edison even got his wish for zero interest.

Near-Equilibrium Trends

On the one hand, much of our analysis is based on equilibrium, a static analysis of an economy over a long period of time. If something is trending, like for example P/E ratios going up or down, then of course it would temporarily influence the equity premium, but it would not be sustainable. In this section we'll take a look at very long-term trends that might not have been excluded by the time intervals considered in historical equity premium analysis. These trends also illustrate how our society and culture and economy are changing as we grow and productivity grows, and what prices we might be paying.

Interest Rates

On the one hand, there is an obvious trend downward in interest rates since ancient times. On the other hand, there does not seem to be any reason to suppose that the relation between interest rates and loan failure due to war or insolvency or business failure has changed. And to some extent, whether we see a long-term trend depends on what start and end dates we pick.

Interest rates were as low as 4% in the core of the Roman Empire in 25 A.D., only to rise again to exceed ancient levels during the depths of the Dark Ages. According to Armstrong,[119] every government has succumbed to the temptation to borrow more than it can repay, and war is most often the cause of excess borrowing. Also according to Armstrong, speculation and inflation are the typical endpoint of cycles, and governments have often tried to regulate interest rates.

It has been our assumption that inflation would indeed end the effectiveness of monetary intervention at lowering interest rates, so we take no issue with these claims. Some clarification of terminology is advisable. Inflation in the historical scenarios was often due to an excess accumulation of gold or other fixed basis money. Inflation in the price of goods corresponds to an equal and opposite deflation in the value of money. In the case of a money supply loosely based on GDP relative to trading partners, the goods themselves are "trade money" and a deflation in the monetary value of the trade goods is somewhat analogous to the historical case of inflation of prices via deflation in the value of the monetary commodity.

In other words, in our model deflation has emerged as a persistent problem in an economy in which productivity constantly increases, but the terminology is masking similarity to historical economies.

Like many economists, and despite my strong arguments in this book, I am wary of an "end of the line" eventually in a government strategy to regulate interest rates. In the remainder of this section we'll attempt to identify other substantive trends that account for the equity premium – trends that allow monetary intervention to be successful for the time being.

---

[119] Armstrong, M. A., "A Brief History of World Credit & Interest Rates," http://armstrongeconomics.com/

Population Growth

Population growth over the last century in the USA is about 1.3% annually, slowing to 1.24% since 1947, or 1.01% since 1974, and about 0.7% in recent years.[120] Population increases absorb production output and also contribute to production output. If business ownership is fixed, i.e. does not grow with population, then excess returns might be expected with population growth. Below we will examine a means by which this might generate some equity premium, but it is not per se a characteristic of population growth, rather the disposition of dividends and capital hoarding.

Productivity Growth

The analysis we have used depends on or is at least enhanced by the introduction of a higher productivity business into an economy – at least once. In fact productivity has been growing at around or just under 2% during the entire history of the US[121] There is a slight decline in recent decades, but the trend once again seems up since the 2009 financial crisis as many automation technologies mature, and business owners implement automation to compete with low cost labor in world markets. In the first quarter of 2013, for example, manufacturing productivity increased 3.5% while labor costs decreased 10%.[122] This is four years into a "recovery" and the deflationary pressure is evident. While future productivity is extremely uncertain, our analysis is valid as long as productivity does not decline. In the very long-term, the decline in importance of labor if productivity increases without limit is something the world economy has not yet addressed.

GDP Growth

GDP in the US has been growing at around 3% since 1929, or around 2.2% since 1947.[123] Let's take 1947 to 2012 as a basis interval for discussion in this section for a variety of reasons, such as data availability

---

[120] US Census Bureau, Population Estimates Historical Data, http://www.census.gov/popest/data/historical/index.html Via: http://www.multpl.com/us-population-growth-rate/table/by-year or via: Wikipedia, Demographics of the United States, http://en.wikipedia.org/wiki/Demographics_of_the_United_States
[121] Shackleton, R., "Total Factor Productivity Growth in Historical Perspective," Congressional Budget Office working paper 2013-01, March 2013
[122] Bureau of Labor Statistics, "Productivity and Costs First Quarter 2013, Revised," US Department of Labor, USDL 13-1101, June 5, 2013
[123] Bureau of Economic Analysis, National Economic Accounts, US Department of Commerce, online data tables revised as of 1st quarter 2013, via http://www.bea.gov/national/index.htm

and avoidance of major wars and major market lows or highs (that we know of, in regard to the end date). It begins just before the modern structure of the Fed in 1951 and should allow full evaluation of any impact of the modern Fed, without difficulties in comparing data to different monetary regimes.

This section was inspired by a comment in Fisher's book (mentioned earlier[124]) claiming that equity returns had no particular relation to GDP growth, and could exceed GDP growth indefinitely. The comment was strong and aroused my contrarian suspicions. Indeed, if one looks at the ordinary way of computing GDP via production, there is little way of identifying how it would relate to equity returns. But there is an *income GDP* which in principle gives the same total result, a kind of book-balancing of GDP, and when we turn to this we find the five components of the table below.

Income GDP since 1947
(Data from the Bureau of Economic Analysis)

Income GDP component	annualized growth 1947-2012
Corporate earnings	2.5%
Salaries	2.2%
Investment income	2.8%
Farm income	-1.1%
Unincorporated non-farm income	2.1%
	====
Total GDP	2.2%

Here we see two factors that relate directly to equity returns. Investment income includes both dividends and interest, and has been growing .6% faster than GDP, increasing its share by 48% (about half) over the 66 year period at the expense of other GDP components. Corporate earnings have exceeded by .3% resulting in a 22% increase in share. Most of the cannibalization has been of farm income, but small unincorporated businesses have also seen their share decline slightly, by 7%.

The BEA data does not distinguish business size, only incorporation status. Large businesses enjoy lower cost of capital due to perceived stability, and should receive relatively more stimulus from a low rate monetary policy. Have they? Shiller provides data on the S&P Composite (1500) which shows a growth rate of 2.65% over this period.[125]

---

[124] Fisher, K., Hoffmans, L., *The Little Book of Market Myths*, Wiley & Sons, Hoboken NJ, p. 15 (2013)

[125] Shiller, R., *Irrational Exuberance*, Princeton University Press 2000, Broadway Books 2001, 2nd ed. 2005, updated data via
http://www.econ.yale.edu/~shiller/data.htm

These 1500 businesses represent 80% of the available equity, and their excess growth rate of earnings over GDP is .45%, increasing their share of GDP by 34.5%. This is 50% higher growth than corporations in total.

Equity returns are price returns plus dividends. Price returns are directly computable as change in earnings (the earnings growth we have just been discussing) and change in P/E ratio. The P/E since 1947 has increased at an annualized rate of 0.9%, also determined from the Shiller data.

Many popular equity premium analyses are based on indices similar to the S&P Composite, or even smaller. If we simply add the excess (over average GDP) growth rates of corporate earnings, P/E, and investment income, we have .6%+.45%+.9% = 1.95% excess return over GDP, a "premium" for holding large corporate entities. Of this, 1.05% is cannibalization at the expense of other GDP components and non-inflationary. The remainder is P/E ratio, a volatile estimate of the stability of future growth, possibly very distant growth, as we have seen. P/E returns are zero-sum, that is, for every dollar realized in a sale, some buyer put up a dollar, so P/E increases do not lead to inflation by themselves. The entire 1.95% is non-inflationary.

Ownership concentration

One component of the equity premium is somewhat theoretical, and that is the full re-investment of dividends. Re-investment has become more practical for small investors with increasing availability of mutual funds and ETFs, both of which come at some non-negligible cost in expenses. This part of the premium necessarily results in a (again theoretical) concentration of ownership, as through re-investment the investor who realizes this return increases her share of ownership of the total market. Obviously if *all* investors followed this policy, per-investor share of the market would remain unchanged, so it is somewhat of a paradoxical component of the EP.

Dividends, like interest payments in the economy of Zo, will have an inflationary effect only if spent for consumption. If re-invested, they have only the effect of ownership concentration. If an investor is "realizing" the full EP, then she must be following a strategy of re-investment, and therefore the dividend payments are non-inflationary. So we can add the average annual dividend of 3.46% since 1947 (again from Shiller) to the above 1.95% to find a justifiable non-inflationary EP of 5.41% over that period. If we accept that 4% of the EP has been equalized through competition and shorter company lifetimes, then a former EP of roughly 9.5% is easily explained.

Relative share of income GDP components

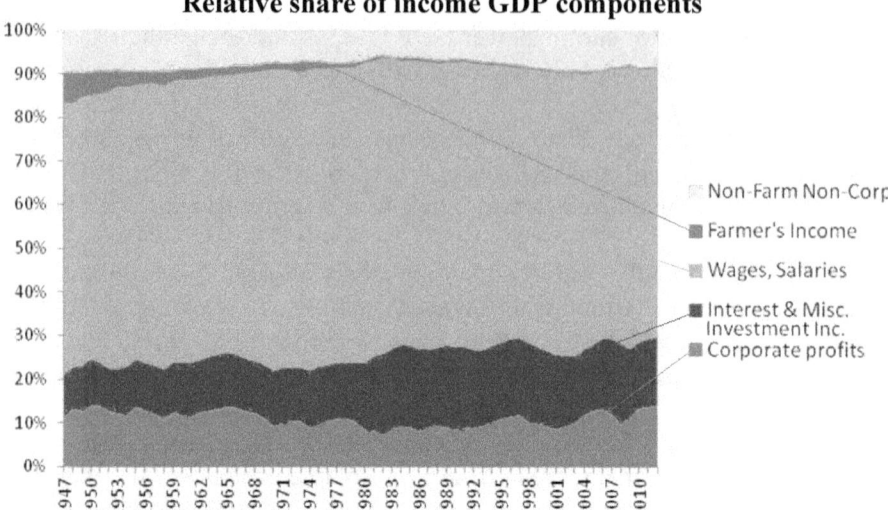

The figure above shows the share of income GDP by its 5 categories. It is evident that while corporate share is increasing, there is a long way to go before investment income dominates salaries, and even unincorporated business are in no apparent danger of disappearing, so cannibalization can continue for a long time (though not indefinitely, of course). Concentration of corporate share among large corporations is not shown by the BEA data.

Conclusions

In market economics the subjects of study are huge (markets), and one cannot just rewind them and conduct a controlled experiment. The experimental process proceeds by trying to formulate mathematical models in which the available data makes sense. When a piece of conflicting data comes along, it is not wise to immediately throw out years of existing theory. The function of a puzzle is to focus attention on a difficult piece of data over time, 28 years in this case, and only then if satisfactory solutions are not found is it advisable to modify theory.

With equities, there appears to be large risk in the short run, but less for market representative indices in the long run. Bonds have little risk in the short run but have some long-term exposure, enough that Mehra and Prescott judged long-term market indices to be deserving of a 1% or less premium over bonds. And studies were done over longer time periods than most investors live.

Intrinsic returns can only equalize in a time window

Equity returns cannot equalize through the mechanism of discounted pricing because, especially when perpetual portfolios are employed, this would result in very high P/E ratios which are unrealistically volatile. And the portfolio-driven valuations would be out of sync with individual equity fair values and subject to attack by arbitrage.

The selection of any particular time preference for investors affects only the P/E ratio. The underlying intrinsic business growth rate re-emerges through re-equalization as new earnings are discovered, formerly outside the time preference window. Therefore, the most likely method of equalization is through rising interest rates, i.e. falling prices of bonds and other debt.

This morning there was an article on BBC Europe about votes in several cities in Germany to buy back electric grids that were earlier privatized.[126] Hamburg has already voted 51% in favor, and Berlin will vote soon. The idea was suggested on a national scale by Merkel's center-right government in January.[127] There are a variety of reasons, from

---

[126] Stephen Evans, "German call to 'undo' energy privatisation amid Berlin vote," BBC News, Berlin, Nov. 3, 2013, http://www.bbc.co.uk/news/world-europe-24763311

[127] *Frank Dohmen and Gerald Traufetter,* "Politician Calls for Nationalization of Electricity Grid," Spiegel Online International, January 16, 2013, http://www.spiegel.de/international/business/member-of-merkel-cabinet-calls-for-nationalization-of-german-power-grid-a-877576.html

citizens wanting more green energy, to the desire to recapture profits that are now going to companies outside Germany to Vattenfall, oddly enough owned by the government of Sweden though it functions like a private company. A big wave of privatizations began about 1990 in developing countries, with 8000 deals in 120 countries worth $410 billion between 1990 and 2003.[128] The German grids were integrated under VEAG in 1991 and sold to a private consortium in 1994, marking the date of full privatization. Vattenfall acquired most of VEAG in 2000-2001.

Is it any surprise to the reader that after 22 years, a period just long enough for the equity premium to be reliably noticed, the ever efficient Germans are noticing they left some money on the table in that deal? Most governments hope to have a lifetime longer than 20 years or even 100. For a long time I have wondered how governments could sell something of nearly infinite future value for what seems like a pittance, a sum of paper money that will soon be squandered with nothing to show for it. Am I saying *every* privatization deal leaves money on the table?

Of course not. I am saying every deal that involves an enterprise *with an economic return greater than bond interest rates* leaves money on the table, no matter what the price. And anyone, individual or corporation or government, who does such a deal without immediately re-investing the money in another activity with equal or higher long-term returns, concrete returns not just indirect benefits, is foolish. I cannot use language strong enough.

Should governments own everything then? That would be ridiculous. But when trading away what they already own, governments should get something of equal or greater value, and cash is not it. Governments can print cash. I will leave it to governments to decide where to focus their resources, probably activities that broadly support the economy and public interest. It may change from time to time, and trades may be in order. We would not want governments to be maintaining and expanding horse trails. Well, actually, in the context of National Parks and in view of the public reaction to the recent government shutdown, I guess we do! It is dangerous to apply one sweeping brush stroke to everything. Even progress.

The trading of one activity for another, rather than cashing out, is the same principle that I elaborated with regard to selling assets you no longer have confidence in. You must buy another asset. Otherwise you will find that in 20 years you are noticeably falling behind, and in 100 years your descendants will be poor while everyone else is rich. You have lost your place in the world, your means of making a living.

---

[128] Sunita Kikeri and Aishetu Kilo, *Privatization : Trends And Recent Developments*, World Bank, November 2005,
http://elibrary.worldbank.org/doi/book/10.1596/1813-9450-3765

Corporations make the same mistakes. HP divested its namesake instrument business, changing the name of it to something no one can remember, and decided to focus on giving away printers and selling ink. Xerox, Canon, Kodak and many others were already equally good at that business and HP lost its place on the Dow. Mergers fail all the time, proving governments have no monopoly on incompetence. Apparently it is not so easy to choose and execute activities that have long-term consequence. That's why we have perpetual portfolios, which rely not on the expertise of corporations or the ability to pick genius leadership, but the resilience of an entire market backed by the will of a people.

Monetary policy does indeed set interest rates

Monetary policy, government borrowing, and the regulation of banking and private borrowing, together with the discriminatory powers and related-transaction interests of rational bankers, are able to maintain an equity premium by lowering, on average, interest rates below equity return rates. As long as business productivity is high and increasing, inflation will permit low interest rates. Indeed, if rates are not held below where investors would equalize them, the economy would be threatened by deflation. As productivity increases, the deflation threshold becomes lower.

The dual action nature of the mechanisms we have described, that is the lowering of benchmark lending interest rates in conjunction with raising the return on equities, suggest that unlike many temporal preference schemes, our mechanism simultaneously contributes to the resolution of both the equity premium puzzle and the risk-free rate puzzle.

One of the most persistent financial news topics since the financial crisis is speculation and guessing about when the Fed will taper down its $85 billion a month bond purchases known as Quantitative Easing. Only some time later would the Fed raise interest rates, but that is considered inevitable as well. Treasury 10-year bond yields jumped from 1.9% to 2.9% in three months from May to August of 2013.[129] That is a profound change of opinion for a ten year security to have occurred in such a short time. It was entirely attributed to expectations of Fed tapering. The Fed hadn't actually done anything yet. Do monetary agents set interest rates? Yes, if they are willing to take enough action. No if like the BOJ they are mostly talk and little pay. The question to ask is, does your central banker have conviction? Is he or she willing to stand and absorb banker-hate from both sides, jealous and fearful of the money creation and destruction power?

[129] http://www.treasury.gov/resource-center/data-chart-center/interest-rates/Pages/TextView.aspx?data=yieldYear&year=2013

Japan is pretty much proof of our thesis that inflation does not automatically follow low or zero interest rates. The Japanese have been praying for a little inflation for 25 years. The US still remembers being haunted by inflation during the 1970s and early 1980s. The solution was ultimately simple. Raise interest rates above the inflation rate, stand firm and take the heat.

Zheng's puzzle is solved

Zheng has pointed out that various preference-based adjustments to the consumption CAPM which seem to work in theory in fact fail when confronted with data regressions. But even worse, they cannot theoretically explain why the equity premium would be large for long periods, and then sometimes negative for long periods,[130] such as the late 1800s. Since our model can move the equity premium and lending interest rates in opposite directions, we don't stand in contradiction to historical data.

In the context of this book, Zheng's puzzle may sound like a small thing. I have not spent much time on it directly, although I did stress that during the period of the early 1800's when there was free banking there was no equity premium. And the increase of the premium after 1933's monetary reforms was a principal clue to the road I took to unravel the EP. But I was having trouble convincing economists, and even myself, that it was really necessary to move beyond the simple concept that risk-reward was all there was to it. I kept looking for ways to justify that stocks were really risky for more than a decade. Six months after first seeing Zheng's paper I looked at it again, and her comment that the equity premium inversions were improbable with any risk model jumped out at me. Then I was confident to go forward.

The equity premium is the result of productivity

We conclude that an equity premium in excess of a traditional "risk premium" is likely to be best understood as the introduction of new high-return business activity into an economy, with a side effect in that the GDP structurally changes, growing toward industries exhibiting the new productivity, and toward large businesses with the lowest cost of capital. However, due to the necessity of maintaining a perpetual portfolio to realize the equity premium there will be a premium on new businesses, and if the EP is fully realized by investors, a concentration of equity ownership through re-investment.

Can productivity continue to increase? Probably farther than we can imagine. While progress in artificial intelligence (A.I.) is frustratingly

---

[130] Zheng, L., "A Survey of the Empirical Difficulties of the Consumption Capital Asset Pricing Models," J. Mod. Econ. Manag., vol. 2, no. 1 (2013)

slow, maybe that is a good thing. No science fiction writer that I know of has been able to envision a future in which our engines of productivity and ourselves remain in peaceful cohabitation if the engines become intelligent. The most optimistic view is that of Isaac Asimov, who wrote a series of novels in which benevolent robots gradually extract themselves from the presence of humans, and become our invisible caretakers.

The real danger present for some time is that so much of humanity lives on in an older state of being while the minority with its obsession with productivity and technology takes over and re-engineers the planet. Humans have a nasty habit of not being able to share the planet with close relatives, either intentionally or accidentally wiping each other out.

Monetary policy must permanently adapt

As a consequence of the findings on the EP, it may be we should not expect a monetary policy which is entirely cyclic. It is likely that over time, if productivity continues to increase, monetary policy needs to *permanently* adapt. Rather than a question of the sustainability of a new monetary policy regime, we find a question of whether it is wise to discontinue an adaptation to productivity increases and associated deflation.

I am writing this book at this particular time partly out of concern that policymakers and, well almost everyone, assumes there is some eternal "normal" value of interest rates, probably set by some market, and all adjustments are temporary. I am hoping I have convinced everyone from central bankers to beginning savers to at least look into the subject with an open mind. It seems to me the evidence is overwhelming that once equity return rates rose above 6%, the equalized market debt rate (and it *will* equalize without a central banker) will create enough deflation to destroy the market and the country and perhaps the world.

It nearly destroyed the country in the 1860's, and nearly destroyed the world in two wars in the 20th century. The role of economics as a cause of war cannot be understated. The Germans had no use for Hitler except that 40% of them were out of work. The Syrians, Egyptians, and Tunisians would not likely have ousted their governments if their citizens were employed. In none of these countries is it over yet, because no one has put the people back to work yet. The Russian Revolution could not have happened in good times.

I should hasten to add that I do not think economic pressure is a sure-fire way to manipulate another country. If Iran falls because of economic sanctions, we might well find they already have nuclear weapons, and whoever grabs power may well use them. And as long as a country feels the threat is from outside, there is a rallying point. The Germans viewed the reparations-extracting allies as the rallying point, and rally they did. The Iranians rallied against the US in 1979, as the US had earlier engineered a coup in that country, and we have given them an external focus ever since that has kept them from falling apart.

Nor is mere aggregate economic growth a panacea. When new high-return businesses are introduced, capital flows to them and all values, such as land values, try to equalize to the new high-return level. Last I checked, the Fed could not create land. At first we just thought everyone needed a high school education. Then college. Now what, a doctorate? With the shortening life of technologies, a doctorate can be obsolete by the time it is obtained. I don't have a solution to this problem for society at large, but I'm going to train my children to live off the equity premium. It seems to be the only thing around with a time horizon greater than 20 years!

Remaining questions

Several questions remain for further research. In the past, it has not always been necessary for monetary agents to supply large amounts of capital at non-market rates. Is this a sustainable situation, or will adaptive forces gradually reduce the low interest capital available? For example, the transfer of wealth from working classes to investor classes might be a long-term adaptive pressure which reduces low interest capital.

Is buying debt, either public (Treasury bonds) or private (mortgage backed securities) always the right way to create money? I do not know. It leaves a potentially useful hook to withdraw the money by simply allowing the debt to be paid and not buying new debt. But if the money does not need to be withdrawn, this might just be building up to a catastrophe. But again, maybe the debt angle keeps the central bank from issuing too much money? What would a central bank even do instead? Other than helicopter drops, I mean.

Risk is still important and issues remain. Logarithmic risk probabilities are very difficult to discover. I have alluded to some long-term concerns about the march of productivity. A separate project of mine posits a mathematical relationship between efficiency and desirability of a process or product, and the "crash rate" that will be experienced while using it. The arguments are economic, not technical or engineering. See "Corporate Risk Compensation" at http://mc1soft.com/papers/ .

Alternatively, we might ask if the working classes embed some instinctive knowledge of the possibility of occasional catastrophic failures which the investor classes are not taking into account. Or will an age of automation and robotics disempower the working class, disconnecting us from historical patterns?

Utopian Visions

Speculation on the Far Future

Looking to the far future one might even ask if, much as during the 19th century corporations enjoyed an expansion of rights culminating in full corporate personhood, perhaps non-human entities will eventually be allowed to enter the investor class, the CEO suite, and the board room?

To become able to travel to other stars, for ordinary people to make ordinary such trips, we would need to double present per capita energy use 30 times. At the (probably unsustainable) 20th century growth rates, that's 2000 years. The energy is available; the sun converts 4 million tons of hydrogen per second to energy, most of which is wasted. We are probably advancing at physics and environmental sciences and space travel quite fast enough to manage it. But can we handle the monetary policy without putting everyone out of work and starting a final war?

A Vision from the Early 1960s

As I was finishing this book, I happened to read an old Science Fiction story from about 1962 which had been re-published. No, this isn't my preferred reading choice. I like to read escapist novels, actually, while I'm tread milling uphill at the gym. The time passes, I'm inspired by the heroes who overcome adversity, and before I know it or have any sense of exertion I have overcome 2000 vertical feet! But alas, I was caught up on all the series and chronicles whose style I cared for, and the authors were either dead or promising their next installments next year.

I found myself suddenly dizzy with déjà vu. There was a direct sales scheme that bypassed retail stores, straight out of a page in Jeff Bezos' Amazon playbook. And a way of comparing products' quality and price and bypassing expensive "telly-marketing" worthy of Sergey Brin and Larry Page's Google. I even thought of Sam Walton and the elimination of distributors and middlemen. The story was "Subversive." By Mack Reynolds.[131] You can read it online[132] if you like. Read it now if you plan to, because relating it to our discussion will be a bit of a spoiler.

Reynolds envisions hover cars, not important to the story, but placing it far in the future. We don't have them mostly because of the enormous energy required compared to other personal transit. Only the very, very rich and the President and military travel by helicopter, the closest thing we have. And eventually you find out the story takes place in the "United States of the Americas," perhaps something like a combination

---

131 http://en.wikipedia.org/wiki/Mack_Reynolds
132 http://www.gutenberg.org/files/23197/23197-h/23197-h.htm

of NAFTA and immigration reform. I can see us headed in that direction. It would be hard to tell when one crossed into Canada if they did not still stop you at the border. Even the money is similar. And to listen to immigration debates one would think most Mexicans had already come to the US

Of course you are led to believe the businessman who engineers the retailing revolution, head of "Freer Enterprises," is the subversive in the title of the story. He is even investigated by an organization calling itself the "Bureau of Economic Subversion." It is unclear if this is a gang of thugs hired by traditional corporations, or an actual arm of the government.

The bureau agent points out that Freer's highly efficient and productive plans will undermine the economy, putting most people out of work. Then no one will be able to buy even his cheaper products. "Exactly!" exclaims the businessman, "Bring it crashing to the ground is the better term." He is fed up with "three quarters of our employed working at nothing jobs, gobbledygook jobs, nonproducing jobs, make-work jobs, red-tape bureaucracy…"

In 1962 Reynolds missed one interesting development. He envisions manufacturing still done in the United States, so the economy can be reconstructed on a different highly-productive basis. He missed the fall and/or transformation of communism and the opening of trade with China. He envisions that the Bureau of Subversion is an agent of the "Soviet Complex" intended to keep us from transforming our economy and racing ahead of the Soviets. The takeover of most of the world's manufacturing by China was not foreseeable, it seems.

But two things were easy to foresee in 1962. Extreme productivity creates massive displacement in the workforce, displacement being a nice word to substitute for "unemployment." And almost all conflicts from WWII to the Cold War to the Arab Spring and the disaster in Syria arise from economic conflict and unemployment. People are tolerant when they are not threatened. And if they are not economically threatened, they are not threatened.

A Vision from the Present

A lot of research into the best ways of producing and marketing print and eBooks was going on between writing sessions in the last days of the manuscript. It was a lesson in the reality of what I had been writing about productivity as I leaned that amid the explosion of options available to authors to cut out middlemen and make the publishing process more productive, one of the largest companies had severely turned the screws on how authors or publishers could set prices.

A technical book is liable to have a small audience, and prices are traditionally in the $75-$150 range. Of course I was going for less than that and hoped to also attract a non-technical audience. But the price of eBooks was effectively limited to $9.99. Now I understand why many technical books do *not* have eBook versions, and why many novel authors have begun to write collections of three to nine books of under 100 pages each, instead of one 300 page novel.

Not only can readers sample their writing at low cost – often the first novel in the series is free – but the authors can more or less maintain a decent per page price this way. The time it takes to write a page hasn't changed much since the invention of the typewriter, maybe a factor of two at most, so writing is mostly limited by the speed of thinking and mulling over what to say. Although, I would not be too surprised to see A.I. composed short stories in the next couple of decades. I saw the first A.I. composed multi-page dialog some 20 years ago.

I needed to download a book from a particular source to verify if it worked to my expectations. It happened to be James Altucher's latest,[133] just because I recognized his name from some market analysis news segments, and I knew he was enthusiastic about this method of publishing. I didn't really scrutinize the subject matter.

There is no inside title page or copyright notice or publisher information (obviously it is self-published). I assume there must be an ISBN and copyright in the print edition. James is the type of guy who has made and lost several fortunes, and thinks he has got it together now. I suspect he just happened to mature, some people do. But he is very well connected with what's going on in the business and financial world, being a multiple serial entrepreneur and commentator, so it's worth noting the pulse he has his finger on.

Altucher says Fannie Mae created an "American Dream" marketing campaign to "convince Americans newly flush with cash [in the 1960s from two-income families] to start taking mortgages," and that it sucked "like a vacuum cleaner," replacing the "peace and quiet of the suburbs with the desperate need to always stay ahead." This led to the expression "keeping up with the Joneses" in the 1970s.

Thus far Altucher's factual account is mostly right. James Truslow Adams popularized the idea of the "American Dream" in a 1931 book.[134] Fannie Mae did equate the slogan to home ownership and still uses it in their public relations.[135] But on matters of judgment the reader will realize I disagree with Altucher on mortgages – they're fine if you put down margin and use the money for production rather than consumption –

[133] J. Altucher, *Choose Yourself*, no publisher or date listed, downloaded 2013
[134] http://people.howstuffworks.com/american-dream1.htm
[135] http://www.hoovers.com/company-information/cs/company-profile.Federal_National_Mortgage_Association.17e905122c580be5.html

while agreeing on the misuse of the liberated money. The problems with housing came in the late 1980s when, confident of inflation, people started accepting "balloon note" mortgages whose payments increased with time. Of course inflation stopped.

Here I have a bone to pick with Altucher's chart:

inflation index

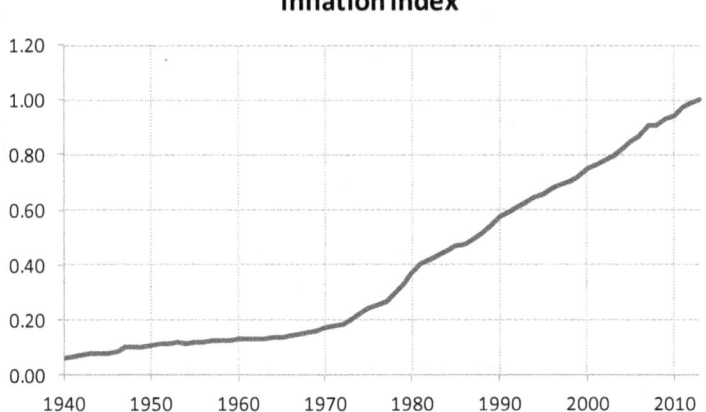

My version is reproduced from BLS data,[136] expressed relative to 2012 dollars as "1," but it looks exactly like his chart. Only the scale at left is bigger so you can read it. What do you notice?

It has a linear vertical scale. That means the change from 0.2 to 0.4 in the 1970s, a 100% change, looks the same size as the change from 0.8 to 1.0 in the last decade, a 25% total change, or 2.2% annually.

Altucher's choice of this chart is probably not deception, but the data selection flaw that I mentioned earlier. He saw a chart that confirmed his beliefs and did not question it. I can't claim any moral high ground. It conflicted with my beliefs so I questioned it. You the reader can decide for yourself. Below is a chart of the same data plotted logarithmically.

---

[136] Consumer Price Index, All Urban Consumers, US Department of Labor: Bureau of Labor Statistics, http://www.bls.gov/opub/hom/pdf/homch17.pdf

inflation index - logarithmic scale

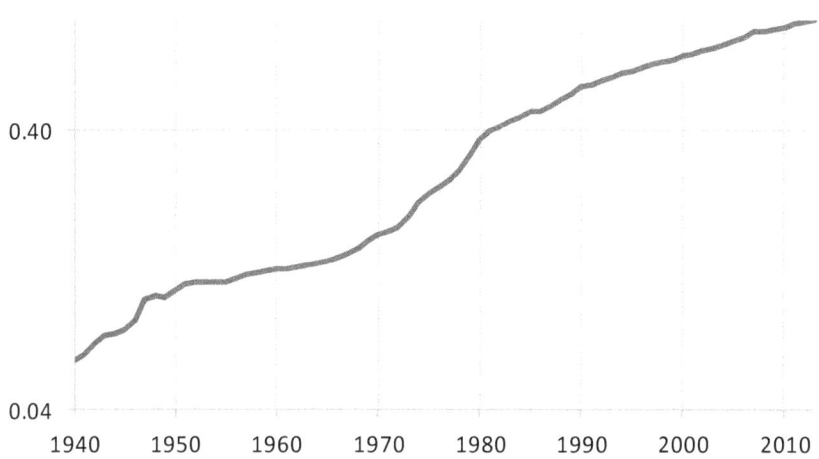

Looks much better, doesn't it? We can do better still. The chart I would choose would portray the *rate* of inflation, which is just the percentage delta between the years for the exact same data as above. This chart is on the next page.

inflation rate

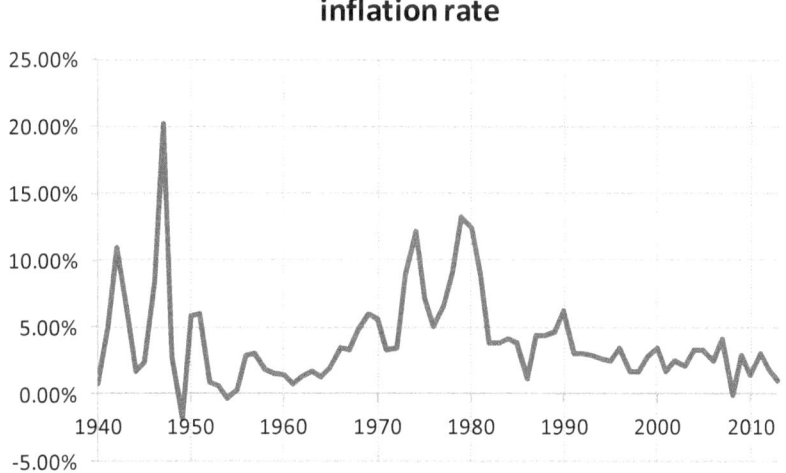

Amazing isn't it? But we're not done. Why did Altucher start at 1940? We did not spend a whole chapter on risk and statistics to make that mistake. Here is all the available data:

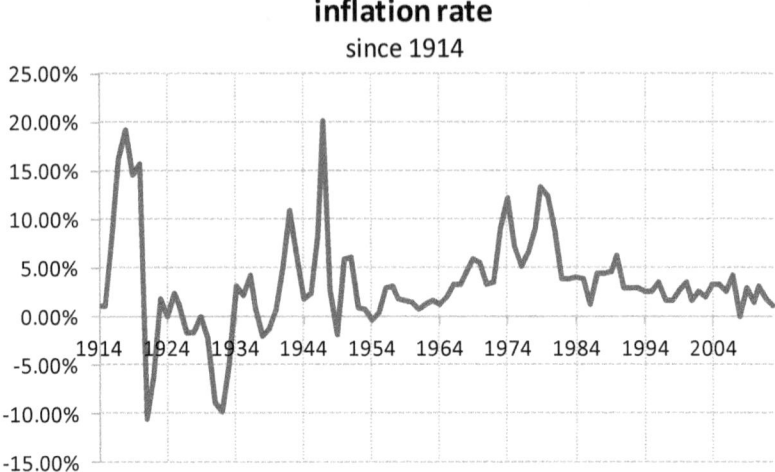

inflation rate
since 1914

Now we get the feeling of some inflation peaks during WWI (even though the gold standard was in effect), WWII, Korea and the Viet Nam War, only the slightest upturns for the Gulf War and the War on Terror, and since then a steady downward trend. In fact there is a dangerous looking cliff right at the end that looks like it might drop out of sight into deflation. Now is not the time to be talking of contracting the money supply (tapering) and steepening that cliff. Altucher, of course, rants for pages about the evils of the Fed dumping money in markets, but the Fed has been struggling against a downward trend in inflation since the mid 1980s.

In case you wanted out of this book some insight into the personality of someone who would work for years on a puzzle in another field considered unsolvable, this is it. I got a sustained euphoric high from turning Altucher's data upside down against him. I didn't cheat or anything like that. You saw every move I made. It's just the facts, viewed from a reasonable perspective, liberated from suppositions.

With the rest of Altucher's rants I quite agree. Real wages are declining, employers used the crisis as an excuse to lay off workers that weren't necessary anyway, and don't plan to ever hire them back. Going even further than I would, Altucher says:

Credit card debt went from $700 billion in 2005 to $2.5 trillion in 2007. Two short years.

... there's a lot more money out there than people let on. It's squirreled away by families who have been hoarding and investing and reinvesting for hundreds of years. And this trillion dollars I speak of belonged to just one family.

... companies don't need to hire as much anymore because technology has reached its manifest destiny from the pulp science fiction novels of the 1930s. Essentially, robots have replaced humans.

... across every industry, technology has replaced not only paper, but people.

Not everyone is an entrepreneur. Not everyone wants to be one.

I agree especially with the last. Altucher's high stress up and down rollercoaster life is typical of every entrepreneur I have known. Some are steadier than others, but it is not for me. However, Altucher's alternative, and he's by no means the only one who thinks this, is that "This is about a new phase in history where art, science, business and spirit will join together ..." where creative people will sell their ideas or art to one another and eliminate all the inefficient middlemen who stand in their way.

Shades! Is Altucher drinking his own Kool-Aid? This is just what he criticized the big corporations for doing. OK, we cannot stop progress. But let's quit worshipping at the altar of a creative utopia and evaluate this objectively. We have the tools.

Return to Zo

It's the future. I can't say exactly when, because this is just the extrapolation of a trend, and humans are good at projecting trends and making choices for things to be different. That's what I'm counting on.

Productivity has continued to increase in Zo, taking almost a life of its own. The engineers now use computers to optimize every aspect of agriculture, which is fully automated. One by one the farmers got bored or died or got bought out and only a handful of farmers are left, with their GPS guided tractors and chemically weeded, genetically enhanced, mechanically harvested crops.

Only the engineers did not spend all their revenue as we had hoped. They neither spent it on personal consumption, nor on employees. Their own operation is largely automated, too. Only a few Ph.D.'s remain to research further improvements. And they can't think of enough new businesses to go into, to deploy their capital for expansion. After all, most people can't afford to buy anything. The epitome of this strategy-gone-wrong is Apple Computer, sitting on the largest un-deployed cash pile in the history of the world, not only in dollars but most likely in absolute terms as well.

The lenders are in one of two situations. Either the monetary agent has failed and allowed deflation, or not. In the case of deflation, the lenders, sitting on cash or contracts for cash, wind up owning everything, so they have as much of a hoard as the engineers. If the monetary agent succeeded in keeping the currency stable by lowering interest rates, then the lenders quit lending and invest in the engineer's technology business.

The rest of the people, let's assume, follow Altucher's advice, and start selling books and music and services and education and inspiration to each other. At first this works, but these people still have to eat, and the only real commodity in Zo is still food.

There are very few engineers and lenders left, and they buy the books and music and inspiration at the same price as everyone else, so the money flow is very uneven, very much toward the engineers, that is the equity partner engineers because they have few employees anymore, and the lenders.

And I suppose now there is a small investor class, which overlaps with lenders and engineers, families who have invested and reinvested broadly in the equity premium for hundreds of years, and have a trillion dollars as Altucher suggested. (What family do you suppose? The top four Waltons have only about $127 billion. Maybe older money more widely distributed, such as the Rockefellers or similar?)

So the money must drain away from the enlightened crowd of ex-employees, liberated from their jobs by robots and automation, because of the imbalance of trade with a very small number of people producing food, and invariably hoarding. The imbalance of trade will be exacerbated by the law of supply and demand. Since there are too many people producing the soft goods, art or entertainment or services, etc., their price will drop.

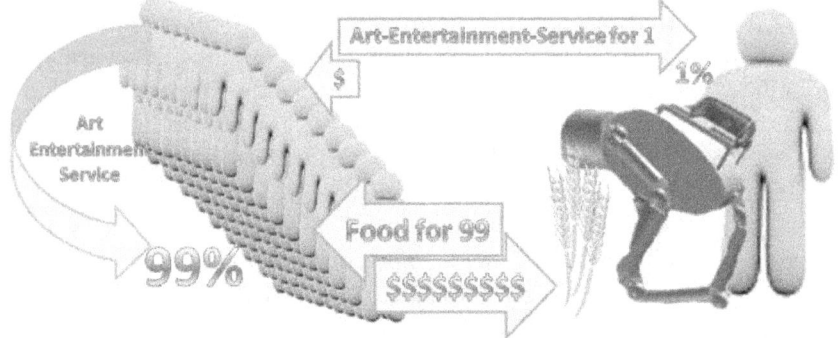

Our model economy of Zo cannot solve this problem. It can only predict what will happen following the actions we choose. Society will have to solve the problem. Maybe it will be easier than I think, but it hasn't been so far. Maybe it will be really hard.

The reader by now surely realizes I advocate people becoming investors, at least as a stop gap measure. Claim some ownership of the giant hoards. Build your own hoard. For every *one* person who has equity, joining the engineers and lenders, then the balance of trade between the artists and the capitalists is improved by *two*! As one side goes down the other goes up. That does not mean you cannot fulfill your dreams as an artist. Investing doesn't take up a lot of time.

By the way, Altucher is himself is also an investor. If you see a person you think is successful, you can do as he says, or do as he does. Sometimes if people are successful, at solving a problem or investing or what have you, they may not really understand themselves how they did it. But if they tell their story and what they think they did, you may be able to figure it out.

Japan is not the only country toying with negative interest rates. As this manuscript was about to go to press, a story appeared on RT.com Venture Capital news saying the European Union Central Bank was considering "punishing" banks for not investing by inflicting a negative interest rate on them.[137] The idea is that money the banks keep on deposit with the central bank will be effectively "taxed" to incentivize productive deployment of the funds elsewhere, i.e. real lending.

Negative interest or its equivalent will not be applied just to bank deposits. Because of "equalization," all safe, non-productive assets which return low rates will come under pressure from the funds thus employed to force higher productivity. Underutilized land, charming older or low-cost sections of cities, family owned and older businesses will be bought up and re-cycled into more of the creeping sameness we have seen in American cities over the last 20 years. The author sometimes finds it hard when traveling to distinguish in which city he has landed. Certainly it cannot any longer be done from the shops and restaurants.

In the video from the RT.com negative interest story there was an interesting analysis of national sovereignty relative to new pro-business "secret" trade courts and fines on both citizens and countries for exposing environmental harm.[138] It appears the model used in the US to protect the food processing industry is now being exported along with the food.

Other Utopian Visions

The labor supply dramatically increased after WWII as women stayed in the workforce, and increased further with the Civil Rights movement as the descendants of low wage workers got educations and better jobs while immigrants (always a factor in the American labor market) took up the low wage tasks. It took a while for the educational

---

[137] Article: http://rt.com/business/european-banks-negative-rate-720/ Video: http://www.youtube.com/watch?feature=player_embedded&v=SO7gJHEpZ74
[138] http://rt.com/op-edge/eu-us-pact-devastating-566/

and cultural pipelines to fill, but this created an oversupply of skilled workers.

The author well knows that industry constantly complains of an undersupply, but the dearth of what they consider qualified resumes is only the result of low wage offerings for high short-term skills, like knowledge of a particular trendy programming language or system. Supply and demand is a cruel law for human supply.

There were widespread predictions in the late 1960s that the number of hours in a work week would decline giving everyone more free time. The emphasis was on the increased free time, or leisure time. The idea kept bubbling around and by the 1980s the concept of job sharing was introduced.

But it didn't catch on. Lowering of barriers to international trade at the end of the 1980s, along with advanced education of foreigners in American Universities and the rising quality of foreign primary and secondary education, created a worldwide surplus of cheap, highly skilled labor. The utopia didn't materialize. Economists and politicians kept hoping the emerging nations would learn to consume their own goods and services, but it is not so easy to re-engineer a society.

Societies decide what kind of economic and political systems they will have, and more mundanely how they will spend their money. Tightly controlled and very free markets have been tried, and in both cases have yielded more toward a middle ground. Certainly the era of free banking was not something people who remember it want to repeat. After that a gold standard was tried, and it too failed. The author is no friend of government bureaucracies, but yet finds bumper stickers proclaiming

"END THE FED"

a little bit alarming. Such views can come from people who might otherwise have sensible opinions, and I have to believe it is because they too don't trust bureaucrats, would like something they can have faith in, and simply aren't old enough to remember failed experiments of the past. Experiments with manipulating currencies unnaturally, and especially suddenly, continue to be disastrous as with the machinations with the Japanese yen in the mid 1980s.

Russia's "sudden" conversion to capitalism was also nearly ruinous and it is just now recovering. Jerry Brown, longest serving governor in California's history, who restored the state's long-ruined finances, in an NPR interview November 6th was asked how he had changed over his 40 year career. He replied:

> "... that gives me a sense of familiarity, clarity about what is needed. I cut to the chase, I get to the heart of things and also realize that change is slow."

Perhaps the Chinese are on the right track with their tiny-steps approach to capitalism.

Stability is like balancing on a knife point. You are more likely to cut yourself than achieve it. As I see it, we either digress into chaos, or move forward into an almost unimaginable future that is certainly frightening for its strangeness.

Every time we use 100 year old ideas to tinker with a monetary policy that in fact isn't that old, but we assume that things like interest rates must be set back where they were because we have always done so, we are stepping out over a cliff and inviting the downslide. As the Japanese are finding, it is a long climb back up.

Bubbles in particular are a transient not based on fundamental value, and if we destroy money when half of it has already been destroyed, the result is a quarter century of deflation. And counting. The monetary agent should look at equilibrium factors.

If off-shoring US manufacturing is such a good idea, why have the Japanese not closed their plants in the US? Is that why their economy is doing so badly? Or alternately, if Japanese off-shoring of manufacturing to the US ruined their economy, why do we think we will escape the same fate?

And if productivity drops, what then, will the monetary agent destroy money to prevent inflation? Maybe higher prices are just the stimulus needed to get production going again. The truth is investors are taking giant risks, and they need to not have money and interest jumping around doing strange things.

And what do we spend all this money we create for? Are government bonds and mortgages adequate? Will the Fed buy student loan backed securities next? You get more of what you pay for. Student loans produce a lot of expensive colleges, but no guarantee of a job, and thus possibly no return on the investment.

Realistic Approaches

Looking for Remedies

Avoiding deflation and encouraging people to join the investor class are stop gap measures. Eventually people have to figure out what they wish to do, and it may be premature to even seriously speculate. The technological and biological underpinnings of our existence have changed much faster than our preferences and emotional makeup are changing.

Artificial limbs controllable by thought have been demonstrated, intense work is proceeding on other neural interfaces, and even a computer emulation of the brain has been proposed of a magnitude comparable to the human genome project. We could possibly do this without first understanding how the brain works and use it as a tool for study. While human lifespan has stalled out in the 80s for now, there is a push to understand aging generally because of healthcare costs. A few people remain healthy until, well, they die, but most deteriorate with age and use up their life savings and potentially everyone else's in medical care costs. Understanding aging could put more people in the former group. But it likely also would create unexpected problems. What do all these retired people do, or do they keep working?

Superficially we can conclude that government and retirement funding and medical care based on taxing wages will not work without a sufficient quantity of wages. Neither will a tax on consumption since the people with most of the money will have inadequate consumption. And a tax on investments might solve the problem by abruptly halting or even reversing our productivity growth, but only a fringe few will really advocate reverse progress.

We quickly will run into conflicts of interest that make healthcare or global warming look like fun and games. For example, we could tax production whether human or automated, based on the value of the production. Notice that this is different than taxing consumption because it hits the investor class as well, but it does not discourage investment. And it does remove the tremendous advantage that employers find now in automation which does not incur these overhead expenses. But the business community will oppose such an idea.

In looking for solutions, the best minds must be incentivized, and continuously so over the coming centuries as things will probably keep changing. Leaving it up to every individual to figure out what they will do without any historical or cultural patterns or reference points is a recipe for disaster. We don't leave productivity and technology advances up to such ad hoc methods. We heavily incentivize them by rewarding the geniuses who come up with the ideas and implement them with billions of dollars and mountains of fame and glory. These few people figure out not only what customers want, they figure out how to mobilize people to provide it.

It is a flaw in our system that now we have switched to rewarding the geniuses who figure out how to serve customers without employing very many of them. Henry Ford already realized that if he didn't pay his employees enough that they could buy a car, that no one else would pay their workers enough either, and soon he would be selling no cars. Where is that kind of deep thought among today's entrepreneurs and leaders? I don't know if it is a cultural change that's needed, or business or tax incentives, but the general direction to look in solving any problem is toward incentivizing the most creative humans to work on it.

Human Value Growth

What we are seeing now is most nearly comparable to the transition from hunter-gathering culture to agriculture 10,000 years ago, which replaced small roving clans with established cities, lords, and eventually the empires that gave rise to modern states. From the Renaissance, mechanical invention liberated the field hands to pursue arts, crafts, trade, exploration, science, and ever more invention. The pace of change, though rapid by historical standards, was slow enough that people easily thought of new things to do, which were of value to each other, i.e. human value, and real wages together with the standard of living gradually rose.

Since 1970, approximately coincident with the mass commercialization of micro and nano technology, initially integrated circuits implementing what were previously room-sized computers, invention of productivity has outpaced invention of human value. We measure, optimize and reward greatly the invention of productivity.

We are not yet even discussing the invention of human value. Since 1990 we seem obsessed with eliminating it, downsizing, outsourcing, off-shoring, and automating. Until we begin to compile data on human value growth just as we do productivity growth, and measure whether value growth is keeping up, we will not even know where to look for a vague problem that plagues us. By comparing the growth of human value and productivity we would have continuous feedback to monetary and political and business and educational policy which would identify divergences early and promote balance between the two metrics.

Human value is non-linear and time dependent. Productivity is simple, just widgets per hour. The value of someone who learns to produce a useful new widget is enormous at first, but declines if the supply of widgets saturates the need, or many other people learn to make them. Using wages as a proxy for human value leads to the following error: maximizing wages without increasing value.

Working directly on value focuses us on creating new careers and pursuits with value that lasts long enough to be worth the investment, preferably a lifetime, but at least 20 years otherwise mobility will be more downward than upward. Maximizing human value may even lead to productivity without unemployment and deflation, since the rewards are distributed widely leading to less hoarding. Maximizing value, like maximizing wages, is inflationary on the one hand, but unlike maximizing wages, it has productivity and deflationary components, which promises better balance and simpler, less volatile monetary policy.

The 20% Solution

Let's see how the stop gap measure of increasing the number of investors would work, how much time it would buy us. According to the World Bank, the market cap of listed US companies is $18 trillion.[139] The labor force is 155,000.[140] Suppose one in five is or will become a self-supporting investor, then that's $580,000 of market cap per such investor. Taking 5% or half of what we have estimated the intrinsic growth might be as income (a little higher than the average dividend rate), that's $29,000 per investor per year. Not quite enough. However, with changes to the tax code to incentivize more REIT and BDC-like dividend structures, we might conceivably get 10% *and even more as productivity continues to increase*. That's $58,000.

Currently, the average 401K size is $75,000. I will use this as a proxy for average account size since I couldn't find that number. 50% of Americans own some amount of stocks, or 2.5 out of 5. We have 2.5×$75k = $187.5k per 5 people, less than 33% of the amount I advocate. The pool of investors is quite top heavy as we are all aware. Regardless of how one would distribute the market cap, plainly there is room for 200% growth (3×) in widely held investments. Combined with the proposed 2× increase in dividends, that's 2×3 = a factor of 6 headroom in investment income available to the general population, the other 99% of us. The *catch* is those dividends have to be at least partly re-invested until the share of market capitalization increases 200%. At a 5% re-investment rate, this is 22.5 years. The top 20% of investors make over $100k a year. Most of us can keep working that long. The imbalance between 20% self-supporting investors and 80% others accumulates *5 times slower than at 99% to 1%*.

---

[139] http://data.worldbank.org/indicator/CM.MKT.LCAP.CD
[140] http://www.dlt.ri.gov/lmi/laus/us/usadj.htm

Inflation adjusted US household income by fifths

http://www.census.gov/hhes/www/income/data/historical/household/

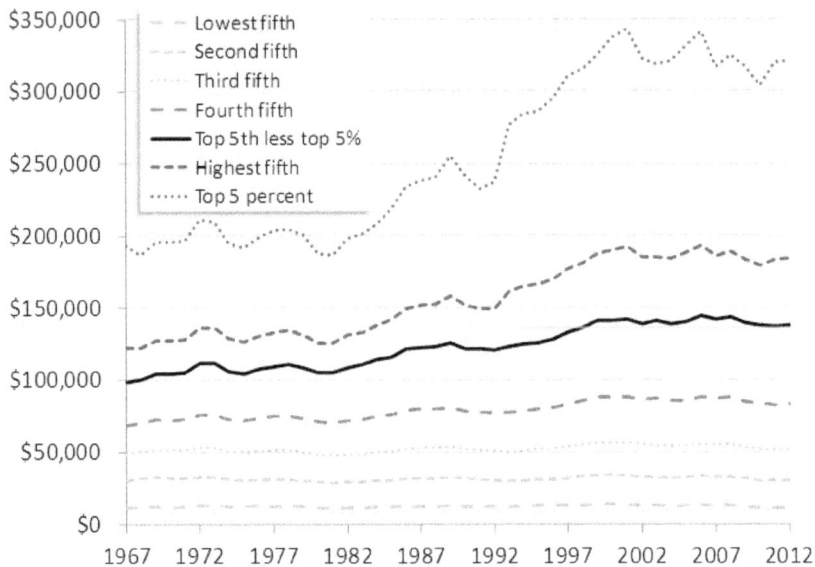

Can or would the top 20% (top fifth) afford to do this? First, I subtracted the top 5% to avoid the average being skewed by the very top, see solid line in chart above. By the faint limit line I added, you can see this group is among the least affected by recent declines in real income. I am not concerned about the decline in the top 5% as they are just coming back in line with historical norms. The incomes of the almost-top 15% then are around $140k. They should be able to save $10k a year, or more if tax deferred contributions are extended to them. Currently this is denied completely for incomes over $129k, eliminating the class of earners who could potentially fix the investor-worker imbalance by switching sides. Even below $129k, For IRAs there is a $5.5k contribution limit. And all IRAs are restricted from using margin which hampers recovery from crises when the Fed is trying to get investors to borrow and invest.

Assuming this (15%) group has only $187.5k in their IRAs and 401k's now, adds $10k annually, and gets 7% geometric mean market growth, they will have $1.3 million in 22 years and can retire from the working class with $92.4k of income. If we take legislative steps to encourage corporations to better share the estimated intrinsic returns of 10%, presumably by dividends, then in 14 years they can retire with $99k income.

A real benefit of having greater ownership of corporations *could be* better corporate governance for the benefit of society. According to the theory under which corporations were chartered, they were supposed to exist only in cases where they clearly benefitted the public, by undertaking some project (such as building the transcontinental railroad) which would not and could not be financed by a private businessman, or wouldn't be in the public's interest to be financed and owned by a private businessman.

However, organizers of a corporation feel like they know what's best. If they didn't, they wouldn't be organizing it. They view shareholders as a necessary source of revenue, but find various ways of preserving as much control for the organizers as possible. The shareholders usually only vote for board members. Corporate bylaws often discourage shareholder ballot initiatives. When was the last time you had a choice of more than one board member, and a policy statement from each of the competing candidates? And if you hold your shares in a mutual fund or index fund, you do not vote them at all. The fund manager does. The fund manager will usually vote only to maximize returns.

This need not be the case. While there are "green" mutual funds, that's not what I have in mind. These are not whole-market representative. If an index fund were created which passed-through voting, it would always have identical performance to any other index fund representing the same market. The logistics of voting could be addressed by having 4 or 5 generic policy affinities from which a fund holder could select, with details of voting handled en masse by the fund management. Such a fund could actively represent environmental and humanitarian positions and even nominate its own candidates for the board without incurring any detrimental performance, because of its index nature.

The transition to investor self-sufficiency is not only doable, I know people who are doing it. Under current less favorable conditions, I know a schoolteacher whose salary never exceeded the mid-$60s at its peak who retired with almost $700k in index funds. If she can do that, what can you do with your $140k income you are currently squandering on mostly material objects that will disintegrate over time?

You in the 15% who are least affected by declining real wages – what are you going to do in your own interest to liberate yourself from a job where you are probably asked to do things you don't agree with, to provide time and energy to share your creative ideas with the world, preserve your health so you will be around to help your children and enjoy your grandchildren? What kind of future are you going to choose for them? See the next page and choose one of the two alternatives!

Final Words

Summing up, you get what you pay for. If you invest in a savings account or bonds, you will get more banks and bond issues. Jobs are great, I still have mine, but if it is all you invest in your employer may take the profit.

If you invest in equity, broadly and over time, you will get earnings growth. Companies are willing to finance with bonds or equity issues, and will issue more of whichever is cheaper for them. When they are issuing more bonds, buy the equity and claim your stake in the future.

∞

Fully dexterous robotic hand offers "V sign" meaning victory, thus also peace.
http://en.wikipedia.org/wiki/V_sign
http://en.wikipedia.org/wiki/Robonaut
photo by author, circa 1999

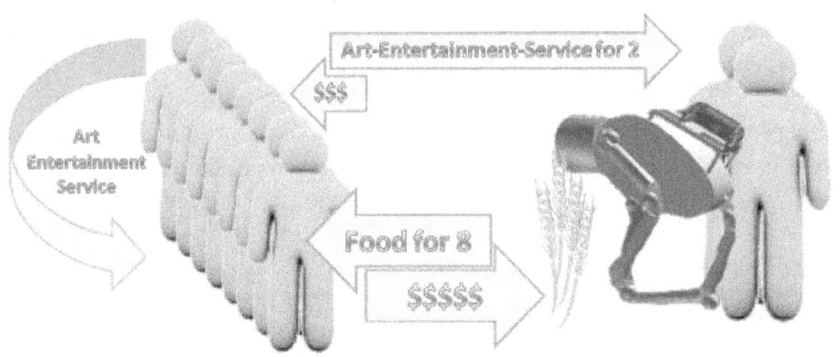

Revised economy of Zo with 20% self-supporting investor fraction.

About Writing this Book

A Friend

This story began a long time ago. I first met Rajnish Mehra in the fall of 1972 as we both entered graduate school at Rice in Electrical Engineering. He was a smart, handsome and friendly young man from a well-to-do family in India, and he and I and my wife at that time became friends and spent some time hanging out. I was disappointed when he announced he was leaving to study finance at Columbia. I could hardly even imagine what that entailed.

There were a number of Indians at Rice at that time, and I was impressed with the friendliness and intelligence of all of them. I remember helping one of them with some assembly code he wanted to run fast. I had spent years mastering 360 assembler, and he picked it up in a few hours. There was a recession going on, and an energy crisis, and Ph.D. graduates were not getting good salaries. I'd been thinking about the economics of career choices since my sophomore economics professor attempted to prove that a college education was not the most profitable choice. Instead the money could be invested and more total return obtained by starting life and earning earlier. It might, of course, not offer the same aesthetic rewards. But multiple factors contributed to my own departure and the start of a career in computers, engineering, management, research and space exploration.

As years rolled by, I was a bit surprised how closely several of the Indians kept up with their friends, not only each other, but also with me. I seldom heard from my high school classmates until later in life, and only from one guy I had known in undergraduate school.

Raj was the most diligent of my Rice friends. Decade after decade the faithful Christmas cards never stopped, and occasionally he might call me especially if he was going to be in Houston. He got an appointment at UCSB in Santa Barbara, and then he got appointments at the University of Chicago, later at Arizona, and recently in Luxembourg. Obviously Raj was going places. I was not sure just what was driving his rise until one day in 2002.

I had been investing for a while, actually for a long while. My father got me started in high school. It seemed to me that money was a number, all investing involved the manipulation or understanding of numbers, and since I was a certified near genius at such matters I should be good at it. But as any of you who have tried it know it's not so straightforward. The market was going nowhere in the 1970s, and interest rates were very high. I spent some time figuring how much money I'd have to save to live off the interest, and how much I'd have to scrimp to save like that, and if we could stand the pain.

The numbers didn't quite seem to work. Then I got divorced and had some other problems, but by the early 1980s I had some money coming in and I was again planning my financial future and had opened a discount broker account. I was trading options during a second mini energy crisis. It seemed to me I could guess as well as anyone what OPEC might or might not do, and I did fabulously well the first year I tried it. It was the worst thing that ever happened to me financially – because I thought I should be able to keep doing it.

I switched to tech thinking I might do better in an industry I knew something about. I managed to speculate on Digital Equipment Corp. just as it succumbed to microprocessor technology. It sounds dumb in hindsight, but that's the way it went down. Because since 1965 the stock market had been relatively flat, my only notion of how to make money from it was trading the ups and downs. I had no clue what was going on in 1983 when the market took off. I pulled out and waited for it to "return to normal." And I invested in some bond mutual funds. By the late 1980s bonds weren't doing so well, and so I went into tech and growth funds, always seeming to enter after the trend was spent.

A Question

In the 1990s I did a little better, learning fundamentals and partly trying to find turnaround companies, which would sometimes work. In the late 1990s I remember adding up my lifetime returns and realizing it was only a few percent. I was horrified. I guess I would have felt better had I known then. I didn't. that this is not unusual for small individually managed accounts with some stock trades and specialized (not index) mutual funds.

If long-term market returns are as good as almost all studies showed, why were most people doing so badly?

This became a question that haunted me for many years. I did keep getting better. I mostly avoided the dotcom bust, having no tech stocks except in a small retirement account (which has never fully recovered). I read many books. I became annoyed with simple rules of thumb based on the unpredictable future. For example, Peter Lynch (and a lot of other people at the time) advocated valuations based on a price to earnings ratio (P/E) which was approximately equal to the annual percentage growth rate of earnings.

As an engineer, this made no sense whatever. It was not possible to find any kind of consistent units or justification for such a formula. Was this the best that the best minds had to offer?

I started doing my own calculations based on what I knew from "osmosis" about the value of equities (stocks) being related to the interest rate, relative to their earnings. It seemed to me that the valuations of companies were all wrong. In the first place, if they were really going to grow as much as predicted the valuations were much too low. But in most cases, the growth didn't really last that long. So how were analysts making precise predictions? It was not until later that analyst predictions became so thoroughly discredited.

The Equity Premium Puzzle
Raj and I were communicating more often at this time, probably due to his schedule being more relaxed and the internet making things easier. For me anyway. Raj didn't type, and he would instead call. I would not always be able to think through everything in a phone call. He sent me his lecture notes on the theory of proprietary returns and how to value a company with a series of future proprietary returns. By 2003 I was reading economics papers for myself, dozens and dozens of them, learning about risk and efficient markets and noise traders (me?). One day Raj asked if I knew anything about his research on the equity premium. What's that?

Raj and his mentor Edward Prescott published a paper in 1985 noting that over long periods of time, longer than twenty years, stock markets on average returned more than bonds. Far too much more to be explained by then existing risk preference models.

It took something like seven years for that paper to be accepted, I later learned. Of course it would not be plausible in the late 1970s, as there had been a flat market and no equity premium to speak of since the mid 1960s. *And more importantly* prevailing economic theory, especially efficient market theory, absolutely forbid that investors might be "leaving money on the table" in such large amounts. The prices of bonds and equities should "equalize" such that returns would be the same. Raj explained that his finding had become known as a famous puzzle that could not be explained, and that he had acquired a certain amount of notoriety.

Raj became an in-demand international speaker, constantly traveling. In 2004 Prescott won a Nobel prize, but not for the equity premium work, something else. Nobel prizes are not generally given until experiment and theory both confirm a thing, and it appears to be both understood and applied.

First Try
I was fascinated, having always been a fan of working on impossible problems. I had been working on the four-color map problem ever since high school. I worked on number theory problems in grad school totally outside my main research area. So of course I tried explaining the equity premium. Raj patiently shot down all my early trials. There were a few points he couldn't seem to explain away in my

arguments, but he convinced me that by themselves they did not solve the puzzle. In particular, I discovered that any return in excess of the risk-adjusted interest rate which could be maintained over a long period of time had an infinite net present value. Economists can easily miss this because they *assume* that the actual long-term return *is* the risk-adjusted rate, and that they just haven't discovered the right model to predict it yet. There is no possibility of a discrepancy to their way of thinking. Raj was telling the world there was a problem, and suggesting solutions such as "friction" that tip-toed around the theoretical problem, but the divergence between his facts and theory are undoubtedly what delayed the publication of his original paper.

I separately discovered some disturbing things about the dispersion of market returns, something I called non-linear returns (which I'll explain in the first chapter). I developed a portfolio theory and started writing a book. I did some reviews of other books on Amazon and got a good response to my writing on economics.

It didn't work out though. As 2008 approached, even before the big crash I realized my portfolio was behaving strangely. It turned out my idea was partly or perhaps mostly a volatility increasing mechanism, maybe not fundamentally "better." I stopped working on the book and turned to other things.

As I watched my net worth get cut nearly in half during the fall of 2008 and early 2009, I was absent-mindedly pursuing some ideas on general relativity and its conflict with quantum ,echanics, another impossible puzzle I was gradually becoming immersed in. I tried day trading. Amazingly, I could make money even when the market was going down, but not a lot and it was tremendously stressful. I needed a long-term strategy that didn't take so much time and energy. I invested in Business Development Companies and REITs which were rebounding, and a lot of other different ideas. By the middle of 2009 when the recovery was obvious I went long on margin, careful not to get close to my limits. By 2010 I was even. I had been burned enough not to assume it due to skill, though. There continued to be portfolio surprises every six months to a year.

By the end of 2011 I had published my first physics paper. In 2012 I finally remarried, and in January of 2013 my paper on quantum gravity appeared. I started intently trying to get an idea on risk management in engineering projects published, an idea I'd been fiddling with on and off for a decade. Finally I started getting a really good reception to it, as I'd learned how to talk about it I think. During a visit to my sister's family in the spring of 2013 I found them socializing with an economics professor, Robert Van Ness, and since my risk theory was more of an economic theory than traditional risk management, I tried it out on him. He immediately said, "Have you tried using this to explain the equity premium?"

Altering the Point of View

Well of course I tried it. There was some peripheral relation. Most explanations of the equity premium have tried to revise and rationalize investor risk preferences to account for the differences in returns. There are a few other types of explanations. It wasn't really working. But I again thought about my earlier idea, about the infinite returns, and realized that no bond return could ever equalize with that. Equity returns could *not* be equalized downward. The risk free rate would have to equalize up.

Why did it not do that? Or was there something I was overlooking? I began to see why economists were so frustrated with this problem. In fact I asked around for help, and could find very few working on it. I turned to Raj again. He was very busy traveling but after a few months he had some time and called me. *"The equity premium can't be explained by risk,"* he told me. I already knew that, but he was confirming it. I pulled a little note card out of my pocket which I had prepared, knowing his call would come at some unexpected time and catch me off guard, and began to go through my ideas. "What is your risk model?" he kept asking. I had to spell it out a second time. "This is not a risk-based explanation. You told me yourself it could not be explained by risk preferences!" Oh. Well, this might be interesting. We'll talk about it again in a few months.

Over the summer I noticed how anxious markets were about tapering of the Fed's program of quantitative easing. This was exactly what I had been analyzing. Productivity, inflation, monetary policy and the equity premium were inextricably linked, and it appeared no one was realizing the inflation trigger level was gradually changing over time. I slowly and carefully wrote a paper and sent it to a journal. Then the government shut down. I had the perfect excuse to write a book, and the time. Thank you Mr. President and members of the Tea Party!

Acknowledgements

Crystal Wolfe helped enormously with the cover layout, colors and fonts. She designs book covers professionally and does editing as well, and you can reach her at

http:// www.crystalwolfe.fineartstudioonline.com

And besides that she encouraged me over many years and let me "practice" on her by following many of my ideas in her own portfolio, even though not all of them were good enough to make the cut for the book. Now that is confidence!

If not for Dr. Robert Van Ness, professor of finance at the University of Mississippi, it likely would have been a long time, if ever, before I got back around to the equity premium, which I had laid aside for several years. He is a friend of my sister's family and we were exchanging pet theories during and after dinner in Oxford one evening, and on hearing about my novel innovation-risk theory he said, perhaps not seriously, that I might use that to explain the equity premium.

In case you skipped the preface, please go back and read about my friend Rajnish Mehra. There is a lesson here for anyone choosing a career and a school. Pick where you go based on the people you want to meet and associate with for the rest of your professional and personal life. Sometimes fate will hand you something you are not looking for. People and friendships are the most valuable assets humans have and cannot be equalized with any amount of money. Money really is just an exchange of favors between friends, but sometimes in its impersonal form we forget it is a favor not an obligation, a symbol of affection not of servitude.

My sister Pauline Lewis set up a small joint account with me to earn income to finance expenses at some joint property, and allowed me a free hand to try my income portfolio ideas. Her husband Mike engaged me in hours of stimulating conversation, and took the devil's advocate position on many market issues which kept me from getting drunk on my own cool aid. He was also very enthusiastic for me to finish the book so he could read it. Mike reads a lot of non-fiction books and makes an excellent marketing test point!

My friend Nat Mosley at UBS provided many insights about banking, provided much early encouragement, and also comments on the manuscript and cover notes.

I wrote the section on how to handle windfalls for my cousin Lee. Unfortunately he didn't win the lottery, but he is getting some money from the sale of family property.

My friend Mark and I have a mutual-encouragement society to promote each other to branch out and try new things.

My friend Scott makes robots for a living, with 5-fingered hands that can do human work. Productivity? The far future speculation is dedicated to him.

John "Buddy" Hyams was the first to ask really substantive questions about the manuscript that prompted major clarifications and additions. Buddy was one of my early mentors in "rational thinking and unexpected outcomes" I see he has not lost his touch!

B.G. Smith expressed fascination with the perpetual portfolio simulator and kept begging me for a draft to read, which was very motivating!

And lastly to my wife who gave me the opportunity to visit extensively in modern Russia, to peer through her eyes at life in the former Soviet economy, and who cheerfully tolerated many late nights of work on this manuscript. I love you, Sweetie!

Appendix – Advanced Data Filtering

You may be wondering how I turned this:

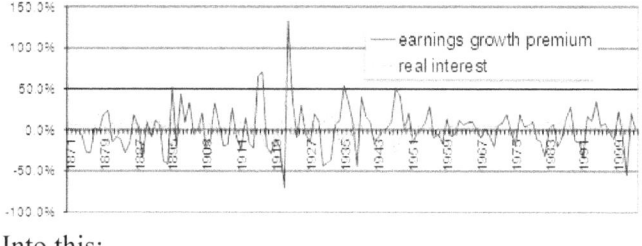

Into this:

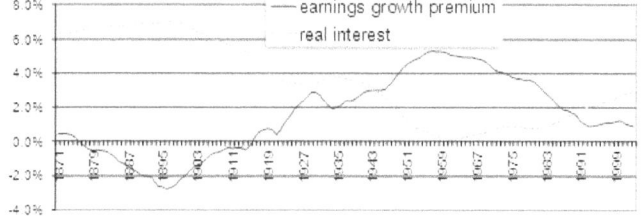

If you tried to do it with standard tricks like moving averages, it doesn't work very well. Financial data are just signals, and the average cell phone pulls signals out of so much noise that you can't even see the signals on a plot, in order to reduce transmission power requirements. I have always been at a loss to understand why such techniques are not used on financial data.

The simplest kind of signal processing is a so-called one pole filter. It can be implemented with a resistor and a capacitor, or it can be programmed on a computer. The capacitor integrates, or sums, data. The resistor bleeds it off so that contributions to the sum from old values eventually decay. The result is a circuit that passes slow moving signals almost unchanged, but blends away fast moving signals. Since it weights recent values, it responds quicker than a moving average while still filtering sharply.

The speed of movement of a signal is described as frequency, and might be measured as cycles per second or Hertz, abbreviated Hz. The reciprocal 1/Hz is just time. So instead of specifying frequency, one can specify a time constant. This is the period of a sine wave that a one pole filter will attenuate to 0.707 of its previous value. (sometimes called the 3 dB half power point, or roll off point, or cut off frequency)

For financial data, we probably want to use years or months, not seconds. A 10 year time constant corresponds to a signal that moves through a cycle, say up and back down, in 10 years. Below is a chart of a sine function input (not a financial function, bear with me!) showing one and two pole filters with roll off periods of 50 years. The one pole filtered signal is 7/10 of its original strength. The two pole is just another one pole applied to the output of the first, cascaded. Plots are sown for 50 and 25 year input data periods.

1 & 2-pole filters, 50 year time constant

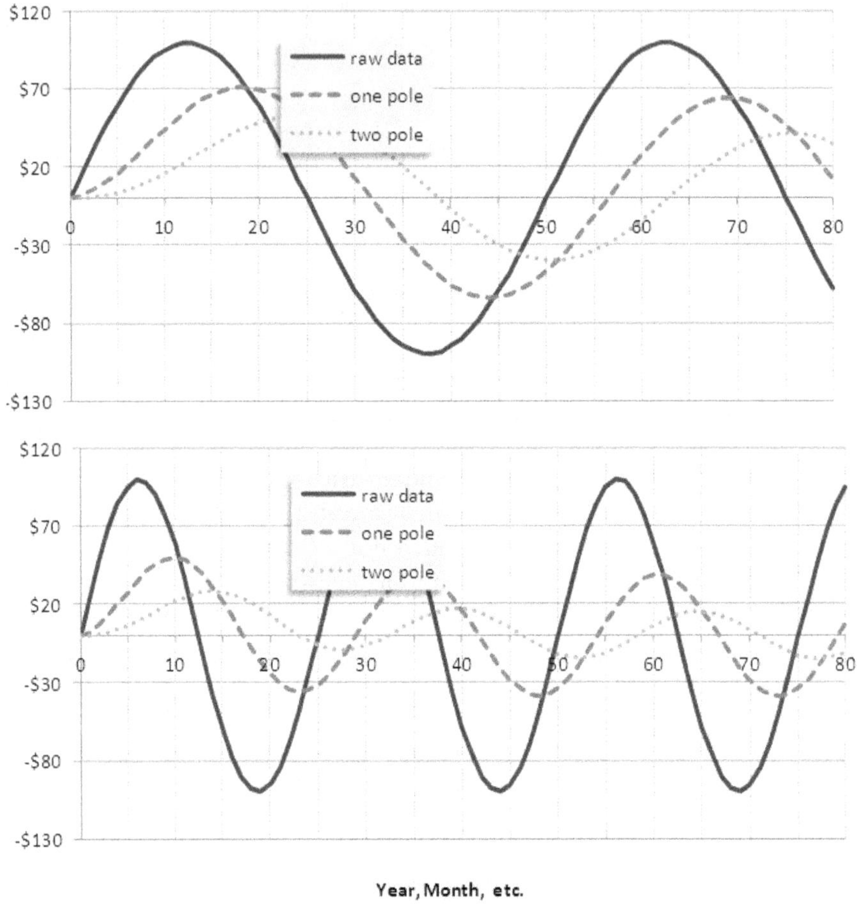

Year, Month, etc.

Below is the response to an input function which jumps around between $0 and $100 at various intervals. The 2-pole filter attenuates the "noise" signals more quickly and does a better job of smoothing without missing changes, c.f. 25 year moving average!

50-year filter response to faster moving input

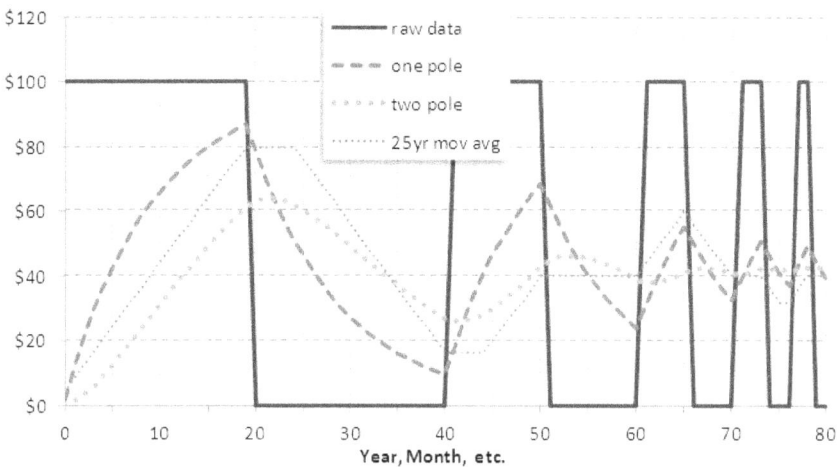

To make such a filter use a spreadsheet formula like this:

	=(E4+F3*($H$1/5-1))/($H$1/5)					
D	E	F	G	H	I	J
					50	roll off period
pole		one pole	two pole		200	input period
$0	$100	$2	$0			
$0	$100	$H$1/5)	$1			
$0	$100	$21	$3		$120	
$0	$100	$29	$6			
$1	$100	$36	$9		$100	

For the first filtered value, assume zero or any initial value for the old summations. Thereafter you are summing the new data input with the previous sum, weighted with the roll off period (time constant) divided by 5. To retrieve this example spreadsheet see:

http://me1soft.com/EquityPremiumBook

On the following page are some examples of different filters.

2-pole filtered @ 12-year time constant

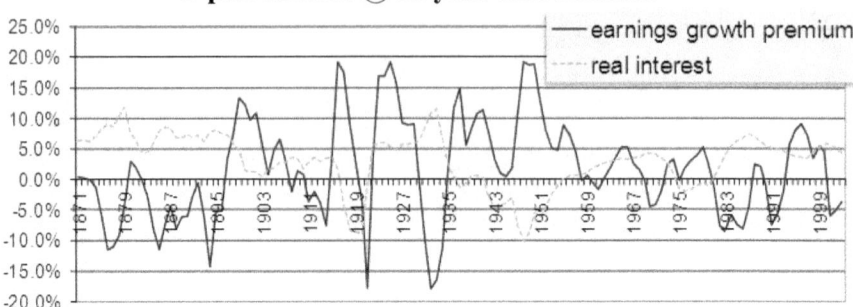

2-pole filtered @ 25-year time constant

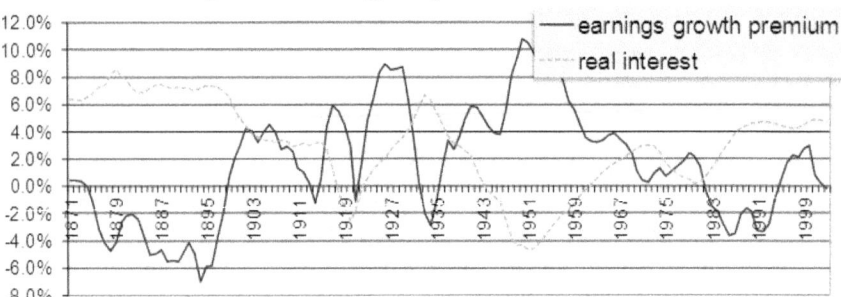

2-pole filtered @ 37-year time constant

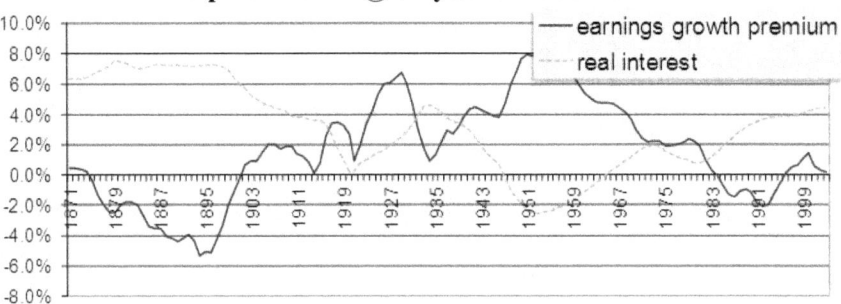

Index

www.ingramcontent.com/pod-product-compliance
Lightning Source LLC
Chambersburg PA
CBHW051903170526
45168CB00001B/218